Republic Studios

Between Poverty Row and the Majors

Updated Edition

Richard M. Hurst

THE SCARECROW PRESS, INC.
Lanham, Maryland • Toronto • Plymouth, UK
2007

SCARECROW PRESS, INC.

Published in the United States of America
by Scarecrow Press, Inc.
A wholly owned subsidary of
The Rowman & Littlefield Publishing Group, Inc.
4501 Forbes Boulevard, Suite 200, Lanham, Maryland 20706
www.scarecrowpress.com

Estover Road
Plymouth PL6 7PY
United Kingdom

British Library Cataloguing in Publication Information Available

Library of Congress Cataloging-in-Publication Data

Hurst, Richard M., 1938–
Republic Studios : between poverty row and the majors / Richard M. Hurst. — Updated ed.
    p. cm.
Includes bibliographical references and index.
ISBN-13: 978-0-8108-5886-2 (pbk. : alk. paper)
ISBN-10: 0-8108-5886-X (pbk. : alk. paper)
1. Republic Pictures Corporation. I. Title.
PN1999.R4H86 2007
384'.80979494—dc22
                                                                    2006100604

∞™ The paper used in this publication meets the minimum requirements of American National Standard for Information Sciences—Permanence of Paper for Printed Library Materials, ANSI/NISO Z39.48-1992.
Manufactured in the United States of America.

Contents

Preface

Almost everyone acknowledges the effects of movies on culture but their specific role in American popular culture varies depending upon the source cited. Writings about film fall into two broad categories—fan and academic. The fan publications are usually unabashedly nostalgic and attempt to revive the pleasures that movies brought to audiences in their youth. Examples would include Alan Barbour's *The Thrill of It All*, dealing with B Westerns, and Jack Mathis' *Valley of the Cliffhangers*, dealing with Republic sound serials.[1] Academically, the cinema can be viewed historically, anthropologically, psychologically, cinematically, or sociologically.

All approaches tend to find a significance in the movies which Hollywood rarely acknowledges. Historically, the importance of film in any given era has usually been recognized but has not often been analyzed since the historian frequently views film as an undeveloped art form whose role in culture is difficult to categorize. Some of the inherent dilemmas caused by this cautious approach are covered in Paul Smith's *The Historian and Film*.[2] The anthropological school is perhaps best represented by Hortense Powdermaker[3] and tends to view film's effect on modern culture as a mass produced technical development filling much the same role as folklore and ancient religions did in past cultures.

From the psychological viewpoint, movies are viewed as unconsciously reinforcing basic cultural patterns and, at the same time, influencing and directing these patterns through the emphases of successful films which affect audience behavior. The main thrust of this approach is perhaps best represented by Martha Wolfenstein and Nathan Leites in their *Movies: A Psychological Study*.[4]

The cinematic approach has gained popularity in the last decade and says essentially that movies are a major force in history and should be studied both as a mirror to the period and as a factor in the overall history of a given time. This approach views film as an art but acknowledges its roots in economics. One of the more successful studies of this type is Garth Jowett's *Film: The Democratic Art*,[5] which is similar to works of a historical nature except that the author is devoted to the study of the cinema and emphasizes film as a major force in modern history rather than treating film as only one incidental factor in the larger pattern of historical development.

Finally, movies can be viewed academically from the sociological approach and, in this case, are usually studied in relationship to what the filmmaker was trying to impress upon his audience through the film. Of course, all films carry some message in the mere act of telling a story but the message film as sociologists think of it is the subject of David Manning White's and Richard Averson's *The Celluloid Weapon: Social Comment in the American Film*.[6]

All of these approaches have two things in common. First, they concentrate on the A film, the major production, and not the much more numerous and far more widely seen B film, that shorter economically produced type of unpretentious entertainment made from 1935 to the mid-1950s to fill the double bill and to enable the small neighborhood theaters to stay open seven days a week and provide an hour or two of diversion for the general moviegoing public. Secondly, these studies normally accept the basic premise that movies influenced their audiences and through them the general culture but they rarely attempt to draw insights from this concept. They do not usually study a genre or a studio in detail and then draw conclusions as to what the effects might be. The failure to take this last step is because sometimes it is felt that the conclusions are obvious and, even more important, because there is no sure way to measure these effects.

This study of the influence and significance of the major B studio, Republic Pictures, on the American scene utilizes aspects from all these schools of thought but probably falls closest to the cinematic historian's approach. By studying certain genres produced by a studio which specialized in the B format, key messages of these films will become apparent and their relationship to and effect upon the American scene will be documented. It will be shown that the studio was not interested in art but in economics, that in order to be profitable the movies had to entertain, and that in entertaining they also influenced and reflected the American culture as they saw it. The results, while unintended, were nonetheless important. Although there is still no way to measure these effects, the following chapters attempt to show that the B film generally and the output of Republic Pictures especially did have a significance to the study of American history from the mid-1940s to the mid-1950s.

To some moviegoers, the collective B film provided a barometer by which they, the individual members of the audience, succeeded or failed far more than the major pictures with a more obvious attempt to moralize—such as King Vidor's *Our Daily Bread* (1934) or Frank Capra's *Mr. Smith Goes to Washington* (1939). Republic was a major producer of quantity and quality B films. Perhaps the studio's quality made a difference in the success of the unintended lessons in their B films. But whether Republic was in a category with other B producers such as Monogram and Producers Releasing Corporation, or whether they were in a class by themselves, their pictures did influence their audience and perhaps to a greater degree of significance than the A picture which is so often discussed in this context. This influence may not have been as immediate or impressive as that of a blockbuster production but it was perhaps of greater depth, longer duration, and thus more substantive as a whole.

To substantiate this hypothesis, the first chapter is devoted to an overview of the history and economic structure of Republic for those unfamiliar with the subject. A more detailed survey of film scholarship as it pertains to Republic follows, while the third chapter develops the importance of various B genres as represented by this studio. The following chapters are devoted to a discussion of significant Republic serials, three representative Republic B Western series, three comedy series from the studio, and finally a brief coverage of non-series B movies from Republic. The last chapter summarizes the messages in the studio's films, their possible relationship to the appropriate eras in American history, and the studio's contributions to the movie industry.

Many Republic files proved to be unavailable though other sources were extensively utilized. Loans from collectors of pressbooks and other studio public relations materials were helpful. Some primary Republic sources existed in the New York Public Library, the American Film Institute in Los Angeles, the Margaret Herrick Library of the Academy of Motion Picture Arts and Sciences in Los Angeles, the University of California at Los Angeles Library, and the library at the University of Wyoming. Over two dozen interviews with Republic personnel and authorities conducted by the author proved invaluable. Also film viewings, taped film soundtracks, and scripts contributed to an understanding of the Republic product. Monographs, newspapers, and other published sources were of course consulted. Finally, fan publications, while not analytical, contained extremely valuable material such as interviews and filmographies.

Acknowledgments are in order but it is hard to know where to begin. Historians and popular culture scholars Professors Milton Plesur, Mel Tucker, and Michael Frisch of the State University of New York at Buffalo, and Frank Hoffmann of the State University College at Buffalo, were very helpful and provided perspective and objectivity. Republic personnel both in front of and behind the camera contributed much as will be seen. Fans and film scholars such as Don Miller, Francis Nevins, and Jack Mathis offered valuable suggestions and materials. The National Museum Act provided a grant which greatly eased the various research trips and purchase of materials. Finally, and most important, there were my wife Jolene and children Ruthann and Michael, who gave support throughout the whole process. All of these people and many others unmentioned have assisted me in trying to show that the Republic B film has an important place in the understanding of American history and culture. Where I have succeeded, they share in the contribution. Where I have fallen short, I, of course, accept responsibility.

Finally, I dedicate this book to Jolene, who has tolerated my interest in serials and B Westerns for nearly forty years. And to Nathan, Alissa, and Benjamin, for whom I have great hopes.

Notes

1. New York: Collier Books, 1971 and Northbrook, Illinois: Jack Mathis Advertising, 1975.

2. New York: Cambridge University Press, 1976.

3. "An Anthropologist Looks at the Movies," *Annals of the American Academy of Political and Social Science*, CCLIV (November, 1947), p. 80–87.

4. New York: The Free Press, 1950; reprinted. New York: Hafner Publishing Company, 1971.

5. Boston: Little, Brown and Company, 1976.

6. Boston: Beacon Press, 1972.

~

Introduction

When the subject of republishing my book on Republic Studios first came up, it seemed to me to be a good idea since I still get occasional inquiries and fan letters. But as I thought more about it, it also seemed like a golden opportunity. The original volume from Scarecrow Press was a verbatim reprint of my PhD dissertation at the State University of New York at Buffalo. In the process of creation, I had been required by my committee to remove and rewrite large portions of material, especially in the serial section, which the committee felt was unnecessary to a dissertation. They felt that once I had illustrated my point with a few examples, additional coverage was unnecessary and repetitive. While this was perhaps true, it made my section on serials incomplete. I felt that something should be said about each of Republic's sixty-six chapterplays. For the dissertation, the committee prevailed but in this new edition of the book, I have retrieved the original material and expanded the chapter on serials threefold, including an in-depth analysis of *Captain America*.

I have also added an epilogue in which I cover what has happened to the Republic archives and film collection over the last twenty-five-plus years. The creation of the Encore Westerns channel on cable has given B Western fans the opportunity to see a wide spectrum of Western movie history including a healthy cross section of the Republic products. Sometimes these are the television prints which have been cut to fit into an hour with commercials. Perhaps the worst example is Roy Rogers' *Bells of San Angelo* which was originally in color and ran seventy-eight minutes. The Westerns channel ran it in black and white at fifty-five minutes! Fortunately, it is available in its original format on DVD. This is an extreme exception as most of the Republic Westerns are shown in their original theatrical release format. And thanks to the voracious appetites of cable television, we do have access to much of the Republic B product today whereas when I was originally writing such was not the case.

We also should thank videotape and DVDs for giving us a clearer view of movie history. Now all Republic serials save one are readily available to the video viewer. Back in the early 1970s, there were only a handful available. To do my research, I had to rely on private collectors, serial and Western film groups, and even written summaries of films for my information. Now, this is no longer the case. Firsthand viewing is possible in most cases. For example, I have sixty-five of the sixty-six Republic serials in my own collection. Why, I even picked up a DVD set of thirty-six episodes of *Stories of the Century* (1954–55), Republic's Emmy-winning Western television series! It starred Jim Davis and was frequently directed by William Witney. It was quite interesting to see how they integrated stock footage from Republic theatrical Westerns in practically every episode. The point is that much of Republic's output is now available to the dedicated and patient video collector.

Moreover, since my period of research in various film collections, libraries, and film societies, many new books and periodicals on films have surfaced as would be expected. The bad news is that most have little to do with Republic specifically and the B product in general. Now, please pay attention if you are interested in the written word because I am not going to add these to the lengthy bibliography at the end of the book. Instead, I'm going to briefly cover those of significance in the next few paragraphs. This should be more useful than burying these more recent sources in the already lengthy bibliography.

First, and of great significance to anyone interested in Republic, Jack Mathis was able to publish three additional volumes in his massive study of Republic prior to his death. First came *Republic Confidential, Volume 2, The Players* (Barrington, Illinois: Jack Mathis Advertising, 1992), covering Republic actors. Second came *Valley of the Cliffhangers Supplement* (Barrington, Illinois: Jack Mathis Advertising, 1995), which provided additional information on the serials. Finally, he released *Republic Confidential, Volume 1, The Studio* (Barrington, Illinois: Jack Mathis Advertising, 1999), which covered the studio, its departments, and the behind the scenes personnel. All of these benefited from Jack's background in layout and advertising and were beautiful works. While Jack's approach avoided the analytical, factually he covered Republic in great depth. Because he had received some criticism, he postponed the last volume, but he was working on the final volume dealing with the films at the time of his death in 2006. The result, about two-thirds to three-quarters complete, was turned over to the archives at Brigham Young University in Utah. McFarland Press published *The Republic Pictures Checklist* by Len D. Martin in 1998 (reissued in paperback in 2006), which seemed to be based on the "Republic Production, Inc. Produced Properties" (a copy of which I have) manuscript in the Republic Archives also located at BYU. While not on a par with Mathis perfectionist standards and flair, it provides much of the information that Jack was assembling.

While not specific to Republic, Don Miller's fine *Hollywood Corral*, a comprehensive survey of the B Western, was reissued in 1993 by Riverwood Press in Burbank, California with sixteen supplemental Western essays edited by M. P. Smith and Ed Hulse. For the sake of completeness, I want to mention that Don Miller had a very good survey of the B movie including a section on Republic entitled simply *B Movies* (New York: Curtis Books, 1976). It is unfortunately out of print.

Continuing on the subject of Westerns, R. Philip Loy did a very nice study including the cultural effects of the B Western entitled *Westerns and American Culture 1930–1955* (Jefferson, North Carolina: McFarland, 2001). It was refreshing since most Western studies in the last twenty years have ignored the B Western. Boyd Magers and Michael G. Fitzgerald issued two collections of interviews entitled *Ladies of the Western* and *Western Women* (both McFarland, 1999) which, while not Republic specific, do include interesting related material.

Of course, both of Republic's Western stars, Autry and Rogers, have written autobiographies since the original research on this book (even though the publication dates are earlier). Autry's *Back in the Saddle Again* (New York: Doubleday, 1978) is a bit self-serving but includes much Republic material. Rogers' (and Dale Evans) bio is entitled *Happy Trails* and is a must for students and fans of Republic Westerns.

In the area of serials, only a few books have been published over the last quarter century. Roy Kinnard's *Fifty Years of Serial Thrills* (Metuchen, New Jersey: Scarecrow Press, 1983) is interesting and obviously includes Republic material but is condescending toward its subject matter for the most part. Not so are the two volumes by William C. Kline. *In the Nick of Time* and *Serially Speaking* (both McFarland, 1984 and 1994) are written by a true serial enthusiast. The first is a history of the subject and the second is a series of positive essays on various aspects of the serials. Also not to be missed is William Witney's (ace Republic serial director) *In a Door, Into a Fight, Out a Door, Into a Chase* (McFarland, 1996) in which he gives his take on his entire serial career. Too bad he didn't live to complete a second volume on the rest of his output. Ken Weiss has also republished his *To Be Continued* in a much improved two volume set (New Rochelle, New York: Loves Labor Press, 2000). Many of the mistakes in the original have been corrected in the new edition. Ken is to be congratulated. Bruce Bennett, Republic serial star, also was the subject of a biography, *Please Don't Call Me Tarzan* by Mike Chapman (Newton, Iowa: Culture House, 2001).

Finally, a few loose ends having importance to Republic's history. Yakima Canutt's autobiography *Stunt Man* (New York: Walker Publishing, 1979) is an integral part of the Republic story since so much of Yak's development took place at Republic. Chuck Roberson's *The Fall Guy: 30 Years as the Dukes Double* (North Vancouver, B.C., Canada: Hancock House, 1980) also covers much behind the scenes activity at Republic. Clayton Moore's autobiography *I Was That Masked Man* (Dallas, Texas: Taylor Publishing, 1996) covered his career as the Lone Ranger but also includes much material on his Republic Westerns and serials. *The Heroine or the Horse* is a rather strange book on Republic's leading ladies by Thomas Burnett. Boyd Magers, Bob Nareau, and Bobby Copeland recently published *Best of the Badmen* (Madison, North Carolina: Empire Publishing, 2005), biographies of 315 Western badmen, many of whom enriched Republic's Bs, Westerns, and serials. Boyd Magers also publishes the only current serial periodical (*Serial Report*, Albuquerque, New Mexico). While there have been several others in the past, they are now defunct (see Bibliography). In passing I might mention Tom Weaver's *Poverty Row Horrors!* (McFarland, 1993), which covers Republic's few horror films, an area which I pretty much overlooked.

If I have overlooked any important material relating to Republic, please feel free to correct and enlighten me through the publisher. Nothing that has been published in the last quarter century relating to Republic has in any way changed my basic hypothesis: Republic made the most effective B films, Westerns, and serials which, although not perhaps so intended, had a positive effect on at least two generations of American youth and rural audiences.

~

CHAPTER ONE

The Rise and Fall of Republic: A Historical Overview

The year 1935 was not an auspicious time to begin a new company and certainly not a film studio. Despite an initial optimism brought on by the New Deal, the country remained in the throes of the economic turmoils of the Depression, a situation that persisted until the sound of military drums in Europe brought economic recovery. Moreover, in contrast to popular legend, the film world did not glide through the 1930s on fat profits from the tickets purchased by millions of entertainment-starved citizens.[1] True, attendance was good but the film industry was affected by the competition of radio and other factors. The big, established movie companies weathered the era, made excellent films for an appreciative audience, solidified their gains, stabilized their business and artistic techniques and laid the foundations for the great profitable and successful days of the early to mid-1940s—at least from the movie makers' point of view. But the Depression era was not so kind to smaller, shoestring, independent film concerns. Many fell by the wayside.

In spite of this, or perhaps partially because of it, in 1935 Herbert J. Yates founded Republic Pictures. Yates, once an executive in the American Tobacco Company, entered the motion picture business in 1915 when he became associated with Hedwig Laboratories, a film processing concern. In 1918, Yates financed Republic Laboratories and in 1924 consolidated several processing plants and crystallized his holdings into Consolidated Film Laboratories, a complete film laboratory service.[2] In 1927, Nat Levine had founded Mascot Pictures and launched a long career with the serial production, *The Golden Stallion*,[3] a ten episode serial with stuntman Joe Bonomo that proved to be a satisfactory entry in the serial genre. From the beginning, Levine's company was financed predominantly by Yates' Consolidated Film Laboratories. During the next eight years, Nat Levine's Mascot Pictures built a reputation for producing competent action pictures and serials.

In 1935, Yates approached Levine with the offer of a consolidation. Yates wished to expand Mascot's ailing feature film and Western program, while retaining its serial production schedule, which led the industry in the genre. Thus, in 1935, the two joined W. Ray Johnston and Trem Carr, both of Monogram Pictures, and other independents to form the new Republic Pictures Corporation. The new company made its headquarters at the old Mack Sennett Studios on Ventura Boulevard at Colfax and Radford Avenue in North Hollywood, which Mascot had leased periodically. By using Levine's production experience and Monogram's exchanges in thirty-nine cities, the new corporation felt that it could dominate production outside of the major companies market.

The pressbooks for the 1935–1936 season were a confusing combination of logos—what with final releases from the combining companies and "new" releases from the parent company—with Republic and Monogram predominating. However, an overview of the situation showed that the cast of Republic's direction was already formed. Twenty-two films, predominantly mysteries such as *The Spanish Cape Mystery*, melodramas such as *The Return of Jimmy Valentine*, and adventure pictures like *The Leathernecks Have Landed*, headed the list. These were followed by "8 John Wayne Greater Westerns," "8 Gene Autry Musical Westerns," "5 Action Dramas," and "4 Republic-Mascot 1936–1937 Serials."[4]

One of the first moves in the campaign to capture the action market was to expand a series of top quality Westerns for which there was a ready audience. John Wayne, under contract to the studio, was put into a proposed series of eight Westerns beginning with a relatively expensive film entitled *Westward Ho*. This was the most costly picture for Wayne since his starring debut in *The Big Trail* (Fox, 1930) and cost nearly $18,000. Some sources credit the film with grossing over $500,000 although this is a much-inflated estimate.[5] On the basis of this and other successes, Republic was now a power with which to reckon.

However, everything did not go completely smoothly. In less than two years, *Variety* headlined, "Carr, Johnston Leaving Outfit."[6] So in less than a year W. Ray Johnston and Trem Carr withdrew from the company feeling that Monogram had gained little in the consolidation. Johnston later reorganized Monogram. Carr's position as Republic's production chief was taken over by Nat Levine. In their first year, Republic grosses were over two and a half million dollars. Flush with the new company's success, Levine was quoted as saying that Republic was spending $6,750,000 on twenty Westerns, twenty-four features, four serials, and eight "special" productions.[7]

But it was Yates who was the guiding force behind Republic from the beginning—both financially and in terms of artistic emphasis and economic patterns. Although Yates and Republic periodically attempted to break free of the B picture mold, they were never really successful and remained first and foremost a B studio—the best perhaps, but nonetheless subject to the fortunes of the B picture.

The B movie was definitely a creation of the Law of Economics. Although the economic organization of the studio is not the major concern of this study, a brief summary of the economics of the B film and of Republic's approach is therefore necessary for the sake of completeness.

Beginning in 1935 and continuing into the early 1940s, the American moviegoing public came to expect the double bill, although small towns would frequently show single films, both A and B. Also, prior to the epochal Supreme Court Decision of 1949, *United States vs. Paramount Pictures, Inc.*, the major studios owned their own theatre chains and knew that they had a guaranteed audience for their products. Now, that monopoly was ended but previously, regardless of the cost and merit of the picture, it had a guaranteed booking. These two factors contributed to the rise of the B film.

The major studios, however, were committed to the A production and, while each maintained a B unit well into the 1940s until rising costs caused them to play down this aspect of production, they preferred to stay with the high quality film which brought in most of the profits because of guaranteed distribution and percentage contracts. But the audience wanted that second feature. B pictures were therefore produced to fill the bill inexpensively and for a fixed rental rate. The profits, while not spectacular, were predictable provided the costs were kept down. The majors were not geared to filling this very real need so the lesser studios led by Republic stepped in to fill the gap. Most of these studios relied on State's Rights distribution wherein film packages, often in blocks of six or eight, were provided to a wholesale distributor who handled them exclusively in a region frequently made up of one or more states. However, Republic and Monogram were large enough to set up exchanges similar to the majors in large cities.[8]

It should never be forgotten that Republic, as well as every motion picture producer, was governed first and foremost by the profit imperative. Time after time, the following chapters will refer to the ideas which Republic films represented. But it must be realized that Republic was not really concerned about ideas in its films. Republic was concerned not about influencing its audience, youthful or mature, simple or sophisticated. Rather the studio was concerned with making an exciting, entertaining, and therefore, it hoped, profitable product for a certain type of theatre and audience, which product would meet with the approval of the Motion Picture Association of America and various religious and local censors. Since Republic's chief market was in the Midwest, the South, and the Southwest, this resulted in the local censors being a bit more demanding and thus made Republic's "message" more conservative and traditional.

The point is that the conscious attempt of Republic to reinforce traditional values can be traced to the simple fact that it was profitable for them and they were in the business of providing good action pictures inexpensively and dependably.[9] Most academic and popular writers have recognized the potency of the profit imperative, but do not give it the emphasis which the industry feels it deserved. For example, Robert Sklar notes it in reference to silent films but, if anything, it increased in the Depression era. "Of the feature films exhibited in such picture palaces, and at every other movie theater large or small throughout the country, no more than a tiny number were produced without the expectation or at least the strong hope of reaping a profit. This made the movies unique among the arts."[10] Sklar also points out that the creators in other fields such as literature, dance, and theatre were often dedicated and willing to break even or accept some losses. Critics used to this approach attacked movies for their lack of aesthetics not understanding their basic commercialism.

Because of this frequent blind spot on the part of critics and scholars, and because of the importance of economics to Republic, it must be emphasized that the studio understood its foundations from the beginning. First, its founder and guiding genius was above all money-oriented. "Yates . . . was interested in a healthy balance sheet. The fact that his studio was considered the horse opera center of the film industry did not matter in the least. He was neither proud of it nor embarrassed by it. He was first and foremost a businessman."[11]

Perhaps the most telling example of Republic's dedication to the profit motive can be seen in a special merchandising section in the *Hollywood Daily Reporter* published separately and devoted to the studio in 1938. Under the headline, "The Stability of Republic Pictures," it is stated, "The people behind Republic have been identified with the financing of motion picture production for nearly twenty years."[12]

> The principle behind Republic is as financially sound as the dollar received from the exhibitor. Just as long as it supplies the exhibitor demand, so long will

be the health of its success . . . Quality Without Waste . . . so long will black ink dominate the red on its ledger.

In fact, there is little about Republic Pictures that is not built upon a cold "business" basis. The barometer of its bank balance is truly the boxoffice.[13]

While disclaiming any ambition to make major epics, the studio argued that it made good pictures but kept the exhibitor's cost in mind. "It is simply a formula whereby every picture must measure up to the Republic standard of consistency . . . the highest point of excellence in production quality, made within a budget cost that will permit the most reasonable of rentals when it reaches the exhibitor."[14]

Of course, Republic expected sound business practices to pay off for the studio as well as the exhibitor. The *Hollywood Reporter* agreed and offered the opinion that, since Republic films had shown steady improvement in the studio's first two years, Republic was likely to become an industry leader within five to ten years.[15] Republic personnel were chosen for their business acumen as well as their artistic sense, the write-up claimed. The technical facilities were described—they were superior from the beginning because of the Consolidated Laboratories and the Sennett Studios—and a typical production scene was included ending with the admonition, "It is all a part of the scheme of things at Republic. Economy—to the nth degree—but without waste. . . . A lost hour, Republic officials know, means many lost dollars. All of which would blast the business slogan and the very basic premise of Republic Pictures."[16] Stressing quality with economy, Republic quickly became the leading B studio.

In order to realize and maintain these heavily emphasized economies, the studio utilized efficient and often clever means to save money. Republic relied heavily and very professionally on such devices as expert use of stock footage (action sequences of merit good enough for multiple reuse), inexpensive character actors and actors on the way up or down, re-releases, strict budgets and shooting schedules, and no-nonsense writing and directing. However, the income factor remained dependent upon flat rentals, and, as production costs rose during World War II and after, profit margins declined. Yates therefore early created four categories of productions to hopefully maximize profits: 1) Jubilee pictures were basically Westerns with a seven day schedule and $30,000 budget (later $50,000). Two per month were normal. 2) Anniversary pictures were Westerns, action/adventure, and musicals with a two-week schedule and budgets up to $120,000 (later $200,000). 3) Deluxe pictures dealt with varied subjects with twenty-two day schedules and $300,000 (later $500,000) budgets. They were frequently directed by house director Joseph Kane. 4) Premiere pictures were directed by top names such as John Ford and Fritz Lang with shooting schedules of approximately a month and million-dollar budgets.[17] Films in the latter category were Republic's premiere productions, meant to compete with the major studios in the A market, and to build Republic into a major studio without surrendering their lead in the profitable but limited B area. Some later well-known examples include: Ben Hecht's *Specter of the Rose* (1946), Frank Borzage's *Moonrise* (1948), Edward Ludwig's *Wake of the Red Witch* (1949), Orson Welles' *Macbeth* (1950), Fritz Lang's *House by the River* (1950), Allan Dwan's *Sands of Iwo Jima* (1950), John Ford's *The Quiet Man* (1952), and Nicholas Ray's *Johnny Guitar* (1954). All of these men were well known creative people who also worked at major studios during their careers and several have even become cult figures in the 1970s.

While it was sometimes claimed that Yates did not understand these films[18] or was not allowed to control them,[19] he backed them because he was hoping to break into the A production percentage rental market while remaining active in the B categories. But the Bs continued as the back-bone of the company, economically as well as artistically and philosophically. The Jubilee and Anniversary categories were consistent and grossed approximately $500,000 each into the 1950s while the latter two categories were variable or sustained losses. Despite Yates' public statements to the contrary,[20] the economic imperative began to catch up with Republic in the 1950s. Audience tastes changed and attendance shrank. Television proved especially competitive to the B market. Production costs drove profits down. Republic also had legal difficulties with the Screen Actors Guild concerning residuals on films released to television, which resulted in a boycott. The expense of the Premiere productions proved a critical monetary drain that was greater than the return either in prestige or profits. In other words, Republic could not compete with the majors in the final analysis. This, and the other factors, broke the studio economically. The following table from *Kings of the Bs* summarizes the economic story of Republic:[21]

In the 1930s Republic's net profit stabilized in the $500,000 to $1,000,000 range. In the 1940s the gross profits increased but, due primarily to economic factors, the net returns actually decreased. Backlog sales to television helped keep up and even increase profits in the early 1950s, but by 1956 Republic was in the red and dying as a film producer.

With the economic organization and the pervasive influence of the profit imperative at Republic Pictures firmly established, it is necessary to describe briefly the studio's early period, its most creative time, and examine the type

Table 1.1.   Republic Pictures, Inc., Financial Data for
Year Ending October 3

Year	Gross Revenues	Net Profit/(Loss)
1958	$33,464,482	$(1,487,337)
1957	37,899,826	(1,362,420)
1956	42,236,206	758,401
1955	39,621,099	919,034
1954	37,962,359	804,202
1953	37,265,035	679,217
1952	33,085,511	759,604
1951	33,409,613	646,404
1950	30,310,748	760,574
1949	28,086,597	486,579
1948	27,072,636	(349,990)
1947	29,581,911	570,200
1946	24,315,593	1,097,940
1945	10,016,142	572,040
1944	11,137,125	561,719
1943	9,465,338	578,339
1942	6,700,358	504,351
1941	6,256,335	513,451
1940	7,235,335	590,031

of product Republic provided and the niche it occupied so well in the late 1930s and into the late 1940s.

Technically Republic quickly proved to be top rated even in its early years. Consolidated Film Laboratories ranked as the best sound laboratory in Hollywood and, together with Radio Corporation of America sound recordings, gave the Republic films a polish that other independent productions lacked.[22] The quality of the Republic product soon came to fill a void between that produced by the major studios and the variable products of the independents.[23] Camera work at Republic was considered to be exceptional. The best camera trucks, good composition, rapid panning techniques, and the use of numerous studio dolly shots all gave Republic productions a feeling of movement that was not found in most of the films of the major studios. In the musical department Republic scored to the hilt. Most of the other companies, even among the majors, let long dramatic and action scenes run without music in the 1930s, but Republic filled most of their pictures including the serials with a nearly complete musical sound score.[24] This attention to detail paid off in a quality product. Republic combined no-nonsense straightforward direction, professional camera work, and skilled editing with these good musical scores to produce a highly competent, attractive set of films.

Republic technicians were considered to be of the highest caliber. Action directors such as Mack V. Wright, Ray Taylor, Joseph Kane, William Witney, and John English all turned out top-rated films for Republic in the late 1930s and early 1940s. In the early 1940s, Lew Landers, R. G. "Bud" Springsteen, and Spencer Gordon Bennet among others joined the Republic directorial ranks. Top stuntmen such as Yakima Canutt, David Sharpe, Tom Steele, and Dale Van Sickel were invaluable given Republic's emphasis, as were special effects geniuses Howard and Ted Lydecker and their able assistants. Cameramen such as Jack Marta, Bud Thackery, John Alton, and William Bradford contributed a great deal which often went unnoticed outside the profession. And the musical scores, already mentioned, were handled by men such as Stanley Wilson, Victor Young, William Lava, Paul Sawtell, Cy Feuer, and Mort Glickman. Finally, credit should be given to staff writers such as Ronald Davidson, Barry Shipman, and Sloan Nibley to mention only a few.[25]

Republic embarked upon an extensive program of Westerns, serials, and second features, or program pictures as they were called. Oddly enough, aside from the serial field where they excelled, Republic never entered the area of movie shorts with any enthusiasm. As film writer Leonard Maltin says:

> Most of the B picture factories had little regard for short subjects, although judging from the speed with which they made feature films, they probably could have turned out a two-reeler in an hour. Republic did have the short-lived "Meet the Stars" series in the early 1940's, but aside from this and occasional one-shots, Republic, Monogram, and their peers steered clear of short subjects.[26]

But in the area of B action features, Westerns, country musicals, and serials Republic found a place. Since most products of both independent and major studios in these areas of programming were lacking in quality, Republic's well planned specialization created a firm and respectable niche for the studio. Whereas the products of the independent producers of this period were often cheap and crude and the films of the major studios which were made to reach the "lower levels" frequently missed the mark, the Republic product found a ready market both among the exhibitors and the audiences, especially among the secondary theaters in large cities throughout the country and in general theaters in smaller cities throughout the Midwest and South.

Moreover, Republic's market was all the more firmly established by the fact that the studio consciously played to the middle America audience. They found their audience not only with the type of material they produced but also with the themes they emphasized. And, as shall be seen in the following chapters, this was to be the importance of the Republic product. They hit a chord. Michael Wood recognizes the significance of this factor for audiences when he says the public can be "extraordinarily resistant both to rubbish and to masterpieces, when they fail to strike the right chord. It is worth recalling . . . the essential structure of the industry in its great days; settled financiers on the East Coast were investing in uprooted adventurers on the West Coast because of their supposed expertise on the subject of what the Middle West really wanted. The movies . . . dreamed up an America all on their own, and persuaded us to share the dream. We shared it happily, because the dream was true in its fashion—true to a variety of American desires. . . ."[27] The dreams had to strike a chord and the Midwest was generally where it—the audience and therefore the chord—was to be found.

This point was especially applicable to Republic. The studio's films were often not reviewed by large city papers at all and when they were, their appeal to non-urban interests were frequently emphasized and not always positively. For example, Don "Red" Barry was a leading star of Republic Westerns in the 1940s who, while appearing in an occasional A film, was basically a cowboy hero with his audience in the Midwest and South. A contemporary New York reviewer of a Barry Western noted this fact with a negative twist when he stated in his review of *The Sombrero Kid* (1942):

"The Sombrero Kid," doubled at the New York Theatre, is a Don "Red" Barry item in which Don does his usual act. He, you know, is the cow chap who frequently has to pretend to be an outlaw himself, thus consorting with the villains, in order to turn them over to justice at the end. He does it here, too, with his usual skill of fist and gun. The picture makes one point, another familiar of the Westerns, which is worth pursuing for an inch or two. The prime or master villain behind the scenes is the town banker. This happens too often in Westerns to be mere coincidence. There is some ground for the belief that the makers of Westerns, operating upon stringent budgets, have deep in their subconscious minds a resentment of people who control money. They take it out in their libelous portraits of that great fraternity of moneylenders, the bankers.

Now, although Westerns in a big city draw their audiences from among the children and like-minded adults, back where the grass grows long the general populace is entranced by them. And since many a Washington legislator hails from these same sticks, the influence of the Westerns on banking legislation in the United States is probably greater than you have ever suspected.

> This is only a thought inspired by "The Sombrero Kid." These Westerns do leave a lot of extra time for thoughts, don't they?[28]

Although these comments are delivered somewhat tongue-in-cheek and with an obvious air of superiority, the big city newspaper was in effect acknowledging Republic's domain.

Action became a class item at Republic and, with its audience and profit ratio firmly in mind, the studio continued to grow throughout the early years. In April 1939, the *New York Herald Tribune* proclaimed: "Republic Pictures Plans 50 Features in Season: Four Serial Films to Complete 1939–'40 Output."[29] Later that year *Variety* stated "30 Writers Working at Repub, New High."[30] And the next year the *New York Times* heralded "62 Feature Films Listed by Republic: Studio's Schedule for 1940–41 Includes 'Deluxe' Releases, Westerns, and 4 Serials."[31] For the next season, the *New York Morning Telegraph* noted, "Republic Sets Biggest Slate: To Spend $15,000,000 During Season for Features, Westerns, Serials."[32] In February 1942 Yates announced plans to spend $2,500,000 to add land and new buildings to the complex.[33] And so it continued throughout the war years and into the late 1940s.

Yet another indication of Republic's success was its decision to join the Hays Office in September 1941. The Hays Office, or Motion Picture Producers and Distributors of America, was the official censorship arm of the industry and membership therein gave a stamp of legitimacy.

In part, the *Times* said:

In the Big Time

Unless blackballed by some class-conscious studio, Republic will become a member of the Hays organization during the coming week. When the independent concern began to show an awesome profit the rushing by the Hays sorority began; on Monday the ten members will pledge Republic. While it is officially gratifying to be deemed worthy of the honor, the elevation provokes a certain distress in the hearts of the studio staff.

Membership implies a dignity they don't like. Republic is one of the few remaining members of the school that operates on the Stern Brothers' theory that "a tree's a tree and a rock's a rock; shoot it in Griffith Park."

Now they will not be able to charge persecution on the part of the Hays group. In the past the publicity department had delighted in dropping bits of information showing how they were being tortured. . . . But the press agents are philosophical about it; they say they might as well be Hays members if they are forbidden, anyway, from carrying on the noble tradition of the elemental life.[34]

As was pointed out in discussing the profit imperative, the fact that Republic had a straightforward no-nonsense entertainment oriented philosophy is one of the points that is crucial in analyzing its influence on its audience.

Republic achieved early success with its serial production program and with series Westerns beginning with the John Wayne, Bob Steele, and Gene Autry series, as well as the group oriented Three Mesquiteers movies, and carrying on with a multitude of similar series into the early 1950s. After the first few years of providing quality action program pictures, Yates decided to actively expand Republic in the direction of large budget major features. Two early examples of this type of production were *Man of Conquest* (1939) with Richard Dix and *Dark Command* (1940) with John Wayne. Republic had hoped for major status from the very beginning but it took a few years to lay the firm foundation of pre-eminence in the B market.

In its very first year the following lead-in to a report on the company appeared in the *New York World Telegraph*:

Film Partners in Quick Rise
*Republic Pictures Corp. Enters "Major" Field
with Capital of $2,000,000*

With many of the so-called "independent" motion picture companies increasing and improving their product so that they are rapidly taking their place in the "major" field—*vide* Columbia Pictures, which started out as an independent producing concern—it is interesting to trace the rise of the Republic Pictures Corp. . . .[35]

In the following year, the *New York Times* reported, "Republic Pictures is aspiring to bigger and better things" and hopes "within the next year, to enter the ranks of the majors."[36]

In mid-1938, Republic seemed to make its first big move. In the New York press, the event merited feature coverage with some depth:

The first problem of the producer . . . is to find some way to take the gamble out of picture making. Perhaps the best formula has not been found, but Herbert J. Yates, founder of the three-year-old Republic Pictures Corp., does seem to have hit upon a thoroughly feasible plan. At any rate, it has worked, and worked well, for Republic.

Concentrated on Westerns

Three years ago, when Republic made its debut in the industry, the company announced a complete program of varied photoplays, feature pictures, Western dramas, and serials. The program was completed on schedule and was generally well accepted, but actually Republic concentrated its greatest efforts upon its Western drama. . . .

Start on Serials

With his first goal reached, Yates turned to new fields in the company's second year. Continuing the policy that made Republic dominant in the Western field, Yates planned to bring his organization to similar eminence among producers of serials. . . .

Now, Republic has declared itself in the fight for leadership among producers of features. "Army Girl" . . . is Republic's most pretentious feature production and is offered as a herald to the company's coming bid for popular acclaim in this new field.[37]

Frankly, *Army Girl* misfired as an attempted A picture but it proved to be a B feature of merit and featured some outstanding stunt work.[38] Moreover, the tenor of the publicity campaign as engineered by Republic represented in the foregoing article did show that the studio was expanding its horizons beyond its beginning borders.

Man of Conquest, a highly fictionalized action oriented account of the life of Sam Houston, was Republic's first real A, and special attention was provided by Rose Pelswick in the *New York Journal American*: "A million dollars is a tidy sum, even in Hollywood, and it's perfectly natural therefore that Republic Pictures should be Pointing With Pride to its first million dollar [the actual cost was somewhat more than half this public relations figure] production—'Man of Conquest.'" She pointed out that in its four year existence Republic had built a reputation for serials, Westerns, and action melodramas, inexpensively but efficiently produced. She claimed that in the process the studio had been the salvation of many small theaters. "But while most of its films are neither intended for nor reach the 'A' theaters, this unpretentious product means a good deal to thousands of small exhibitors throughout the country. Many a mortgage has been saved for a small town operator." Pelswick concluded that Republic was expanding but appreciated its already established market:

As a matter of fact, the company has no intention of departing from its present distribution. It is proud of its reputation as the "King of Serials" and the good will it enjoys. Only by this time Republic figured it was time to step out, to produce a couple of million dollar items and widen its distribution to gain *class as well as mass response.* [Emphasis added.][39]

Actually, as Pelswick implied, Yates had already determined to straddle the fence. He and the Republic organization wanted the status and respectability of A productions but he realized that Republic's foundation lay in producing good Bs. Previously *Variety* had stated, "Yates Wants Better B's from Republic,"[40] and the *New York World Telegraph* reported Yates' prediction that "Republic Will Turn Out Escape Films."[41] In this very telling article Yates gave in its basic form the essential philosophy on which the Republic success story (and eventual demise) was based. He stated, "The kind of entertainment that we, at least, will stick to will veer away from heavy dramatics or pictures of war. They will have to provide an escape . . ., and until new things develop the company will stand pat on its present plans."

Yates conveniently overlooked Republic's commitment to one service serial per year and its various patriotic and preparedness films which were frequently war pictures. However, "its present plans included continuing A productions on a limited basis," Yates concluded. In another interview, Yates elaborated on his policy as well as his problems concerning A films:

> And about twice a year . . . we will come forth with our big-scale contributions. . . .
>
> [I]t's especially difficult for an independent studio to cast important films because the "name" players, for some reason or other—even if we pay them top salary and our money is as good as anybody else's—feel as though they're lowering themselves by working for us. Once they get going, however, they change their viewpoint.
>
> Many a fine actor has gotten his real break through working in independent pictures. At Republic, we don't attempt to develop personalities. We'd rather farm out our promising players to other companies and let them do the experimenting. Take John Wayne, for instance. He's in our Westerns—which are cleaning up doubly because we loaned him to Wanger for "Stagecoach."[42]

Republic's own house organ, *The Republic Reporter*, reflected Yates' ambivalence. During this same period, it noted "Republic's Rise in Industry," ran newspaper quotes on Republic as a major studio, proudly emphasized Republic's competition with other film companies for advertising space, and trumpeted both *Man of Conquest* as a major production according to famed Hollywood columnist Louella Parsons, and headlined *Dark Command*, a fictional treatment of Quantrill's Raiders as an A picture. At the same time, the company periodically pushed its serial production values, stressed Gene Autry's popularity, openly acknowledged the importance of Republic Westerns to the studio, and pointed out the family entertainment values of the B ranked Higgins Family series.[43] Republic, quite reasonably, wanted the best of both A and B worlds.

In retrospect, Yates' decision to stay with Republic's strong areas at this point and venture only occasionally into A productions seemed wise. *Man of Conquest* was a good beginning but a flawed one. Released in 1939, it was Republic's first serious attempt at the A movie and press releases from their house organ reflect this. Nonetheless, *Man of Conquest* retained a kinship with Republic's major line of productions. The music was good but reminiscent of countless action films released and to be released by Republic. The action sequences were spectacular but strangely enough seemed to lack the personal involvement, frenzy, and spontaneity of the B Westerns and serials. The cast with Richard Dix, Gail Patrick, and Joan Fontaine, along with several non-studio character actors was adequate, but even here Republic stock players such as George "Gabby" Hayes and Max Terhune plus many bits by people like Ernie Adams, the small "weasel" of countless B films, were in evidence.

And the plot, despite any pretensions, boiled down to action/adventure melodrama with even more patriotism and honor than in the B Westerns thrown in if anything. About three-fourths of the way through, Andrew Jackson is confronting Sam Houston who is on his way to take over Texas; Jackson delivers a no-holds-barred speech about his relation to the United States, Houston's relation to Jackson, and Houston's relation to the United States which, although a bit longer and more pretentiously written, matches any morality speech given in lesser Republic productions.

Later, the film includes a bit of unconscious male chauvinism. Margaret, Houston's love interest, complains soulfully that Houston is riding off to battle and she wishes she could do the same to which Houston romantically replies that if she did so, he would not be able to ride back to her!

Perhaps Otis Ferguson, noted film critic for *The New Republic*, best summed up both the failure and significance of *Man of Conquest*:

> Its story of Sam Houston and the grabbing off of Texas is perhaps less prettied up than is true of the run of screen epics, but its importance to the trade is that it was made by one of the "small" companies. Republic is, of course, getting larger, but there is always the dazzling hope that someday some outfit too small to tremble with such mighty fears as shake Metro will take on a subject that is not good movie taste, and do it up brown. *Man of Conquest* is done brown enough—it scandalizes history with the best of them.[44]

The film was recognized for its attempt to break into the majors but possessed the same "flaws" of the majors' productions without really being unique. And like the majors, Republic and Yates had the same "fears"—or perhaps beliefs—that the majors had. Republic could not have handled the story of Houston any differently. It was flag waving and patriotism to the hilt as were Republic productions on all levels. That was a major part of Republic's style.

Thus, Republic in its first time out really failed to break free of the strictures of the product at which it did best. *Man of Conquest*, for all its merits and its high budget, remained essentially in all aspects a good, expensive B production.

And the same held true for a great many Republic A productions through the years. John Wayne felt that Republic could not deliver a true major production.[45] Sloan Nibley, a writer at Republic, offered the following opinion to the author: "Republic was never considered a 'major' lot although they did make three As, *Wake of the Red Witch*, *Sands of Iwo Jima*, and *The Quiet Man* (which was entirely the product of John Ford and the writer Frank Nugent). . . . What Republic did better than anyone else was good, fast action shows for a price."[46] While the statement is a bit harsh, perhaps it has an element of truth. Republic-controlled As usually lacked the class of As produced by others and released by the studio.

Throughout the life of Republic Pictures until a final lingering illness in the late 1950s Herbert J. Yates ruled the studio with an iron hand.[47] To his credit, the fact remains that his studio was a success for nearly two decades within the parameters of its endeavors.[48] Nat Levine, the serial genius, left within eighteen months of the merger to go to Metro Goldwyn Mayer Studios and thence into relative obscurity.[49] However, it is Levine who established the serial format which helped make Republic the important action studio that it was and for that contribution he retains credit. Neither Carr nor Johnston had any lasting effect on either the Republic philosophy or production techniques and emphases, although the Monogram exchanges undoubtedly helped establish Republic distribution.

Perhaps the best way to gauge the progress, success, and hopes of Republic is to look briefly at the rather magnificent and somewhat overpowering Tenth Anniversary brochure the studio published on itself in 1945.[50] This was the year before the motion picture industry as a whole hit its zenith in attendance and perhaps popularity. Like the entire industry, Republic was buoyant and full of high hopes. The sixty-four page booklet covered the whole spectrum of movie production, promotion, and distribution but obviously emphasized the "stars." Republic listed eighty-nine, running the gamut from John Wayne and Susan Hayward to character actors such as Tom London, sheriff, grandpa, or badman in over four hundred movies, and Edward Everett Horton, bewildered comedian of sophisticated farces. Republic candidly recognized the fact that their list of "stars" included contract players and lesser lights and stated under the heading "Read Your Fortune in the Stars":

> A box office name is a name that attracts people to your theatre or a name that adds to the value of a production or a name that grows greater with each new appearance. In the eighty-odd pictures on the following pages, you will find some in each group. A few have pulling power on their own, such as John Wayne, Roy Rogers, Gene Autry, Ann Dvorak, Constance Moore, Vera Hruba Ralston, Joseph Schildkraut, Tito Guizar, names which go above the title . . . real marquee names now. Then there are the featured players, the addition of whose names to any billing adds selling value to the picture. And finally the young players, the shooting stars of tomorrow. In the past Republic discovered many young players only to lose them to bigger studios. Today in our 10th Anniversary Year Republic is a "bigger" studio in its own right . . . and today Republic will discover new stars . . . and hold them for Republic pictures.[51]

The company recognized the importance of its foreign markets—serials and Westerns were very popular overseas and in South America where the action easily surmounted the language barriers—and pointed out, "Europe . . . Asia . . . South America . . . Pan-America . . . the Middle East . . . everywhere Republic's 10th Anniversary is a big event. . . . Hundreds of picture-wise people in every department, all bound together by the common language of the American motion picture in general and Republic pictures in particular, enthusiastically face a future of brightest promise."[52]

In the area of product, the copy acknowledged the studio's past successful year in the area of general releases. "Last year, Republic Pictures turned out sixty-six full length feature pictures, including such honeys as 'Brazil,' 'Earl Carroll Vanities,' 'Flame of Barbary Coast' and others.

Most of the scenes . . . indoor and outdoor . . . musical and dramatic . . . costume or western . . . were shot on these 135 acres . . . every costume and property passed through Republic's shops and property rooms."[53] But they quickly zeroed in on the two areas for which the studio was best known.

The first was of course the serials:

> But wait . . . we almost forgot the boys and girls who add so much bounce and zest to your theatre program . . . those action-mad menaces, those thrill-tingling tanglers, those cliff-jumping, daredevil, death-defying deemsters who make the hair stand on end and the hero get the gal . . . the serial makers. To be specific, the Republic serial makers. The lads and lassies who put serials back on the "come-hither" map when they went into the lush comic strip field and came up with "The Lone Ranger" and "Captain Marvel" and "Dick Tracy" of hallowed ticket-selling fame.[54]

Oddly enough, Republic had made its last serial using a comic hero, *Captain America*, the year before. But the writers had no way of foreseeing that Republic was to forsake comic characters and turn its serials to other areas for sources so they pointed with pride to an accepted successful development.

The second area of strength was obviously the Westerns:

> And you and your box offices know that it is Republic which dominates the western field. With Gene Autry, we started westerns back on the high road to fame and fortune. Now with Roy Rogers at the top of his stride, with Wild Bill Elliott, Allan Lane, Sunset Carson, "Gabby" Hayes, Bob Nolan and The Sons of the Pioneers, and others, we mean to keep them that way . . . one small but very profitable part of Mr. Herbert Yates' 10th Anniversary Plan to put Republic at the top of the heap in 1945.[55]

The anniversary booklet concluded hopefully and forcefully:

> Watch Republic. Watch its list of big directors grow. Watch its list of star box office names grow. Watch its list of top-flight pictures grow. For we're headin' for the top spot in the motion picture industry in 1945.[56]

Ironically, while Republic specifically and Hollywood in general had every right to expect an expanding and prosperous future, events were to take them in the opposite direction within another decade. The next few years did seem to justify their optimism. But forces were in motion which would affect the whole moving picture field and Republic was not destined to be an exception. Some production cutbacks in the late 1940s were only a slight indication of what was to come in the 1950s. Although adverse factors were to change the entire motion picture industry, Republic, which was a borderline case, was one of the first to feel the tremors which were eventually to prove fatal.[57]

In the 1950s, Republic suffered a series of setbacks, which eventually led to its demise as a producing unit. One fact was undeniably the emergence of Vera Hruba Ralston (later Vera Ralston). Herbert Yates attempted to make Ralston, who became his wife, into a leading star. While she was not as poor an actress as some critics felt she was, she simply did not have star caliber and the attempt to push her pictures upon the exhibitors gradually discredited Republic to some degree.[58] One author summarized the situation: "From 1941 to 1958, a Miss Vera Hruba Ralston, the wife and perennial protégée of Republic's President, Herbert Yates, made twenty-six indescribably inane pictures, all for Republic, a feat of conjugal devotion (on her husband's part) romantically credited with dispatching Republic into

receivership."[59] Ralston also influenced Yates to back at least one class production per year, such as Orson Welles' *Macbeth* and John Ford's *The Quiet
Man.*[60] These prestige productions were not always financially successful.
Ralston herself admits that, "We [she and Yates] attempted to upgrade . . .
to do better things . . . but it didn't always work out."[61]

It all began in 1941 when the *New York Morning Telegraph* began a story,
"Figure Skating Bug Hits Republic Head."[62] Ironically enough, the tenor of
the article was that Yates was interested in making ice pictures after seeing
the "Ice Capades" starring a Dorothy Lewis. While "Vera Hruba" was mentioned, she was not the main thrust of the article and her future position of
influence was unforeseen. However, she was a Czech refugee and ice-skating
star who became the favorite of Yates[63] and he set out to make her a star. By
1946, the *New York Post's* Screen News and Views identified her as, "It's Vera
Ralston Now—Republic's Queen Takes 'Rib'"[64] in reference to the dropping
of her Czech last name which she had been using as a middle name. The
same article cited her as "Queen of Republic Pictures. She's the high-budget
gal, and the big box-office bambina." Ralston's favorite director was Joseph
Kane. "He is so gentle and so understanding—and I don't react well to tem-
peramental people—directors, players, or anybody else." By 1953, when she
had become Yates' wife, columnist Louella Parsons queried her, "Has being
married to the owner of Republic Studios made any difference in your career?" She replied, "No, I don't think so . . . I've always worked hard because
I knew I had a lot to learn."[65]

Unfortunately, Republic stockholders felt differently and in 1956, the
New York Times noted, "Investors Sue Yates: Charge He Used Film Company
Funds for Wife's Career."[66] The *Herald Tribune* was even more specific and
stated, "Allege 18 Vera Ralston Films Flopped."[67] At this point she had appeared in twenty films. The *Daily News* chose to headline the odds, "Suit
Calls Film Tycoon's Wife 9-1 Floperoo."[68] Ralston was to go on to make six
more pictures through 1958 when another suit was instituted charging that
Yates operated Republic "as though it were a private family-owned business."[69] This he had done from the beginning although during the years of
profit, it was accepted. These lawsuits were symptomatic of the problems Republic faced. While Ralston's lack of box-office appeal did contribute to the
situation, it was only a part of the setbacks that beset the studio.

It is true that many actors resented working with Ralston and that super-
star-to-be John Wayne even then had the clout to refuse additional pictures
with her. This oft repeated charge was commented on by Maurice Zolotow,
Wayne's biographer: "Determined to make his movie about the Alamo,
Wayne was beset by problems with Yates. Already Yates was looking for ways

to make his dearly beloved, Vera Hruba Ralston, a co-star of this epic. Wayne rebelled at making pictures with Vera Ralston. She had made twelve pictures for Republic since 1945, and only two showed a profit, the ones with Wayne."[70] Ralston did not appear in *The Alamo*, made later and away from Republic. But she did appear in the Wayne produced *The Fighting Kentuckian*, which hastened the break between Wayne and Republic. Wayne is quoted as saying, "Yates made me use Vera Hruba. . . . I don't want to malign her. She didn't have the experience. She didn't have the right accent. . . . Yates made me cast her. It hurt the picture. . . . I've always been mad at Yates about this because we lost the chance to have one damn fine movie. . . . Yates was one of the smartest businessmen I ever met. I respected him in many ways, and he liked me. But when it came to the woman he loved—his business brains just went flyin' out the window."[71] It was the last picture Ralston made with John Wayne.

Nonetheless, Ralston was not the sole downfall of Republic. She herself feels that she was the victim of poor material.[72] Perhaps the last word on the Ralston controversy belongs to director Joseph Kane who helmed nine of her twenty-six pictures:

> She was very nice to work with. She was in the same sort of position with Yates as Marion Davies was with William Randolph Hearst. So, if she'd been that sort of person, she could have made it rough for everybody. Naturally, when you're in that kind of position with the boss, you can do anything you want. She never took advantage of that situation. She was always very cooperative, worked very hard, tried very hard.
>
> But, you know, the public is a very funny thing. The public either accepts you or it doesn't, and there's nothing you can do about it. If they don't go for you, well, that's it.[73]

Another factor in Republic's demise was the competition of television. Republic had the knowledge, the facilities, and the technical ability to make good competitive television series. In fact the company won an Emmy for its *Stories of the Century* television series.[74] This was one of the few television series that the studio attempted. Utilizing years of exciting stock footage, the series offered Western action in a pseudo-historical setting with different famous desperadoes meeting justice each week. Nonetheless, Republic really failed to meet the competition of television. The popularity of *Stories of the Century* proved to be an exception and, after a few less successful series, Republic used its television arm as a means of releasing old movies to television. When the studio did not develop an active television production unit in its own right to any appreciable degree, other television units took over Republic's specialty.

Complicating the problem was the fact that Republic also sold its extensive library of old films to television in the 1950s.

Yates early realized the potential advantages of selling Republic movies to television. He used the Hollywood Television Service (Republic's television division) not only to make series for the medium but also to handle the leasing of Republic's old product, which was a natural for the youthful industry. However, difficulties quickly arose. In October 1951, Roy Rogers sued to ban the showing of his old features on television for commercial purposes arguing that it implied product endorsement and therefore damaged his professional name. The courts found in his favor. But then in May 1952, the courts decided against Gene Autry in a similar suit thus throwing the whole controversy into a state of total confusion.[75]

However, Republic went ahead with plans to make its product available to television and late in 1952, *Variety* reported, "200 G Rep Deal Releasing 104 Pix for TV Seen Breaking Log Jam," but noted that the Autry-Rogers films were still questionable.[76] (It was not until 1960 that the complete package was made available.)[77] But, in making this move, Republic was one of the first large, active studios to make a deal with television.

Three years later, Republic went the rest of the way. In a story entitled, "Republic to Rent Top Films to TV: Studio to Offer 76 Features, Valued at $40,000,000—Plans No Outright Sale," it was pointed out that, "the studio has made some 300 of its old "B" products and low-budget Westerns available to TV in the past."[78] Ironically, four months later the same source included a story, "Republic Starts Cutback in Staff."[79] This undoubtedly contributed to the next development.

In January 1958, the Screen Actors Guild and the Writers Guild of America threatened to strike Republic over the question of residual payments to post 1948 films released to television.[80] The next month the writers did vote to strike and Republic was eventually forced to give way on the issue of residuals.[81]

The decision to provide their old films to television proved a misjudgment on Republic's part in yet even another way in retrospect. This sale represented one of the first such major packages to be sold to television. Unfortunately, this move tended to discredit Republic in the motion picture exchanges so that their theatrical productions did not get proper circulation.[82] Another competitive factor was that the major studios, noting the success of Republic over the years, finally began to compete with that studio on the same ground in making low budget action films utilizing the techniques, the lessons, and sometimes even the personnel of Republic.[83] The majors were always better able to circulate their now competitive product in the theatrical markets than Republic, especially given Republic's mishandling of the television issue.[84]

The final factor in Republic's collapse is more difficult to document but perhaps ultimately it was the greatest factor of all. Scholar Francis Nevins hits on it briefly. "My conversations with Bill Witney and Dave Sharpe, my reading of such reminiscences as those of Joseph Kane, and my general *gestalt* of what was going on at Republic have led me to conclude that what killed Republic was not competition from the majors; it was Herbert Yates' obsession with sinking all his profits from the action picture into super-productions starring Vera Ralston, combined with the fact that the rise of TV *ended the traditional Saturday matineegoing habits of America's children* combined with post-WWII inflation and union demands [emphasis added]."[85]

Besides providing a nice summary, Nevins also voices an additional important point. Republic was tops at escapist fare—Westerns, serials, series, and country Western musicals—and this was what the audience thrived on in the Depression 1930s and the war years of the 1940s. By the 1950s middle American values prevailed, luxuries were more abundant, and the audience preferred harsh realism and downbeat excitement in their movies. Interest in the old escapist fare was relegated predominantly to television. The Saturday Matinee died.

Republic just did not adapt. The need for change in B film subject matter to meet audience demands was covered by Joe Solomon, active B and exploitation film producer of the 1970s, in an interview in *Kings of the Bs*.[86] To survive, the B film producer anticipated or quickly followed the latest audience fads in what had become a market with accelerating changes in popularity, Solomon felt. With a few exceptions, Republic tried to continue to provide the same quality, but outmoded, entertainment to an audience who had either outgrown it in the 1950s or absorbed it for free on their home television. By way of illustration, Ed Bernds, who directed Bs for Columbia, Allied Artists, and American International during his long career, and who has provided valuable contrasting viewpoints said that he and other Columbia directors referred to Republic "as the home of entrenched mediocrity" and felt that "Yates made the Republic personnel so conservative that they didn't adapt" thus leading to the failure of Republic. Bernds felt that Yates was very loyal but stifled initiative in his staff.[87]

Needless to say, Republic workers interpreted the situation somewhat differently. Albert S. Rogell, Republic director and leading cameraman/second feature director from the 1920s to the 1950s, felt that Yates' tight budgets caused his people to be very imaginative and to create good films under adverse conditions and rigid deadlines.[88] Others voiced variations on the opinion that

Republic was resourceful in its day but acknowledged that Republic played it-self out in the early 1950s. Perhaps Sloan Nibley, Republic writer after World War II, best capsulized it when he said that "Republic had the right formula at the right time . . . it was an unconscious success . . . Republic had it at the right time but didn't even know it."[89] When the times changed, Republic did not change the formula—at least not enough. Perhaps the studio was too busy try-ing to cope with other more concrete problems it faced in the 1950s. Perhaps it just lacked imaginative leadership.

The decline was of course a gradual process, and there were continuing hopeful signs but it was just so much whistling in the wind. The following headlines from the *New York Times* are indicative of Republic's prolonged "last Hurrah":

Republic Is Adding Four Sound Stages
Republic to Offer Independents Aid
Republic Studios Continue to Grow
Republic Raises Production List
Republic Studios to Resume Work
Republic Studios Expanding Plant.[90]

Production was suspended several times in the mid-1950s and periodically announced as resuming thereafter but finally ceased in 1956. Republic had produced and released approximately fifty to sixty pictures a year in its prime but only twenty-six in 1957, seventeen in 1958, and five in 1959. Most of these were produced elsewhere.

Herbert J. Yates authored a column in 1953 in which he summarized Re-public's position and his plans for the future. In view of Republic's increasing difficulty concerning the competition for distribution and exhibitors, as stated above (p. 20), the article takes on an added interest.

> There is no one person who has all the answers to the problems which must be faced in 1953; but, at least from Republic's viewpoint, I have formulated a def-inite program for our business platform.
>
> Republic for the past two years has streamlined its production organization. We have economized in our studio costs, but not at the expense of entertain-ment values appearing on the screen. In fact, our cost-per-picture-produced is higher than ever, because of increased production magnitude, best casts, and the public demand for pictures in color. We will make at least 20 deluxe pic-tures for the new season, at costs ranging from $750,000 to $1,500,000. Our production budget will be triple the amount that Republic has ever spent on any season's product.

From our experience with pictures like "The Quiet Man," we know that few pictures gross what is regarded as abnormal business. However, the average deluxe picture, costing up to $1,000,000, has a hard time recouping its negative cost. A few super-grossing deluxe pix can't keep the producers in business, nor can they sustain the large number of 'A' theatres that depend upon this type of product.

Thus, the problem represents a triple responsibility for producer, distributor, and exhibitor. If the producer makes marketable 'A' pictures that the public will buy, and the distributor merchandises the picture in such a way as to arouse audience interest, it still remains for the exhibitor—the most important link in the Hollywood to the public chain—to bring people into the theatre by solid promotion which takes advantage of intrinsic audience value and national preselling.

The production of a program of 'A' pictures is the gamble that Republic is taking in 1953, and it is the gamble that every other producer in Hollywood will have to take. How many pictures will be produced in 1954 and how many theatres will continue to operate will depend on what returns the producer and the theatre will receive on the majority of 'A' pictures produced for 'A' houses in 1953. We are selecting our stories not only for their entertainment but for exploitation values as well.

Competition from television will increase. In areas that have television, more stations will be added. In many cities that have not had television competition in 1952, there will be stations in 1953. But I believe Republic's large investment in 1953 is justified and reasonable business risk. If I weren't, I wouldn't be in the picture business.[91]

His assessment of the condition of the motion picture industry was accurate for the time. His projection of Republic's future was not.

In late 1957, Republic resigned from the Motion Picture Association and the Motion Picture Export Association. *Variety* noted, "Republic bowout is said to be based on economical considerations since the company is folding its overseas setup and plans to retain only a few territorial operations."[92] Considering the popularity of its product in the foreign market, this move was especially indicative of what was developing. In February 1958, it was rumored Republic was going to close its remaining domestic branches and it was pointed out that it had "virtually dissolved its distribution organization" and had lost $1,362,420 in 1957.

At the annual stockholders meeting in 1958,[93] Yates announced, "We have one problem—getting out of the motion-picture business." One anguished stockholder inquired, "What happened to your vision, Mr. Yates?"[94] But Yates, who was tired and ill, no longer had the interest or the vision.[95] He had lost his enthusiasm for filmmaking and with his exit the producing end of the business ceased.

On July 1, 1959, Yates relinquished control of Republic to Victor M. Carter, California banker and real estate operator. For all practical purposes Republic was declared dead as a motion picture studio. An article in *Variety* headlined, "Fading, Fading—One-Man Rule, Yates' Republic Exit Latest Instance," and indicated that Carter and his associates paid Yates and his family "slightly under $6,000,000."[96] The Carter administration decided not to continue to make new films for theatres or television. The Consolidated Film Industries would be operated as in its beginning. It would be a processing and releasing organization, and the studio would be made available for television and theatrical production rentals from other firms. The studio's first major rental was Dick Powell's Four Star International, Inc., a major television producer.

With new administrative operations in effect, the company was once more on solid ground. Old films were made available for television and theatrical releases. But the Carter regime was not committed to film. The conglomerate had other priorities as indicated by the following headline from *Variety*: "Plastics the Charmer in Bettered Earnings Picture for Republic."[97] Under those circumstances, it comes as no surprise that on May 4, 1963, it was reported "C. B. S. Gets 10-Year Lease on Coast Republic Studio."[98] The property valued at close to ten million dollars had been taken over by the Columbia Broadcasting System with a ten year lease and an option to buy after that time, which was exercised in February 1967.[99] The studio, now known as Studio Center, is presently the West Coast production headquarters for the C.B.S. television network. Republic still exists on paper but the past glories of the studio are no more except in ever increasing revivals. National Telefilm Associates, the legal owner, repository, and distributor of most Republic films and related material, reports that not only are Republic packages for television in demand, but Republic pictures are also continually circulating in foreign theatres throughout the World.[100] (See Epilogue for changes over the last twenty-five years.) Interestingly enough, after the deal with the Columbia Broadcasting System was concluded it was generally confirmed and acknowledged within the industry that the technical facilities of Republic Studios were still far superior in all respects even to those of the major studios.[101]

Opinions on Republic seem to vary and frequently reach extremes. Those who are critical give Republic and Yates no credit. Fans tend to be overzealous, nostalgic, and defensive. Walter Abel, well known character actor and Paramount contract player active in movies in the 1930s and 1940s, was a professional of wide experience and some objectivity. He did a two-week B feature, *Who Killed Aunt Maggie?*, at Republic in 1940. As an outsider without an axe to grind or special interest in the studio his opinion represents a reliable middle ground. Abel contended that Yates did not regard himself or his studio as inferior in the Hollywood system, noting that he did not keep a stable of name actors but produced his own kind of pictures and had his own small distribution setup. Abel regarded Republic as "better than poverty row" and Yates as "a small scale Harry Cohn . . . [however] he was considerate of actors but he had to work like hell." Abel did not resent his stint at Republic and indicated, "It was just another job." The picture was "a great hit in the South," and "a damned good little mystery . . . but would have been great at another studio." Abel also credits Yates for urging him to accept the Paramount contract offer.[102] His characterization of Yates and Republic sums both up well—a successful Hollywood executive whose studio made a quality product within limits which was aimed at a specific audience to make a profit with no further pretensions.

Notes

1. Robert Sklar, *Movie Made America: A Social History of American Movies* (New York: Random House, 1975), p. 162.

2. *1956 International Motion Picture Almanac* (New York: Quigley Publishing Company, 1956), pp. 446–447.

3. Gene Fernett, *Next Time Drive Off the Cliff* (Cocoa, Florida: Cinememories Publishing Company, 1968), p. 143.

4. *Republic 1935–36 Attractions Now Available!* (Los Angeles, California: Republic Pictures, 1935).

5. Sam Sherman, "Hollywood Thrill Factory, Part I," *Screen Thrills Illustrated I* (January, 1963), p. 28. Allen Eyles, *John Wayne and the Movies* (Cranbury, New Jersey: A. S. Barnes, 1976), p. 45 lists the cost as $37,000 but agrees with Sherman on its profitability and significance to the Wayne series.

6. December 18, 1936.

7. *New York Suns*, May 4, 1936.

8. The birth of the B picture is covered in depth in *King of the Bs: Working Within the Hollywood System: An Anthology of Film History and Criticism* edited by Todd McCarthy and Charles Flynn (New York: E. P. Dutton and Company, Inc., 1975), pp. 13–32.

9. Republic personnel consistently played down the artistic aspects of their films preferring to emphasize that they did their best to provide entertainment for profit. Of the twenty-four persons interviewed only one played down the profit motivation but she acknowledged its existence. Telephone interview with Vera H. Ralston, Republic actress, Santa Barbara, California, May 10, 1976.

10. Sklar, pp. 86–87.

11. Roman Freulich and Joan Abramson, *Forty Years in Hollywood: Portraits of a Golden Age* (Cranbury, New Jersey: A. S. Barnes, 1971), p. 114.

12. "Republic Pictures Studio," *The Hollywood Reporter*, 1938, p. 5. Extensive correspondence with the newspaper failed to uncover the actual date of publication although the supplement is clearly identified as a product of *The Hollywood Reporter*. The supplement was located in the Republic clipping file at the Margaret Herrick Library of the Academy of Motion Picture Arts and Sciences.

13. "Republic Pictures Studio," p. 5.

14. "Republic Pictures Studio," p. 5.

15. "Republic Pictures Studio," p. 17.

16. "Republic Pictures Studio," p. 21.

17. Sample budgets in each category are reproduced in McCarthy and Flynn, pp. 26–29.

18. McCarthy and Flynn, p. 30.

19. Letter from Sloan Nibley, Republic writer, January 19, 1976.

20. See the Yates authored article, pp. 26–27, *supra*.

21. Source: *Motion Picture Almanac, 1949–1959* cited in McCarthy and Flynn, p. 32.

22. Sherman, "Part II," p. 28. Morris R. Abrams, while admitting the technical excellence, has an interesting viewpoint. He feels that the quality of Republic's Bs was strictly an economic factor. The studio developed technical sophistication because speed was needed to compete in the low budget field. Thus a need to "keep jobs" caused the studio to improve techniques to best the competition and incidentally led to a quality product which resulted in a "brand identification"—that is, Republic's Bs stood out. (Interview with Morris R. Abrams, Republic script supervisor and assistant director, Los Angeles, California, May 17, 1976.)

23. "Republic Pictures Studio," p. 25. "Republic fits that unique niche of being a coordinating, producing company rather than a competitive one." In other words, Republic took up the slack and filled a need ignored by the majors.

24. Don Daynard, "The Film Music of Stanley Wilson," *The New Captain George's Whizzbang*, no. 17 (n.d.), p. 5.

25. Most of these men were craftsmen who remained active in their fields following the demise of Republic. Most moved into television and some remained active at the time the book was originally written. The latter include William Witney, David Sharpe, Bud Thackery, Barry Shipman, and Sloan Nibley. A few such as Yakima Canutt, Victor Young, and Cy Feuer achieved fame in their areas of expertise beyond Republic.

26. Leonard Maltin, *The Great Movie Shorts* (New York: Crown, 1972), p. 27. Although essentially accurate in spirit, Maltin's statement does overlook a brief series of world travelogues from Republic entitled *This World of Ours* (32 entries, 1950–1955), a similar series of United States travelogues entitled *Land of Opportunity* (four entries, 1950), and other diverse short subjects. Republic's total for short subjects has been listed as 78 and few more have been discovered in recent years.

27. Michael Wood, *America in the Movies, or Santa Maria, It Had Slipped My Mind* (New York: Basic Books, 1975), p. 23.

28. *New York Post*, September 30, 1942.

29. April 6, 1939.

30. August 16, 1939.

31. May 30, 1940.

32. March 4, 1941.

33. *New York Times*, February 18, 1942.

34. September 7, 1941.

35. April 7, 1935.

36. August 30, 1936.

37. *New York Herald Telegraph*, July 13, 1938.

38. Bob Thomas, "Hollywood's General of the Armies," *True* XXX (July, 1966), p. 87.

39. April 23, 1939.

40. February 22, 1939.

41. September 9, 1939.

42. *New York Post*, May 2, 1939. Compare this statement as it concerns contract players with the Republic philosophy on the same subject six years later (see p. 16).

43. *The Republic Reporter* I (April 25, 1939), p. 1. I (May 16, 1939), p. 3. I (August 19, 1939), p. 4. I (September 6, 1939), p. 4. I (January 9, 1940), p. 1. I (June 28, 1939), p. 2. I (August 4, 1939), p. 2. I (September 18, 1939), p. 5.

44. Robert Wilson, ed., *The Film Criticism of Otis Ferguson* (Philadelphia, Pennsylvania: Temple University Press, 1971), p. 259.

45. Maurice Zolotow, *Shooting Star: A Biography of John Wayne* (New York: Simon and Schuster, 1974), p. 154.

46. Letter, January 19, 1976. Republic did make other A films of course. Vera H. Ralston claims that Yates did have input into the scripts for all major Republic productions. (Telephone interview, Santa Barbara, California, May 19, 1976.) In the case of *The Quiet Man*, however, Ford did retain more control than normally allowed at Republic.

47. *Variety*, July 8, 1959.

48. Sam Sherman, "Hollywood Thrill Factory, Part 2," *Screen Thrills Illustrated*, I (October 1, 1963), p. 13.

49. Fernett, p. 137.

50. *10 Years of Progress: Republic Pictures Corporation 10th Anniversary, 1935–1945* (Los Angeles: Republic Pictures Corporation, [1945]), unpaged.

51. *10 Years*, [p. 24].

52. *10 Years*, [p. 39].

53. *10 Years*, [p. 49].

54. *10 Years*, [p. 51].

55. *10 Years*, [p. 51].

56. *10 Years*, [p. 51].

57. These events, which are covered to some extent in the text, are covered more in detail in "Exit (As Expected of Republic From MPEA [Motion Picture Export Association] First in O'Seas Body's History," *Variety*, December 11, 1957 and "Fading, Fading—One-Man Rule: Yates; Republic Exit Latest Instance," *Variety*, July 8, 1959. A copy of a short history of the studio prepared as a five-page manuscript in 1963 for publicity use in studio rental and leasing was provided to the author by Ernest Kirkpatrick of National Telefilm Associates and previously in Republic's business division. In covering the studio's switch from active production to rental to outside producers, the document refers to the early decline of Republic as a movie producer. *History of Republic Pictures*, p. 3. Mr. Kirkpatrick did not know who wrote the manuscript.

58. Harry Sanford, "Joseph Kane: A Director's Story, Part 1 and Part 2," *Views and Reviews*, V (September, 1973), pp. 21–28, and V (December, 1973), pp. 17–25.

59. McCarthy and Flynn, pp. 50–51.

60. Interview with Anthony Slide, then of the American Film Institute, January 18, 1975.

61. Telephone interview with Vera H. Ralston, Santa Barbara, California, May 10, 1976.

62. June 14, 1941.

63. Diane Scott, "Memory Wears Carnations," *Photoplay* LXXII (May, 1949), pp. 34–35.

64. June 4, 1946.

65. *New York Journal American*, February 8, 1953.

66. October 30, 1956.

67. October 30, 1956.

68. October 30, 1956.

69. *New York Post*, August 20, 1958.

70. Zolotow, p. 251.

71. Zolotow, p. 252.

72. Telephone interview with Vera H. Ralston, Santa Barbara, California, May 10, 1976. She said in part, "I was satisfied with Republic as a studio but not satisfied with the material. I had no decent chance. The material didn't fit me. . . . Yes, the writing was not good but I was under contract and [had to] do what was required."

73. McCarthy and Flynn, p. 322.

74. Sherman, "Part 2," p. 15.

75. *New York Times*, May 15, 1952. The *Times* headlined, "TV-Movie Tie-ins Remain Confused." On June 9, 1954, the *Wall Street Journal* noted, "Republic Pictures Upheld in Autry, Rogers Suits."

76. December 17, 1952.

77. *Variety*, October 12, 1960.

78. *New York Times*, January 13, 1956.

79. *New York Times*, May 23, 1956.

80. *New York Times*, January 22, 1958.

81. *Variety*, February 19, 1958.

82. Sherman, "Part 2," p. 16. Also *Variety*, June 13, 1951. In an article entitled "Myers, Renbusch Blast Rep on Plan for Selling to TV," Abram F. Myers, Chairman of Allied State Association, is quoted as saying, "No doubt, exhibitors will be very bitter toward Republic." Truman Renbusch, president of the exhibitor organization, expressed similar opinions calling Republic's move "foolish."

83. It has been already noted that Republic personnel often went to major studios upon leaving Republic. However, some Republic personnel worked major studios simultaneously with their work at Republic. Mark Hall interview with David Sharpe, Republic stuntman, August, 1976. American Film Institute Oral History Program, American Film Institute, Los Angeles, California.

84. Interview with Anthony Slide, then of the American Film Institute, January 18, 1975. See also footnote 82.

85. Letter, January 20, 1976.

86. McCarthy and Flynn, p. 144.

87. Interview with Ed Bernds, B film director, Los Angeles, California, May 6, 1976.

88. Interview with Albert S. Rogell, Republic director, Los Angeles, California, May 5, 1976.

89. Interview with Sloan Nibley, Republic writer, Los Angeles, California, May 4, 1976.

90. June 16, 1953; September 11, 1953; August 7, 1954; February 3, 1955; January 8, 1957; June 14, 1957.

91. "Top Cost Pix Shed," *Variety*, January 7, 1953.

92. December 1, 1957.

93. *Variety*, February 12, 1958.

94. *Time Magazine*, LXXXIX (April 14, 1958), p. 56.

95. Interview with Albert S. Rogell, Republic director, Los Angeles, California, May 5, 1976; Roland "Dick" Hills, Republic office manager, Los Angeles, California, May 13, 1976; and Morris R. Abrams, Republic script supervisor and assistant director, Los Angeles, California, May 17, 1976. All indicated that Yates was ill, that his attitude changed in the last years of Republic, and that this was a major factor in the studio's failure to adapt.

96. July 8, 1959.

97. October 12, 1960.

98. *New York Times*.

99. *New York Times*, February 24, 1967.

100. Interviews with Rex Waggoner, National Telefilm Associates, Publicity Director, and Ernest Kirkpatrick, National Telefilm Associates, Technical Services, May 12, 1976. Also, *Variety*, July 17, 1974.

101. Sherman, "Part 2," p. 16.

102. Interview with Walter Abel by Milton Plesur, Professor of History, State University of New York at Buffalo, New York, New York, March 1, 1976.

CHAPTER TWO

~

Film Studies and Republic

The predominant theme of the following chapters is basically that the movies during their period of greatest strength were not interested in art or influence but in profits, that quality productions nonetheless did have a very basic impact on the audiences, and that the B films, which were routine programmers inexpensively produced, by the very fact of being unpretentious and extensively viewed especially in the rural and urban neighborhood areas, did carry more effectiveness in reaching the audience with straightforward messages than has been previously acknowledged or credited to them.

This hypothesis relies on primary material relative to Republic Pictures, perhaps the best of the B studios, and on film writing in both scholarly and fan publications. With this in mind, a survey of these works as they relate to the theme to be presented will be helpful. The goals, methods, and capsulization of the conclusion will be outlined in conjunction with a survey of previous studies.

First, there are the popular or fan treatments which tend to emphasize some combination of nostalgia, reminiscences specifically on Republic Pictures, B movie recollections, or anecdotes on serials and Westerns. These are normally non-academic, enjoyable, sometimes quite factual and informative but completely unpretentious and should be used guardedly due to varying standards. The second category is scholarly works which stress the place of the movies in history, the influence of the cinema, and which tend to emphasize the A picture or occasionally the "sleeper" B—a "sleeper" B being a routine inexpensive program filler which due to critics and unrecognized quality is elevated to the position of a classic film after release. While some film scholarship strains for significance, several academic works do reach conclusions, which can be applied to the B film in general.

Small as the Republic Pictures Studio was and limited as its product emphasis chose to be, there is enough of interest in the Republic story to fill a multivolume series dealing with the history, production techniques, limitations, personnel, and goals of this leading smaller studio. This study is aimed at explaining the audience influence and the industry significance of Republic as represented in the studio's most successful products. To accomplish this goal, appropriate ideas from both fan and scholarly publications have been combined with information from the files of Republic as well as contemporary observations.

Rapid movement became the key to Republic's success. Despite scripting deficiencies, the headlong pace and exemplary action sequences were soon realized as the crowd pleasers, and the sort of thing the Republic crews accomplished best. Nor was it a small accomplishment. Action sequences are tough, time-consuming to stage, and were usually not fully appreciated by audiences for their worth. A film without lags, even an action film, is a rarity; pacing is one of the hardest aspects of film making to overcome. Credit or blame is shared by writer, director, cutter, and producer. And to their credit, Republic pictures began early to move, and fast.[1]

Republic had moved up fast to become contenders. Their more elaborate films were good and solid. But the studio subsisted on the bread-and-butter movies, and after the attempt at versatility in the beginning, turned inexorably toward the action, mystery, adventure type of mass-audience budget job, sure to please the paying customers if not the critics. None of them were world-beaters, and more than a few would have been better off buried in quicklime in the dark recesses of some back lot. However their average was good and the pictures accomplished what they set out to do.[2]

These two quotes perhaps best summarize the mystique of Republic Pictures Corporation both for the fans of action films and students of the B cinema. There has been a series of volumes, both amateur fan publications and commercial professional treatments, which pertain at least peripherally to B films, action pictures, or Republic. And Republic was synonymous with B films and action pictures. Yet none of these really captures the flavor of Republic productions, which gave them their significance. The preceding statements neatly capsulize the essence of Republic, but the work from which they were taken is an overview of the B film with only two chapters devoted to the studio in question and the author does not attempt to delve into the potential significance and influence of the best of the B studios.[3]

Alan G. Barbour, an ex-businessman turned fan and commercial publisher of film material, has for many years been attentive to Republic.[4] But his works are basically photographs, ads, pressbooks, and other studio releases flavored with brief, nostalgia-laden, introductory texts which, while they occasionally turn a good phrase or hit lightly on an important point, are not meant to be scholarly cinema studies—nor has he ever claimed otherwise. They do have the merit of preserving intact and making available valuable studio material.

Gene Fernett has written two episodic studies relating to the B films. The first, entitled *Next Time Drive Off the Cliff*,[5] was on Mascot Studios, an immediate predecessor of Republic responsible for the studio's serial emphasis, and contained some interesting information concerning Republic's pre-history. The second, called *Hollywood's Poverty Row*,[6] was made up of individual chapters on various studios who located at least temporarily along the famous, or to the elite studios infamous, Gower Gulch—so named because independent producers of Westerns located often on Gower Street in Hollywood. Here again, the section on Republic contains a few informative statements. However, Fernett's books lack depth and consistency and must be used cautiously.

Several publications have been completely devoted to serials—often with emphasis on Republic serials. The journals and books range from good to poor but all are intended to be popular and are aimed at the fan market. Robert Malcomson, a fan publisher, put out twenty-nine chapters of *Those Enduring Matinee Idols*,[7] totaling well over four hundred pages. Although *TEMI* was a "fanzine," it was well done and published a great deal of value including the transcripts of interviews with and panel discussions involving Republic personnel. However, with only a few significant exceptions, *TEMI* was not analytical or interpretative.[8] The same can be said of Jeff Walton's *Serial World*.[9] It was a newer fanzine and lacked the polish or even depth of *TEMI*. It did, however, include valuable information and interviews. Boyd Magers still publishes *Serial Report* in Albuquerque, New Mexico.

Kalton C. Lahue has published two books on silent serials which refer only occasionally to Republic.[10] Jim Harmon and Donald F. Glut wrote *The Great Serial Heroes*[11] and, while the book is an undocumented popular treatment aimed at the general audience, it makes some telling criticisms of individual Republic productions. The same cannot be said of Ken Weiss' and

Ed Goodgold's volume, *To Be Continued. . . .* This is an encyclopedia approach, summarizing all 231 sound serials, which unfortunately is riddled with errors and poor editing.[12] There is no interpretative coverage save a short introduction. (Ken did republish this volume with corrections and new material in two volumes in 2005. It was a vast improvement.) The sole book dealing with sound serials which lays any claim to the scholarly approach, is Raymond William Stedman's *The Serials: Suspense and Drama by Installments.*[13] Stedman covers not only movie serials, both silent and sound, but also radio and television serials. While having scholarly pretensions, the work is a surface treatment and ends up more popular than academic. It still has some merit for light reading purposes and as a very general overview.

In many respects, the most interesting book in the area of Republic serials is Jack Mathis' *Valley of the Cliffhangers.*[14] Privately published, this book is massive, oversized, and expensive ($66.00). In 2005 copies were valued at $1200. It is sumptuously laid out—Mathis was in the advertising profession—and includes an abundance of information on Republic serials. Mathis interviewed numerous Republic people, did extensive research in primary sources, and developed a detailed chronological coverage of Republic serials. Mathis had access to the Republic business files and extensive references are made to them. The major drawback to the Mathis study is his inclusion of excessive detail on minor points in the serials and too much emphasis on source materials such as historical incidents, novels, and comics, rather than the serials themselves. Still, his volume provides a wealth of primary references and he and his collaborators have salvaged important data before they were destroyed by time, neglect, and disinterest on the part of their owners. The work is objective, documentary, and apparently aimed at the hard-core fan as opposed to subjective, interpretative, and scholarly. He includes nothing on the influence or significance of the Republic serials except by inference. Mathis later gathered materials for an objective history of Republic entitled *Republic Confidential.* These were published in two volumes, *The Studio, Volume One* and *The Players, Volume Two* in 1999 and 1992 respectively. (Jack published them in reverse order.) Jack told the author that these volumes had little on the significance of the Republic product—and were not interpretative.[15] They were a magnificent contribution to Republic scholarship nonetheless. A third volume on the films of Republic was almost complete at the time of Jack's death, but this has not been published.

There are of course innumerable books devoted to the Westerns but none exclusively to Republic. A series of B Western filmographies which frequently relates to Republic Westerns has been edited by Les Adams and is entitled *Yesterday's Saturdays,*[16] but these are basically documentation without any analysis. The various volumes devoted to the Western in general either ignore Republic save for an infrequent A production or acknowledge the studio's superiority in brief chapters devoted to the B Western. Most tend to go no further than to mention the Gene Autry-Roy Rogers musical Western series, often in a critical way. Don Miller's *Hollywood Corral*, mentioned above (p. 32) is one exception. William K. Everson, a film scholar equally at home with popular treatments, is another outstanding exception in clearly singling out Republic for its production values.[17] Everson's acknowledgment of Republic stems from his willingness to accept the importance of the serial and the B film to the general history of cinema development especially in Hollywood. Other writers on the Hollywood Western prefer to emphasize the art of the A production. These general treatments on the Western film are included in the bibliography and where appropriate in the text but will not be individually covered in this introduction since their importance to this study is peripheral at best.

There are also many articles relating to various Republic series, actors, directors, or other personnel in such diverse periodicals as *Views and Reviews*, *Screen Facts*, *Captain George's Whizzbang*, *Film Collector's Registry*, *Film Fan Monthly*, and even *Playboy* to mention only a few. These are invariably popular pieces and with the exception of an occasional article by a fan, fail to consider the importance of the studio or even to pinpoint its uniqueness in the B film field.

Even the frequently praised anthology of interviews, essays, and filmographies compiled by Todd McCarthy and Charles Flynn[18] fails to do justice to either Republic or the value of its output. While there are several references to and acknowledgments of the general superiority of Republic, this anthology was aimed more at defining, explaining, and analyzing the philosophies of B films and recording the opinions of B film personnel. There are some perceptive statements concerning the importance of the Bs in McCarthy and Flynn which will be utilized in the present study but essentially the drift of their book is broad, and as such, it does not really focus on Republic satisfactorily.

The influence of the motion picture industry as a whole and the artistic and sociological interpretation of various aspects of the Hollywood film have been frequently treated from the academic viewpoint increasingly in the last decade although some of the better studies came earlier. None of these studies, early or recent, has concentrated on Republic or any phase of the B film. In fact, they have made no more than passing mention of Republic or its type of product in most instances. Nonetheless, they have provided points of discussion relating to the Bs and Republic just as have the popular treatments discussed above.

Disregarding for the moment most of the psychological interpretations of the movies (these are more appropriate to Chapter 3), one of the earlier academic studies which related heavily to film falls more into the common sense school of thought and is quite sympathetic in tone to the general themes which are to be developed. Robert Warshow's *The Immediate Experience*[19] makes much of the point that when the critic places psychological, sociological, or other intellectual interpretations between himself and the film, he is missing the impact. Lionel Trilling aptly summarizes this most important point in introducing Warshow's posthumous book in pointing out that "Warshow speaks . . . of those critics who deal seriously with film either in the aesthetic way or in the sociological and psychological way and who, by one intellectual means or another, forbid themselves 'the immediate experience of seeing and responding to the movies as most of us see and respond to them.' . . . He meant, of course, that the man watches the movie with some degree of involvement and pleasure in it. . . . And of himself as the man who watches the movie, Warshow says that in some way he takes 'all that nonsense' seriously."[20] A man involves himself in the fantasy of the movie and not in an analysis of it. As shall be seen, a great many film historians and critics fall prey to this analytical approach which Warshow criticizes and it undoubtedly has contributed to a near universal blindspot among film scholars regarding the strictly entertainment oriented B picture as epitomized by Republic.

Warshow himself zeros in on the dispute between "fans" and "intellectuals" in discussing the primacy of the "immediate experience":

> This is the actual, immediate experience of seeing and responding to the movies as most of us see them and respond to them. A critic may extend his frame of reference as far as it will bear extension, but it seems to me almost self-evident that he should start with the simple acknowledgement of his own relation to the object he criticizes; at the center of all truly successful criticism there is always a man reading a book, a man looking at a picture, a man watching a movie. Critics of the films, caught in the conflict between "high culture" and "popular culture," have too often sought to evade this confrontation.[21]

He specifically criticizes the sociologist's emphasis upon the audience and the aesthetic's emphasis on art as missing the personal importance of the film to the individual involved in viewing it.[22] To Warshow the movies are not something apart to be dissected. "The movies are part of my culture, and it seems to me that their special power has something to do with their being a kind of 'pure' culture, a little like fishing or drinking or playing baseball—a cultural fact, that is, which has not yet fallen altogether under the discipline of art."[23] This is the position, which any fan and most workers on a Republic picture could applaud. Their B pictures were made to entertain and to reach certain basic emotions. Sociological and artistic implications were totally secondary, if that. Republic pictures were indeed "the immediate experience."

Warshow also makes a subsidiary but telling observation concerning negative versus positive values in the movies. In his opinion, the elitist critics assume that art must involve social criticism and thus "negative social images" are more important as a "truer reality," while the lower cultural levels emphasize "positive images" of home and religion to obtain automatic approval.[24] Warshow concludes, "So much of 'official' American culture has been clearly optimistic that we are likely almost by reflex to take pessimism as a measure of seriousness. Besides, the element of pessimism is often for educated people an aid to identification."[25]

Although the point is made using A films' big budget with intellectual pretensions as his example, the appropriateness to the B film is obvious. The Republic B film was on the lower cultural level, stressed positive images, and was optimistic in tenor. These factors frequently automatically cut off the Republic product specifically and the B film in general from serious consideration by the educated upper levels of culture—hence the academics' frequent failure to even consider the Bs. But in doing so these same students of the film were missing the contributions which these films were making to the lives of the viewers because of their positive images, their optimism, and their basic understanding of "the immediate experience."

Andrew Bergman's *We're in the Money: Depression America and Its Films*,[26] a study of the film in the Great Depression, brings forth another theme to which Republic and the Bs were to make a significant contribution. One of Bergman's basic ideas is that Hollywood helped America survive the Depression. "Hollywood would help the nation's fundamental institutions escape unscathed by attempting to keep alive the myth and wonderful fantasy of a mobile and classless society, by focusing on the endless possibilities for individual success, by turning social evil into personal evil and making the New Deal into a veritable leading man."[27]

While Bergman goes further and contends that the Depression films of the major studios unconsciously reflected the needs of the people regardless of their surface intent, were subtly critical of the system, and without realizing it provided complex answers to their criticisms which require deep analysis, it can be pointed out that Republic's goals were straightforward and contributed much to the comfort of the Depression audiences. Bergman does not mention Republic but the studio did just what his basic theme implies. Republic films, due to Herbert Yates, President of the studio, various organized pressure groups, and the prevailing concepts of the writers, supported the traditional American ideals and reflected what the studio felt their audience needed and wanted on a conscious level. Republic's policy was a consistent reinforcement of the American way of life and the values of heroism. They were very much the "guys in the white hats" for reasons which will be examined in detail in the following chapters.

In a related vein Bergman points out that the movie audience is given more of the type of film which it accepts and comes to expect.[28] This factor—generally acknowledged and in many respects a truism—was especially true of the B studio like Republic where formula and generic films make up the preponderance of production. Hence when they found a message which was acceptable to their public, they hammered it home in film after film as long as the audience bought it.

In discussing G-men and cowboys, Bergman again develops an idea, which is representative of Republic's philosophy and contributed to the studio's success. "And simultaneously with the emergence of the federal lawman as hero came the re-emergence of the cowboy as a vital force in the movies. . . . As for the westerns, their epic nature unleashed some powerful, if elderly, myths about the law as a great national, creative force . . . cowboys making the West a 'fit place to raise a family.' . . ."[29] The year he is discussing is 1935, the year that Republic came into existence. That Republic contributed to the revitalization of the Western as a force for law and order and to the audience acceptance thereof is discussed in Chapter 7.

On the other hand Bergman also makes much of the concept of shyster throughout his book[30]—that is the plot motif wherein the villain is someone in a position of authority—the lawyer, the banker, the sheriff, the mayor—who is using his power to take unfair advantage of the average citizen. This was a favorite theme in Republic pictures and was a natural plot device given the audience acceptance of the situation. The villain had to be powerful to be a fit adversary for the hero—which seemed to be a continual crowd pleaser in that the average viewer preferred to think the worst of the power figures and enjoyed seeing them brought to justice.[31]

In his conclusion Bergman sees Hollywood at the end of the Depression as having "made a central contribution toward educating Americans in the fact that wrongs could be set right within their existing institutions. They did so . . . by reflecting aspiration and achievement. They showed that individual initiative still bred success, that the federal government was a benevolent watchman, that we were a classless, melting pot nation."[32] That conclusion applies not only to the efforts of the major studios but also to the B film as represented by Republic.

Stephen Louis Karpf's *The Gangster Film: Emergence, Variation and Decay of a Genre 1930–1940*[33] is sometimes contradictory in its coverage of the films it emphasizes and somewhat more negative in its interpretation than Bergman. However, it has some application to a study of Republic especially in providing contrast. That is to say it emphasizes some negative factors involving gangster pictures and A productions, which can provide a positive insight into Republic films. For example, Karpf feels that the gangster picture as a genre was extremely critical, even subversive, of the American way of life: "The gangster film questioned the very foundations of American society. It was and is popularly held that an individual can become a success in America by studying and working hard, being thrifty and having respect for family and institutions. . . . Mixed in with this general outlook is an adherence to the Ten Commandments or some similar set of moral values. The gangster film in its fullest development represents anarchy in the above scheme."[34]

It is of interest to note that Republic made very few gangster pictures and that the genres wherein their strength existed—serials, Westerns, country musicals—tended to neutralize the message which Karpf sees in the gangster movies.

Along the same lines, Karpf does explore four films produced by Warner Bros., which have positive values. "These films are optimistic in tone. . . . They have a quality which points to a problem in American society and suggests solutions based on traditional values already inherent in the country."[35] His examples include *The Story of Louis Pasteur, The Life of Emile Zola, Juarez,* and *Dr. Ehrlich's Magic Bullet* and his discussion delves into political implications in the films. The point is that these were all A budget, historical biographies, long on dialogue and possible political parallels, but short on action and pacing. Therefore, whether they were positive or not, whether they really had an intended message or not, it is likely that they were not seen by the youth and young adults and where they were seen they made little or no lasting impressions. In comparison, as shall be discussed in Chapter 3, the effect of a Republic action piece would be to make an impression on the younger audience even if such were not the original intention. And the impression was generally positive.

Basically then, both Karpf and Bergman were frequently negative in their interpretation of the messages and themes imparted to audiences in major productions.[36] In comparison, Republic was both consciously and unconsciously positive in stressing the traditional standards of the audience at which they aimed and unconsciously reinforced these standards by an un-failing reiteration over a long period of time in series films.

Michael Wood's *America in the Movies*,[37] an interesting volume on the significance of the film, is similar to Warshow in some respects and adds yet another interpretation which can be applied to the Republic type of movie. Wood early expresses his conviction that the movies are overdone inten-tionally and that this must be taken into consideration when analyzing their effect: "This sense of the overblown is not a question of hindsight or changing tastes. . . . It is a question of the exact tone of these movies, of their being simultaneously hammed up and just right, pitched at their own chosen level of swagger and exaggeration. It is the movies, an independent universe, self-created, self-perpetuating, a licensed zone of unreality, affec-tionately patronized by us all. . . ."[38] This description is again particularly true of the B film as represented by Republic wherein certain ground rules were recognized and accepted by the audience. In the chapters on Repub-lic serials, Westerns, and series, it will be seen that Wood's "licensed zone of unreality" is immensely recognizable and efficiently effective. It will be shown that such ready acceptance and recognition of the Republic style and pacing made the audience even more receptive to both the story and its implied moral.

Wood also sees the film as having an unconscious effect on the audience but not in the deep symbolic meaning psychological studies frequently claim. "We translate and interpret and transfer from films back to life, but we do it instantly and intuitively, working at a level of awareness somewhere just be-low full consciousness."[39] This is probably a good description of where the lasting impact of Republic films hit the audience. The messages did not nec-essarily lie on the surface in the stories. Nor were they deep and complex. But they did make an impression in this area, which Wood describes, and in much the same way, by an intuitive transfer—especially when absorbed ef-fortlessly over a long period of time as in series films.

In essence then, Wood feels that the movies did mirror the American mind, "that virtually any Hollywood movie, however trivial . . . can be seen as a text for a rather special kind of social history: the study of what might be called the back of the American mind."[40] And this is one of the major hy-potheses to be developed in the following chapters—namely that the Re-public product did represent certain values accepted by the American audi-ence and that this helped explain the success of Republic. Moreover, this "mirroring effect" made these films all the more effective in their influence on the viewer—it was a two-way street.

In concluding his small volume, Wood summarizes his position—"the movies, then, offered structures of thought and feeling to an almost inconceivable quantity of people . . . especially when we didn't give them a second thought."[41] This is indeed the way that the films of Republic were viewed. The youthful audience rarely gave their exciting entertainment a second thought for it was just that—entertainment. Yet the message was there. Wood's work sees all Hollywood films as a force in America's social history.

The same can be said of Robert Sklar's *Movie Made America*.[42] But Sklar's approach is entirely different and his conclusions vary, so that the value of his book in regard to understanding the significance of Republic Pictures lies more in his concern with economic factors.

Sklar's book is a general treatment of the history of American cinema with a heavy emphasis on the industry being controlled economically and philosophically by the underdogs, the minorities, and by men who came out of the lower and lower-middle classes. Such men thus understood the traditional values of the moviegoer and appealed to the mass audiences. At the same time, these men feared criticism from the upper classes and elitist critics and defended themselves at various times against charges of catering to the basest instincts of the lowest common denominator, of films espousing suspect political philosophies, or of any emphasis by critics on the disproportionate power of movie leaders. Sklar is concerned with the influence of the movies, which controlled that influence, and some of the implications of the influence. However, Sklar, like so many other scholars, continues to emphasize the major productions and personalities and gives only a passing nod to the factor of the B picture. Nonetheless he makes some telling points, which are equally applicable to the Bs.

For example, Sklar emphasizes the importance of the profit motive in the film industry and from it the ultimate power of the public over film content.

> One reads with skepticism the many works written by movie-industry insiders that claim the movie-going public holds the real power over motion pictures. Yet there is some truth in it. . . . Awesome as the power and profit of the movie moguls became in the 1920's, they never ceased to depend on their ability to please the public.[43]

Sklar is actually speaking of the silent era in this statement but it proved to be just as true in the 1930s and 1940s. Republic realized it was governed by just such a consideration and found a product and an audience and put them together. Republic was doing the right thing at the right time for a segment of the audience and it gave the studio a significance, which was unrecognized at the time.

Sklar also summarizes the traditional view of movie historians, critics, and popularizers concerning the upsurge of the influence of the cinema in the 1930s.

> The heavenly gates swung open, and American motion pictures, so their chroniclers have universally proclaimed, entered their golden age: Hollywood took center stage in the culture and consciousness of the United States, making movies with a power and élan never known before or seen again. Not only did the movies amuse and entertain the nation through its most severe economic and social disorder, holding it together by their capacity to create unifying myths and dreams, but movie culture in the 1930s became a dominant culture for many Americans, providing new values and social ideals to replace shattered old traditions.[44]

Sklar then goes on to point out that this interpretation has many salient points but that it is oversimplified since Hollywood also was severely influenced by the Depression. Sklar's summary of the era differs from Bergman's in that it emphasizes the creativity of Depression Hollywood. This fact is important in that Republic was indeed founded in this unstable but creative period, that they of necessity quickly found an approach which suited them, and that, whether it was intended or not, their product did serve as a unifying force and did uphold traditional values, shattered or otherwise. Republic's role in the movie culture as "a dominant culture for many Americans" is worthy of exploration.

While not referring to Republic, Sklar further isolates yet another factor which contributed to the success of the studio and the good timing with which it came into existence. "So in 1933–1934, spurred by the changes in national mood brought about by the New Deal and prodded by the Legion of Decency, Hollywood directed its enormous powers of persuasion to preserving the basic moral, social, and economic tenets of traditional American culture."[45] This, on the eve of the founding of Republic, could well be the tenet upon which Republic was to base its existence. When these circumstances changed after the war, Republic did not, and that began the decline of the studio. Sklar declares the peace between Hollywood and its political critics was accepted because it gave the motion picture industry more opportunity for profits and prestige. This too could be applied to Republic's wholehearted acceptance of the role of cultural guardian. However, there were also other factors.

Sklar provided yet one more theme, which is important to the success of Republic. In analyzing the change in the movies in the late 1940s, he recognizes the importance of the formula picture:

> What Hollywood had learned to do supremely well—comedy, musicals, genre Westerns and crime pictures, melodramas, popularizations of classics—did not provide many lessons for a new era of seriousness and responsibility. Hollywood's triumph had been overwhelmingly a triumph of formula, and the novelty and freshness of American commercial movies had come from the inventive new ways in which formulas were reshaped to meet the times. Formulas worked beautifully in their place—and continue to do so—but formulas and significant social themes did not mix effectively. . . .[46]

This point is also seminal to an understanding of the Republic contribution. With one exception, all of the people connected with the studio who were interviewed for this study acknowledged that Republic was strongest in the area of the formula picture.[47] Also significant is the fact that the decline of Republic dates from the late 1940s and early 1950s.

In discussing the various background works, both fan and academic, several themes relating to the role and significance that Republic and its pictures had in the pattern of American social history have emerged. How do these themes fit together to form the hypothesis, which will be developed throughout the following chapters?

Film as art is a legitimate topic. However, the studio product of the 1930s, 1940s, and 1950s was rarely concerned with film as an art form. This was true of all studios, but especially of those which specialized in the B film. Of these studios, Republic was undoubtedly the finest. This type of motion picture was created to entertain in order to be profitable. The B picture and the serial, especially at Republic, were, however, frequently quality products and, as a result, had more influence on the industry and the moviegoing public than was intended or realized at the time but not because of artistic or sociological pretensions. Of course many Bs even at Republic were of lesser quality but the overall average was better than has been realized. Conversely such films did have artistic merit occasionally but such occurrences were accidental and of minimal interest to those involved.

Republic learned early to produce economical films which had top quality and which appealed to the small theatres in large cities and to a variety of outlets throughout the Midwest and South. Other small studios could not match the Republic quality and the major producers normally viewed such films as throwaway products upon which they spent little time. They each had their B units but were committed to A products first and foremost. However, Republic's success in the B area resulted in the smaller studios attempting to upgrade their films while the majors took notice by upgrading their Bs and by utilizing Republic personnel. Thus Republic did have an effect on the film industry, which is worthy of examination.

However, Republic's position within the industry was secondary to the other and perhaps more important role of the studio. The general quality of the Republic product proved to be important in the studio's relationship to its motion picture audiences. The Republic "attention to detail" resulted in a greater public acceptance of the type of film in which the studio specialized. This positive effect in turn increased the significance of the Republic product on American social history in that it contributed to, reinforced, and/or reflected the audience viewpoint. In other words, the films influenced the "public mind." The films of Republic were seemingly especially important to young audiences in the Midwest and South. The extent of this influence is difficult to measure but its existence should be acknowledged, documented, and examined. The audience was entertained but at the same time it was painlessly influenced.

In order to examine these suppositions with an emphasis on the second point, this work will concentrate on 1) the Republic serials, 2) the Republic B Western series, and 3) other less genre oriented Republic products such as the country musicals and general action features since these were really Republic's bread-and-butter and where their greatest success occurred. A passing examination of a sample of the Republic A films was made in Chapter 1 on Republic's history for the sake of completeness, but since this area is not the source of Republic's significance, further reference to Republic As will be only in relationship to the Bs.

In no way did Republic's occasional venture into A productions pose a threat to the majors. Although these big productions did not directly hurt Republic until the declining years, they rarely benefited the studio greatly either in terms of profit or prestige, ironically the studio's greatest area of concern. This budgetary drain plus the other factors, which were examined in Chapter 1, proved too much for Republic. Perhaps under different guidance, the studio would have survived and adapted. For example, Monogram did just that, becoming Allied Artists. However, Republic was besieged by a variety of problems in the late 1940s and early 1950s and did not adapt.

Regardless of the causes for the passing of Republic as an active studio, the fact remains that the care and quality of its technical facilities and its personnel especially in the 1930s and 1940s resulted in a superior product of its kind. The importance of this superiority will be the main thrust of this study. The movies of the period under discussion had a direct influence on the life styles, moral codes, and ethical patterns of the viewers. These films gave them a simplified but quite consistent, understandable, and usable life model couched in the terms of period pieces and fantasy to increase the entertainment value and therefore the profit ratio. Moreover, since the audience was more frequently and consistently exposed to the B movies, serials, and shorts, these products, while not as "significant" as the larger and classier major productions, had an appreciable influence on several generations of young and impressionable minds. And the surface messages of these productions, because they were formula pieces, were easily and painlessly absorbed by their willing audiences. There may have occasionally been deeper and more disturbing messages, but the major import of these films does not lie in subliminally subversive interpretations—rather if these interpretations were accurate or inaccurate is immaterial. Finally, because of their appreciably higher quality as well as their admitted quantity, the Republic Pictures products are perhaps the best and leading example of the importance of this type of film on the regular moviegoing audience of the period which was the heyday of the sound film.[48]

Notes

1. Don Miller, B Movies (New York: Curtis Books, 1973), p. 113.

2. Miller, p. 112.

3. Miller has also published an interesting, unpretentious but reliable survey of the B Western, Hollywood Corral (New York: Popular Library, 1976), which devotes considerable space to Republic. Later republished as Don Miller's Hollywood Corral (Burbank, California: Riverwood Press, 1993), with additional material.

4. Barbour's fan publications through Screen Facts Press can be found in the bibliography. The commercial volumes include Days of Thrills and Adventure (New York: Macmillan Company, 1970), A Thousand and One Delights (New York: Collier Books, 1971), and The Thrill of It All (New York: Collier Books, 1971). His recent Cliffhanger: A Pictorial History of the Motion Picture Serial (New York: A & W Publishers, 1977), is basically a continuation of Days of Thrills and Adventure and unfortunately repeats much of the same material.

5. Cocoa, Florida: Cinememories Publishing Company, 1968.

6. Satellite Beach, Florida: Coral Reef Publications, 1973.

7. Mt. Clemens, Michigan: privately published, 1969–1974.

8. One exception was Jon Tuska's "Overland with Kit Carson—A Cinematography" in Those Enduring Matinee Idols, II (June–July 1971), pp. 146–148 and II (August–September 1971), pp. 163–165 in which Tuska finds significant symbolic parallels between this Columbia Western serial starring Wild Bill Elliott and Moby Dick among other literary works.

9. Los Angeles: privately published, 1974–1984.

10. *Continued Next Week: A History of the Motion Picture Serial* (Norman, Oklahoma: University of Oklahoma Press, 1964) and *Bound and Gagged: The Story of the Silent Serials* (New York: Castle Books, 1968).

11. Garden City, New York: Doubleday & Company, 1972.

12. New York: Crown Publishers, 1972. Don Daynard in the letter column of *TEMI*, II (June–July 1972), p. 246, states "The book is so full of errors, omissions, and false information that I spent one full hour making corrections in the picture captions and even then, I didn't get them all!!!"

13. Norman, Oklahoma: University of Oklahoma Press, 1971.

14. Northbrook, Illinois: by the author. Jack Mathis Advertising, 1975. This book is a valuable reference work.

15. Letter from Jack Mathis, April 26, 1976.

16. Lubbock, Texas: privately published, 1972.

17. *A Pictorial History of the Western Film* (New York: Citadel Press, 1969), pp. 140–153.

18. *Kings of the Bs: Working Within the Hollywood System* (New York: E. P. Dutton & Company, 1975).

19. Garden City, New York: Doubleday & Company, 1962.

20. Warshow, p. 19.

21. Warshow, p. 19.

22. Warshow, p. 27.

23. Warshow, p. 28.

24. Warshow, p. 179.

25. Warshow, p. 181.

26. New York: Harper & Row, 1972.

27. Bergman, p. xvi.

28. Bergman, p. xvi.

29. Bergman, p. 83.

30. See especially Bergman, Chapter Two, "The Shyster and the City."

31. Interview with Sloan Nibley, Republic writer, Hollywood, California, May 4, 1976.

32. Bergman, pp. 167–168.

33. New York: Arno Press, 1973.

34. Karpf, pp. 212–213.

35. Karpf, p. 237.

36. For example, Karpf sees the gangster as finding himself more honest and less hypocritical than his betters who cheat within the law. Karpf feels that this was a basic message of this type of film, p. 151.

37. New York: Basic Books, 1975.

38. Wood, p. 8.

39. Wood, p. 16.

40. Wood, p. 126.

41. Wood, p. 193.

42. New York: Random House, 1975.

43. Sklar, p. 148.

44. Sklar, p. 161.

45. Sklar, p. 175.

46. Sklar, p. 280.

47. Interview with Morris R. Abrams, Republic script writer and assistant direc-tor, Hollywood, California, May 17, 1976. Mr. Abrams felt that there was continu-ous change in Republic pictures to adapt to the audience and the formula designa-tion is oversimplified.

48. Due to the fact that the story of Republic has not been previously documented or its possible significance even acknowledged beyond fan oriented publications and because the Republic "bread-and-butter" product was infrequently discussed by the critics, this study relied on over two dozen interviews and extensive correspondence with Republic personnel and others knowledgeable on the subject. In addition some Republic records and press releases were available as well as newspaper and periodi-cal reports on the company, its president, and its business affairs. The repository for the remaining Republic files is National Telefilm Associates, Los Angeles. (Both the papers of Republic and Jack Mathis' material relating to Republic were given to the Brigham Young University Library under James D'Arc in 2005. They are being in-ventoried and should be available in 2007.) Fortunately, much Republic material has been deposited in and collected by three major theatrical libraries—the University of California at Los Angeles, the Margaret Herrick Library of the Academy of Mo-tion Picture Arts and Sciences, and the American Film Institute, Los Angeles. A quantity of additional material of merit is in the theatrical section of the Library and Museum of Performing Arts in the New York Public Library at Lincoln Center.

~

CHAPTER THREE

Influence, the Motion Picture, the B Movie, and Republic

As has been discussed, the B picture was low budget, intended to make money with a minimum investment, and usually relied on a generic structure and formula plots. This is not to denigrate such films—many had more value than major productions, they are worthy of study, and as Charles Flynn says in *Kings of the Bs*:

> Finally, we go to the movies for great experience, not for great ideas. Our aesthetic response to a movie is inevitably linked to our movie experiences. And, for quite a while, the s/k/h [schlock, kitsch, hack—read B movies] movies *were* America's movie experiences.
>
> Obviously, today's moviegoer may find it difficult to develop a taste for the s/k/h movie. But these movies constituted the preponderance of Hollywood's output for so long that they are not only a part of movie history, but also of American cultural history.[1]

The movies as a whole were a force in American history. The Bs were a major aspect of that influence. And Republic began and remained a B picture studio.

Historically, the influence of the movie industry was increasing during the 1930s. Doubt and discouragement induced by the Great Depression generated the psychological imperatives, which gave the movies a new role in the nation's emotional economy. There was a need for distraction and entertainment as well as for reassurance. As Arthur Schlesinger, Jr., put it, "With the American dream in apparent ruins . . . people longed to hear again an affirmation of individual identity, to see again a chance for individual possibility, to feel again a sense of individual potency."[2] Movies were not always better in the Depression but they were important to the audience.[3]

Movies may have had more importance than ministers in this era. In their well-known sociological study of "Middletown" in the 1930s the Lynds even go so far as to impute the movies with more influence than that of the local preacher.[4] And, it can be pointed out, "Middletown" or Muncie, Indiana, was in the heart of Republic's distribution stronghold—the Midwest. Frederick Lewis Allen, the journalist and popular historian, also comments on the popularity of the movies in the 1930s and attributed it to their escapist themes: "The movies took one to a never-never land of adventure and romance uncomplicated by thought. The capital invested in the movies preferred to steer clear of awkward issues, not to run the risk of offending theatregoers abroad or at home."[5] He feels that these escapist themes represented the desires of the moviegoing public and that the movies actually neutralized the immediate goals of social reformers. He points out that, after all, there were eighty-five million moviegoers a week. Hollywood advanced the Horatio Alger myth of individual success and this dream helped these same moviegoers accept the economic hardships of the 1930s.[6] As will be seen, Republic Pictures contributed regularly to the Alger myth as well as related positive myths. However, regardless of which myth or myths Hollywood provided, its presence was felt in the Depression era.

With the gathering war clouds in Europe, the nation began an economic recovery but the influence of Hollywood did not slacken although attendance declined temporarily. The new uncertainties of potential involvement increased the interest in diversions and Hollywood, always sensitive to the mood of the times, began to move away from pacifism toward preparedness. Senator Champ Clark of Missouri, ever wary of foreign influences, feared that the 17,000 movie houses were nightly becoming "17,000 nightly mass meetings for war."[7] Clark's fears were not totally unjustified. During wartime the need for entertainment did not abate and Hollywood's importance increased. Geoffrey Perrett, journalist/historian, in his book on the home front, emphasized both the popularity of the movies and emotionalism of the audiences. "In 1942 it [the movie industry] fell heir to sudden riches. Movie attendance jumped 50 percent over the 1940 level, reaching 80,000,000 paying customers a week. Boomtown movie theaters stayed open twenty-four hours a day to accommodate the swing shifts. No more free dishes, bingo, breakfasts, and other gimmicks. The customers packed in regardless of what was being shown. But these were also the rowdiest audiences in memory, booing, hissing, cheering and leaving demolished seats and tattered draperies in their wake."[8] True, the emotionalism was perhaps more due to the period than to the immediate experience of the film being shown but the reactions were there in any case.

Moviegoing, especially among the young, became a casual but persistent habit.[9] The war mood undoubtedly contributed. It was "a curious atmosphere that wartime is to some extent vacation time, a time in which life is not quite the same as it has been before."[10]

The movie industry prospered as the movie theatre became a social experience. More than 90,000,000 people went to the movies every week and grosses were over a billion dollars per year even though admissions increased 33 percent on the average.[11] War pictures seemed to predominate although most films were profitable. During the war, the emotional effects on segments of the audience remained high. "Morale was the excuse for Hollywood's wartime product—an elusive word if there ever was one. Probably, the morale most frequently energized was that of small boys and teen-age girls who sat in darkened theaters, their hearts quickening to the phony war on the silver screen."[12] The point is that in a great many films morale and patriotism did continue to have a place for the youthful audiences.

After the war, during the late 1940s came the decline of the movie industry. Nonetheless, the movies were indeed a major force in American popular culture from the Depression until after World War II. The historian, while usually acknowledging that the movie medium had some influence on American society and the American "way of life" during this period, has not really delved into what this influence was to any great extent. In order to analyze the influence of the medium or to place it in the broader aspects of American historical studies it is necessary to consider film not as art or as history but as a part of American life.

Michael T. Isenberg, historian at the University of Colorado, has recognized and summarized the historian's dilemma. He points out that popular art, in this case the film, should not be considered only for artistic values, especially by the professional historian, since it also reflects society.[13] Instead of recognizing the film's contributions, historians have used the movies as a whipping boy because of their commercialism.[14] Isenberg feels that the film industry has been criticized unfairly because elitists faulted its business/commercial orientation because it addressed itself primarily to "puerile audiences," and finally, it was seen as an intrinsic leveler, even degrader, of the national culture.[15]

In his conclusion, Isenberg makes a strong point, which is particularly applicable to the historical study of the B movie and its influential role in the lives of its audience.

> Historians who have become comfortable with the concepts of "symbol" and "myth" within the last quarter century have balked at extending these concepts from the literary to the visual media. History has been slower than most of the other social sciences in realizing the social dynamism hidden in such concepts. The movies operate on both symbolic and mythic levels. One ardent proponent of the film even claimed that this situation was ideal for the historian. "It is not the man who describes what actually happens who best tells history," wrote Harry C. Carr in 1918. "It is the genius who symbolizes it for us, who puts it into doses we can take without mentally choking."[16]

While some film historians such as Michael Wood and Robert Sklar have indeed emphasized the mythic proportions of Hollywood's product, none have seriously considered the contributions of the B genres such as the Western and the serial to the American attitude over a long period of exposure. While the historian has indeed had an anxiety concerning the role of the film in history, the relationship of the two is being recognized.

Perhaps Garth Jowett, whose *Film: The Democratic Art*, stresses that motion pictures are a major social phenomenon which continually interrelates with the changing mores and attitudes of American society, best sums up what the historian faces. "It is my contention that we historians must see the movies as commercial products—but products that had a tremendous and unknown influence on American Society as a whole. It was because of the 'unknown quality' that the movies were subject to forms of social pressure and censorship never before seen in the U.S. . . ."[17] To the historians then, the influence of the film, while recognized, remains an "unknown quality."

If the historian has been hesitant about this influence and how to approach it, other disciplines have been less so. The well known and articulate anthropologist Hortense Powdermaker readily accepts the significant role of Hollywood in American culture—that the movies reflect the audience and the audience is influenced by the film. She states, "Through the study of American movies we [the anthropologists] should likewise contribute to the understanding of American society . . . we assume that movies will reflect values and goals, as folklore, the theater, and literature (both 'fine' and 'popular') have always reflected them. In a period of rapid change and conflict within the value system it will be of interest to note which values are most stressed by the movies."[18] In other words, the movies emphasize selected values over others based upon audience preferences as a major factor and these emphases change with the historical situation. Since we live in a rapidly changing world there is some time lag involved but the movies still provide a gauge by which to observe the changing social patterns.

In recognizing the influence of the movies on the populace, Powdermaker specifies that the movies are often examined for their effects on the abnormal audience but that they also impress the general viewer. "As anthropologists, we are more interested in the normal than in the pathological. What is the effect of the movies on the vast audience who are not criminals, delinquents, or drunkards? How do movies influence their concepts of human relations, their value systems, their notions of reality?"[19] In the long run the more subtle long-range effect on the general multitude is more significant than any aberrant reaction on select unstable members of the viewing group.

Powdermaker sums up her viewpoint on the relationship of movies and society: "There is almost no important American pattern that is not reflected in Hollywood. Frequently, it is exaggerated, sometimes to the point of caricature."[20]

Psychologists and sociologists tend to agree with anthropologist Powdermaker that the cinema is influential although the interpretation sometimes varies. Psychologist Hugo Münsterberg was convinced that the movies influenced the minds of the audience and, unaware of the future commercialism and profit motivation of the medium, he projected a big idealized picture of the good effects movies would have.[21] He enthused, "No wonder that temples for the new goddess are built in every little hamlet."[22] Later students of the film were not so positive although they too recognized the motion picture as influential.

In the early 1930s, the potential influence of the movies was of concern to many, and a series of scientific studies, predominantly psychological and sociological, were undertaken. These were the famous Payne Study and Experimental Fund studies, eleven volumes of which were published, and while the techniques used and the social perspective from which the researchers operated have caused the entire body of work to be viewed cautiously, the Payne Fund volumes do include some interesting material and do recognize the influence of Hollywood on society.[23] This project and others of the period tended to find that the film product of the times was undermining or even destroying American society without recognizing that the movies were in reality reflecting and reinforcing the culture. They were in effect propaganda against the movies but they did increase our awareness of the import of the screen.

Herbert Blumer and Philip M. Hauser, authors of one of the clinical studies and one of the most critical of the series, summarize the approach of the

Payne Fund volumes. "While primarily a form of recreation, they [motion pictures] play an appreciably important role in developing conceptions of life and transmitting patterns of conduct. They may direct the behavior of persons along socially acceptable lines or they may lead, as has been indicated, to misconduct. They may be, therefore, an agency of social value or of social harm."[24] Both authors at least admit that the movies can contribute to acceptable behavior and can have value. It was just that, given the slant of their beliefs and approach to the subject, these psychologists failed to realize that there was more to the films than sex and crime.

The summary volume for the series was undertaken by Henry James Forman, a journalist whose role it was to popularize the scientific studies. He acknowledges the pervasiveness of the movies. "A good motion picture, briefly, with its peculiar and inherent capacity to circulate throughout the globe, to penetrate into the smallest town and even into rural areas, represents a social force which may be described as nothing short of a godsend."[25] Forman also comments that the results of the Payne Fund project have indicated that the young are the most subject to the messages of the film.

> The screen is the most open of all books. And when the young see pictures presented in a certain way, it is small wonder that the vividness of the reception of those scenes, owing to the youth and freshness of the spectators, makes of the movies a peculiarly incisive and important factor in schemes of conduct. The less experience the spectators have, the less selective they naturally are. Coming to the young, as pictures do, in the most impressionable years of their life, the effect becomes of extraordinary weight and potentiality, and amounts often to a shaping and molding of their character.[26]

Based on this finding, Forman pleads for the guidance and presence of adults in order to counteract the potential negative influence of the movies on children.[27] Despite their apprehensions, the Payne Fund studies did provide evidence and arguments that the film, including that fare which would become known as the B film, was indeed a social force with which to reckon. The Payne Fund volumes were a tentative attempt to identify how the influence of film might work specifically.

Later film studies stressing the psychological viewpoint were not as critical as those in the early 1930s and were more objective in their approach. For example, a later study of the Hollywood movies of the 1940s credited them with reflecting the daydreams of the culture in which they are produced. "The common day-dreams of a culture are in part the sources, in part the products of its popular myths, stories, plays and films. Where these productions gain the sympathetic response of a wide audience, it is likely that their producers have tapped within themselves the reservoir of common daydreams."[28] It is the power of these dreams, which give the movies their influence.

Dore Schary, who was a major writer-producer at RKO, then headed Metro Goldwyn Mayer, and later became an independent producer sums up the truism of the influence of motion pictures in his introductory remarks to a sociological study. "Of course, the fact is that you simply can't make a picture without content or, more candidly, without a message."[29] Every film then carries some message. The entire film industry was unavoidably intertwined with society. Fritz Lang, famed German and American film director who worked once at Republic, asked, "Do you realize, by the way, what really made propaganda for the American way of life? American motion pictures. Goebbels understood the enormous power of film as propaganda, and I'm afraid that even today people don't know what a tremendous means of propaganda motion pictures can be."[30]

Thus, traditional historians, anthropologists, psychologists, and sociologists, working from slightly different approaches, serve to concentrate the arguments for the film as an influential factor in American society. However, perhaps Robert Sklar of the University of Michigan best summarizes the dilemma of attempting to isolate the influence. "This is perhaps the most vexing and murky area of all for social historians of the movies. We know movies have a profound impact on cultural life. But it's hard to provide specific evidence to support broad generalizations."[31]

And to add to the perplexities, most of these academic treatments of the film including those from scholars trained in university film departments are predominantly concerned with the role of the A film. Although most gave some credit to the B film as a part of the general motion picture scene, they normally studied and cited specific A productions on a regular basis. However, much of what authorities from various disciplines say about the A picture or the motion picture in general also can be applied to the B field. Some of their conclusions are particularly appropriate to B pictures.

Powdermaker, the anthropologist, comments on the importance of formulas to successful filmmaking, "The movies have some resemblance to it [folk art] in their repetitive use of well-known themes or formulas which is so characteristic of primitive folklore. . . . Many times the latest 'scoop' is set within a well-known formula used in the past."[32] As will be seen, Republic specifically and the B film in general made good use of formulas with slight updatings and variations to meet the tastes of their audiences for something different. Republic writer Sloan Nibley has illustrated this point in commenting on the fact that in the Roy Rogers pictures he wrote, the character of the hero and his supporters as well as the formula were fixed factors. Therefore, Nibley and other B writers always turned to the villains' characterizations and the different devices upon which the standard plots hinged for their variations.[33]

The psychologists, Wolfenstein and Leites, also consider the formula picture important and, at the same time, strengthen Nibley's point. "Within the limits of a code and a general plot formula there remains a choice of a considerable range of possibilities."[34] They feel that the use to which the formula is put reflects the desires of the American people, that the themes are drawn out of society.

The acknowledgment that Hollywood, and especially the B productions, relied on formulas brings up the fact that the Bs emphasized melodrama and violence. Wolfenstein and Leites put this in perspective. "Violence in American films may be fast moving and noisy or technically intricate; it is less apt to be emotionally involved. . . . Death is not very real in American films. . . . A murder is the starting point of furious activities (setting off the process of investigation), or marks the end of such activities (when the murder is eliminated), thus leaving the hero free to take a holiday."[35] While aimed at the general Hollywood movie, this statement is very descriptive of many B movies in general and is particularly related to both the intricate stuntwork and special effects and the typical plot of most Republic serials and Westerns as shall be seen.

Melodrama also served a useful function in the motion picture by providing an external danger as opposed to inner conflict.[36] But melodrama, a staple of the Bs, has its place. As sociologists White and Averson admit, "Whether melodrama per se is necessarily inferior art begs the question . . . the movies very often have used the melodrama form to sustain audience interest. The moving picture has generally stressed physical action, sudden plot reversals, and unexpected outcomes—a kind of instinctive bow to the operation of chance in human life."[37] The B films frequently used this same violence and melodrama to reflect and enhance the value system of their audiences.

Still, many film analysts from all disciplines are critical of the Hollywood value system. Powdermaker, for example, feels that the movie industry should stress certain cultural patterns. "There are, of course, other patterns in the U.S.A. which Hollywood could elaborate. They are the democratic ones of the dignity of man, the concept of freedom, a belief in man's capacity to think, create, and to exercise some control over his life—a belief that man is more important than property—all part of our cultural heritage."[38] This latter set of values is essentially what the Bs in general and Republic specifically did emphasize, although frequently in an action format and often with a blatancy of which Powdermaker might not approve. But the fact remains that a B film studio was indeed providing material for the audience representing the values, which this anthropologist advocates. Hollywood could emphasize positive values and the Bs produced by Republic often did just that.

As an example of positive values, White and Averson emphasize a major theme in the message film as being one of the individual's fight against the conformity of the system. "The struggle of the individual to preserve his integrity against those forces in society which would diminish him—whether tyrant kings, political demagogues, or labor racketeers—has been a continuing dramatic subject of the American message film."[39] This was the message, sometimes obvious, usually subtle, of countless B films and was a continuously employed theme in many Westerns as well as some serials produced by Republic. In fact, Republic and the other B producers without conscious intentions gave us many "contraband-message" films. "The critical comment in the contraband-message film is incidental; in the message film the social viewpoint is overt and dominant."[40]

The important factor is that a film need not be specifically aimed at topical social issues to serve as an index to popular thought—the B films and serials in general and the Republic product specifically also reflected mass beliefs and even dealt with social issues both directly and indirectly although the topical aspect of the subject matter was often disguised or at least secondary to the action/adventure motif so popular in escapist entertainment. But both the message of the particular issue at hand in any given film and the relationship of the film to popular social thought was still there in a great many Republic Bs.

Thus, film analysts, utilizing various disciplinary approaches, agree that the motion picture industry in general was influential, but their conclusions often bear direct relationships to the B film as well as the higher quality production.

Other film scholars of course have specifically concentrated upon the B field. Some of these writers are defensive, noting only the merits and influences of the B productions. But perhaps Professor Russel B. Nye of Michigan State University is typical of those who hold a negative point of view. He dismisses the Bs as routine, cheap, melodramatic, transitory, and utilizing minor players. He admits they formed a greater body of films than the major productions but claims, "their titles and the people who played in them are long forgotten, and appear in none of the many histories of the movies."[41] Nye admits that by their very quantity and playing time, Bs did have extensive audience exposure. And it has been shown that even cheaply made, simplified melodramas do carry messages. Moreover, sleeper Bs and occasionally less remarkable B movies illustrating a particular point have shown up with regularity in film histories and cults have grown up around certain B actors and series.

Other writers viewing the B phenomenon put it in context and acknowledge the merits of Bs. Don Miller feels that the coining of the double bill was the signal for the B picture to become an important factor in the motion picture industry. In 1935, the structure of exhibiting films gave way to "the second feature" and in the process Miller states that Bs came to stand, "not for budget or Class B, or bad, but in many ways signifying 'better.'"[42]

Miller is not alone in acknowledging a debt to the Bs. Peter John Dyer, film critic for the journal *Films and Filming*, considered Bs as "Those first rate second features" even prior to the demise of the B film and pointed out, "They can sharpen our critical senses. Many of them [have] good story telling and direction, ingenious plotting, expert photography and more than competent acting."[43] The director of the film program at the Los Angeles County Museum of Art provides the major clue to their potential influence. They filled needs inexpensively. "These films fulfilled an emotional need for American audiences; that of sheer entertainment and total escape, all for the price of a quarter."[44]

These films developed imagination in the moviegoer, which was coupled with a receptive mind. "The B movie . . . was a known quantity. . . . These were uniquely American stories, and audiences of the Bs didn't want to be stirred but entertained, perhaps stimulated, and certainly, comforted. They knew that in the formula films of the Bs they could relax and feel at home."[45] Because they were so dependable and so comfortable, these films were accepted wholeheartedly by viewers and that included a life pattern and a moral, ethical framework. "They [the Bs] were plucky, predictable and often pedestrian, yet they touched a chord in American life. . . ."[46] The B films successfully reached their audience not only because they were comfortable and dependable but also because they were often energetic, well paced, and exciting. "[D]espite the insane working conditions, the output of the best B directors had a raw crude energy and viscerally powerful quality that remained unnoticed by most critics until recently," says one critic.[47] This seeming contradiction is explainable. While the B picture was formula and normally predictable, it also had room for improvisation within the form, the budget, and the schedule. Creative men worked on these pictures—sometimes on their way up, sometimes down, and often just working to do the job as best they could—and these pictures did have some variation in plot and techniques.

Moreover, since they lacked big stars and massive sets, they had to rely on movement or gimmicks. They were efficiently produced but they could have imagination and challenge. The best were fast paced, good story telling with an impact—even if it was predictable. When various authorities refer to the films or the Bs striking a chord, it need not be the same reaction. The B movies could thrill, could have an immediate impact, as well as lull and be comforting to their audience. Either way, they had an influence.

In essence then the B movie was the most prolific form of movie making in Hollywood's most successful period. It provided a training ground for professionals, be they stars, directors, writers, editors, or cameramen. The Bs occasionally resulted in a product superior to the A film due to the fact that their creators were given more artistic freedom as long as they brought in a marketable film on schedule and within the budget.[48] These films could alternately excite and comfort their audiences and as a result could be an extremely significant part of the moviegoer's life style. With the coming of television as a major entertainment force, the B film with its philosophies, formats, and impact was absorbed by that medium. The personnel and the formats transferred often intact over to the television screen where the B film as television series and movies maintains a continuing existence.[49] And, as most critics and authorities agree, these television products are also a major influence on American society.

Republic was the largest and best of the B studios. The styles, techniques, and messages of the Republic product led the B field. Chapter 1 on the history of the studio provided the basic philosophy behind Republic Pictures as represented by the studio and its head, Herbert Yates. In respect to this point, Hortense Powdermaker singled out as significant, the importance of the studio leader and pointed out how his values might affect the end product and ultimately the audience. She noted that the personalities of the movie people who are in positions of power and have the responsibility of making decisions have a continuous and cumulative effect on millions of people.[50] The values of Herbert Yates were the basic values of the time in which he lived.

Albert S. Rogell, pioneer director who spent several years at Republic, noted these values when he stated that in his Republic films "when we could wave the flag we did." He remembers that Yates was a proud American who frequently asked his moviemakers to get the American flag on screen even when there was no reason.[51] The actress and wife of Yates, Vera H. Ralston, confirms that Yates was consciously patriotic and very moral where Republic pictures were concerned. "We specialized in B pictures and their message was leading the good life, the clean life. This was consciously put into every picture. Mr. Yates . . . was very strict on this."[52] The significant factor here is that the studio head did have control over his company and thus did influence the audience.

If Yates considered Republic's espousal of the good moral life important, how then did contemporary sources view the role of Republic and its methods of reaching its audience? To begin with, *The Film Daily Cavalcade* in 1939 credited Republic with successfully reviving the action drama and thus gaining an important place in the Hollywood studio structure. While admitting that Republic's four year rise in a depression period had not been expected, the *Cavalcade* acknowledged that the studio had "fulfilled its promises of reviving and revivifying the forsaken field of outdoor and action films" and had gained "the respectful attention and good will of [the] industry. . . ."[53] The article went on to point out that Republic created Gene Autry and the successful image of the singing cowboy. Autry was praised as "America's Number One Singing Cowboy, emulated by many, rivaled by no one."[54]

Republic was also credited with giving new life to the serial genre. "In giving new life to the serial picture, a phase of production that had lost its identity in Hollywood's rush toward more sophisticated film fare, Republic's purchase of radio's popular 'Lone Ranger' proved to be another 'coup de theater.' . . . Republic, as it fully intended, found itself with a pre-sold, pre-publicized episodical production that became so popular and important as to find bookings in Class A theaters throughout the nation."[55] All of these successes went to prove that Republic knew "the pulse of the film-going public."[56]

What is the significance of all this obviously public relations oriented copy? Seemingly, Republic knew its market, picked its area, and handled the product well. The studio was of course interested in profits but in creating generally acknowledged, documented successes in their fields of specialization, they were also creating products which influenced their audiences. And they were trying to do just this, not for the power of influence but because they understood the importance of understanding and reaching the audience to insure continued profit.

That Republic fully understood the import of audience contact and acceptance is also shown in its insistence that its stars tour the country. Major stars from the big studios rarely toured but the B film stars at Republic were frequently on the road. Comedienne Judy Canova, Western stars Gene Autry, Roy Rogers, and Don Barry, hillbilly performers the Weaver Brothers and Elviry, all were big attractions for Republic and all made frequent audience contact. Republic's strength was in grassroots audiences so its stars went to the grassroots level with regularity. And the approach proved effective. In order to stay in business, Republic needed to produce good pictures and make them cheaply enough to earn profits within the organization's sphere of influence. Republic's effective formula for making itself and its stars known to audiences—the personal appearance tour—encouraged its stars to keep up the good work and Republic never shared in the proceeds from their outside engagements.[57]

Republic also utilized local radio talent for guest appearances in pictures whenever possible. Here again the motive was profit but the results were to make the films more effective in influencing their audiences. "Republic's faith in these acts is based on the premise that they add box office value to pictures in particular localities at a price far less than . . . ranking specialty performers. . . . [B]ack home they plug Republic and their forthcoming pictures."[58]

Regardless of the reason, Republic recognized its audience and consciously catered to the market for which the studio was most qualified. With the coming of the Second World War, Republic's patriotic escapist entertainment strengthened its position with the moviegoing public. A feature on the studio announced that "Republic Aims Its Films at Heart of America."[59] The Republic audience and its tastes were well suited for films with a wartime emphasis. Because the product of the studio had always aimed at the American masses, its themes needed little alteration.[60] In other words, the Republic product already reinforced the traditional values of patriotism, conservatism, self-reliance, and justice.

The war also effected a temporary broadening of the Republic market. By shifting the population from the Republic small town strongholds to industrial centers, wartime increased the demand for Republic films in the cities. The Republic audience physically moved and enlarged to some degree while remaining the same in their entertainment habits.[61]

As illustration of this point, it was noted at the height of the war that Republic and its audience were still in harmony. "One reason why the company stands on such a firm basis is because . . . Republic always has stressed the adventure type of story, and for this reason it had a ready-made audience awaiting every picture it turned out in this field. . . . Even had it not participated in the inflated box-office, due to war conditions, Republic then would have continued enjoying the best of box-office health with the same type of pictures it has made for years."[62] Republic was to continue to meet the demand for this type of entertainment, to fulfill the needs of its large and identifiable audience, and to influence them in the process throughout the 1940s.

In a discussion of influence, the impact of the Republic stars must also be recognized. The three best examples are John Wayne, who soon left the Bs, Gene Autry, and Roy Rogers. The audience reaction and the influence which these three stars had as B actors at Republic will be included in Chapter 7.

Another good example of the Republic actor is Don Barry who was rated as number four or five in the list of Republic top Western stars for many years. His success was noted by a Hollywood columnist who compared him with James Cagney as a moody violent hero and noted that in one year he rose from an unknown to become one of the top ten Western stars in the movie industry.[63] Well-known newsman Lee Mortimer admitted in a review of *Remember Pearl Harbor*, a patriotic piece rapidly rushed out by Republic, "This quickie will have a better box-office potential in the sticks and suburbs than on Broadway. To much of the hinterland population, the hero of this film— 'Red' Barry—is as well known as Clark Gable."[64] Barry's pictures followed the clean cut formula to the hilt; Barry was tougher than most of his Western rivals, he killed off seven to fifteen villains per picture, and fans preferred him as a bad man who reforms. He followed the Western formula of abstinence from tobacco and sex.[65] Barry was quite proud of his career as a cowboy hero and feels that he did influence the audience positively. While he denies any deep meanings in Republic films—"they were made to entertain and to get people away from their problems"—he feels that the audiences "loved Republic and loved its stars" and that he and other Western series stars therefore did provide an effective positive behavior model for the audiences.[66]

Other Republic personnel view the question of the studio's influence on the moviegoing public in much the same way. Among the interviews conducted for this study, there was near unanimity that Republic did not set out to influence the citizenry, either positively or negatively, for any goal beyond profit. Nonetheless, upon reflection many Republic workers did comment upon the studio's role in this area, identifying its contribution to the American scene as either secondary to the entertainment factor or recognizable mainly in hindsight. But they do grant that the influence existed.

Sol Siegel, Republic producer who went on to bigger efforts at major studios and as an independent producer, feels that Republic "produced the best or worst of the Bs depending upon your viewpoint." He maintains that Republic was the best of the independents but that Bs produced by the majors were better. However, Siegel also commented that everyone at Republic did his best and that "every writer set out to write the best story possible within his limits." In this regard he concedes a possible influence and observes that while "we were very commercial, Republic did preach traditional morality, the American success story, the Horatio Alger story."[67]

Albert S. Rogell was more adamant and feels that the impact on youth was intended. He states that the Republic product was aimed at "John Q. Public and family" and that, while he and others were just "doing a job," he always knew that "films are education." Because of this, he and his coworkers "didn't have the dollar but did have the dream of doing something better." As a result, in his opinion, "to concentrate on the big A pictures is to miss the quality of the Bs. They were the heartbeat of the industry."[68]

Bruce Bennett, successful character actor who was known as Herman Brix in his leading man days at Republic, indicates that most Republic personnel did not think in terms of influence. "No, absolutely not, they were bread-and-butter jobs for everyone involved—no thought of anything but entertainment to please the Saturday matinee crowd. However, with the increased interest, nostalgia, and request for interviews and appearances, I can see that they were more influential than we realized. They included and reinforced American values."[69]

Robert Livingston, Republic leading actor best known for his role in the Three Mesquiteer series and as the second filmic Lone Ranger, responded forcefully to the question of nostalgia versus academic interest and in the process expressed the opinion that the Republic influence was simple and direct. "The nostalgic interest is phenomenal and has a lot of reasons. I don't think the academic interest is real. Perhaps it is. . . . Freudian complexity in these films is bullshit. . . . It was good guys versus bad guys. Simplicity [of interpretation] is fine and they [the academics] should stick with it. It [the influence] worked, it was there, but it wasn't deep."[70]

Vera H. Ralston's belief in the quality and influence of Republic has been previously noted in relationship to her husband's position of power. She feels Republic's influence was a real one and a good one. While not all Republic films were good and "some were very bad," she notes the increased quality of the pictures which made them both attractive and helped account for the renewed interest in them. She concludes, "Our pictures were aimed at the youth and we were very aware of it . . . we tried hard, did a good job, and made pictures we could be proud of. I'm sorry that it didn't end better."[71]

Barry Shipman, Republic writer later active in educational films, was of the opinion that Republic movies did indeed have an impact and that the influence was sometimes consciously intended by the writers. However, generally speaking the influence and any symbolism was unconscious but positive. As he puts it, "Does the apple know it's nutritious?" He also commented that his writing at Republic was deliberately juvenile and that he had to work to overcome this upon leaving the action field.[72]

Rowland "Dick" Hills, head of the Republic script (reproduction) department and office manager, while not involved in the creative end of the business, proved very perceptive on the subject of impact. He felt that the recognized Republic morality reflected the times more than the wishes of either Yates or the Hays Office. The end product was also reflective of the times and the writers simply wrote the way they felt. They intended no symbolism because they were journeyman pragmatic writers. It was Hills' contention that Republic's "class appeal was to the common man" and that whatever influence the studio had was on that level.[73]

Morris R. Abrams, Republic script supervisor and assistant director, responded more thoughtfully to the questions on Republic's role. In regard to influence, he states that he "is unable to say since he was concerned with survival and not Republic's philosophy." This statement in itself is valuable as an accurate indicator of the realities of working within the Hollywood system. Nonetheless, Abrams does make some interesting observations. He feels that the "good guy philosophy was basic in films" and that the concept of "virtue triumphant was taken for granted" in the era of Republic and was not unique to the studio. However, "the industry and Republic did better than it [sic] knew in affecting Society . . . [they] tried to study audiences and to meet expectations but did not consciously try to provide a mythology or symbolic approach."[74]

Perhaps Peggy Stewart, Republic actress, makes the most telling point. She attends many Western movie conventions and states that when the products of Republic, Columbia, and Monogram are compared in showings, "Republic's Class A stands out." She feels the interest and the market are still there, pointing out that Republic was the "Master of Bs" and that people raised on these films were influenced and have a continuing interest. She claims that private Saturday matinees are still being set up on a family basis in the South utilizing the Republic product and that she is frequently told of these projects at nostalgia conventions. She feels that the current interest is indicative of the lasting Republic influence.[75]

The significance of Republic in relationship to its contributions to the B film was perhaps best summed up on the occasion of the studio's tenth anniversary: "It can take credit for the introduction of a new type of screen entertainment in the singing western; the use of popular song titles as film titles; the invasion of the comic strip field for serial background; the policy of using radio and record talent in musical entertainment; and showmanship in both the selection of exploitation screen material and in national promotion to sell both its pictures and its stars."[76]

These contributions to the world of the Bs also apply to Republic's influence on the American scene and the *Zeitgeist*. Just as Republic revitalized the Western, the serial, and the country musical and aggressively sold these products, so too by the same means did it make an impact upon its chosen audience. In the case of the movies, the B film and Republic, three factors are logically and irretrievably intertwined—entertainment, marketing/profits, and influence. Republic was predominantly interested in the first two but out of these the third followed.

It appears that Republic's B films were more influential on regular movie audiences than film scholars have heretofore acknowledged. In various works they have analyzed many films in depth concerning their influence on the American public. In almost all cases, the movies analyzed were top grade major productions or sleeper artistic cult films. However, a great many of these films were never seen by a major segment of the moviegoing public or were seen only once. These films were also a minority of the total output. On the other hand, the B film was legion. It was mass produced in six days to three weeks usually by a dozen poverty row and independent companies and played and replayed the neighborhood and small town theatres during the week, on Saturdays, and sometimes even on Sundays. These were the films that the impressionable youth, the young adults, and the mass adult audience saw and re-saw on a regular weekly basis.

For every *Grapes of Wrath* (Twentieth Century Fox, 1940) or *Citizen Kane* (RKO Radio Pictures, 1941) that came along and may or may not have made an impression, most children and even their adult counterparts saw a dozen Judy Canova, Higgins family, or Three Mesquiteers films. The same was true of the serials, which by their very construction came to the audience in twelve and fifteen week doses. And these films made an impression—perhaps even greater than the A productions as a group. Even when there was no message, these films had a long term, subtle, and unconscious effect. To today's audiences they are transparent, wide-eyed, unrealistic, and naive. To the immature, defenseless, and more innocent audience in those darkened theaters waiting to be entertained, a total life style or at least ethical system was often pieced together from countless B films which, unrealized by them, influenced the way they conducted the rest of their lives. If film is truly significant as an effective force on society, it was achieved both directly and indirectly through the pervasiveness of the B as well as the A film.[77]

Notes

1. McCarthy and Flynn, *Kings of the Bs*, p. 12.
2. "When the Movies Really Counted," *Show: Magazine of the Arts* (April, 1963), p. 77.
3. Schlesinger, p. 125.

4. Robert S. Lynd and Helen Merrell Lynd, *Middletown, A Study in Modern American Culture* (New York: Harcourt, Brace and World, Inc., 1929), p. 381, n.6.

5. *Since Yesterday: The 1930's in America* (New York: Harper and Row, 1939), p. 222.

6. Allen, p. 224.

7. Geoffrey Perrett, *Days of Sadness, Years of Triumph: The American People 1939–1945* (New York: Coward-McCann-Geoghegan, 1973), p. 162.

8. Perrett, p. 239.

9. Sklar, *Movie Made America*, p. 269.

10. Manny Farber, "Movies in Wartime," *New Republic*, CX (January 3, 1944), p. 19.

11. *Film Daily Yearbook of Motion Pictures: 1944* (New York: Film Daily, Inc., 1944), p. 44.

12. Richard R. Lingeman, *Don't You Know There's a War On? The American Home Front, 1941–1945* (New York: G.P. Putnam's Sons, 1970), p. 206. Lingeman goes on to cite a Republic production, *The Fighting Seabees*, as illustrative of the Hollywood patriotic film of the period and its effect on youth.

13. "A Relationship of Constrained Anxiety: Historians and Film," *The History Teacher*, VI (1973), p. 553.

14. Isenberg, p. 557.

15. Isenberg, p. 561.

16. Isenberg, p. 568. A book length treatment, Paul Smith, ed., *The Historian and Film* (New York: Cambridge University Press, 1976), covers much of the same ground, comes to many of the same conclusions and includes historical and geographical surveys of the subject as well as a look at resources. Most contributors conclude that the import of a film, "the film fact," is more than just the factual material in a film and what it is about. It is the sum of the film, where it was made, how it was made, how the audience perceived it and accepted it, and what it can add to an understanding of the society out of which it came. Film as a reflection of and influence of society is where the importance of film to the historian lies, seems to be the general conclusion of the book.

17. Letter from Garth Jowett to author, December 2, 1975.

18. "An Anthropologist Looks at the Movies," *The Annals of the American Academy of Political and Social Sciences*, CCLIV (November, 1947), p. 80.

19. Powdermaker, p. 81.

20. Powdermaker, p. 87.

21. *The Film: A Psychological Study: The Silent Photoplay in 1916* (New York: Dover Publications, 1970), p. 100.

22. Munsterberg, p. 95.

23. Sklar, pp. 135–139.

24. *Movies, Delinquency, and Crime* (New York: Macmillan Company, 1933, reprint, ed., New York: Arno Press, 1970), p. 202.

25. *Our Movie Made Children* (New York: Macmillan Company, 1935, reprint, ed., New York: Arno Press, 1970), p. 2.

26. Forman, p. 177.

27. Forman, p. 277.

28. Martha Wolfenstein and Nathan Leites, *Movies: A Psychological Study* (New York: Free Press, 1950, reprinted, New York: Hafner Publishing Company, 1971), p. 13.

29. David Manning White and Richard Averson, *The Celluloid Weapon: Social Comment in the American Film* (Boston: Beacon Press, 1972), p. x.

30. Peter Bogdanovich, *Fritz Lang in America* (New York: Frederick A. Praeger, Inc., 1967), p. 16.

31. "A Broad Mosaic on the Social Screen," *American Film I* (June, 1976), p. 73.

32. Powdermaker, p. 80.

33. Interview with Sloan Nibley, Republic writer, Los Angeles, California, May 4, 1976.

34. Wolfenstein and Leites, p. 14.

35. Wolfenstein and Leites, p. 178.

36. Wolfenstein and Leites, p. 304–305.

37. White and Averson, p. 107.

38. "Hollywood and the U.S.A." in Bernard Rosenberg and David Manning White, ed., *Mass Culture: Popular Arts in America* (New York: Free Press, 1964), p. 292.

39. White and Averson, p. 207.

40. White and Averson, p. 25.

41. *The Unembarrassed Muse: The Popular Arts in America* (New York: Dial Press, 1970), p. 387.

42. Miller, *B Movies*, p. 34.

43. "Those First Rate Second Features." *Films and Filmmaking, II* (September 1956), p. 17.

44. Joan Cohen, "The Second Feature: The Rise and Fall of the B Movies," *Mankind, V* (June, 1976), p. 26.

45. Cohen, "Second Feature," p. 29.

46. Cohen, "Second Feature," p. 35.

47. Francis Nevins, *Review of Kings of the Bs, Films in Review, XXVI* (October, 1975), p. 499.

48. William Everson, *Review of B Movies, Films in Review, XXV* (November, 1974), p. 564.

49. Sklar, p. 282.

50. Powdermaker, "An Anthropologist Looks at the Film," p. 86.

51. Interview with Albert S. Rogell, Republic director, Los Angeles, California, May 5, 1976.

52. Telephone interview with Vera H. Ralston, Republic actress, Santa Barbara, California, May 10, 1976.

53. David B. Whalen, "Republic Pictures," *The Film Daily Cavalcade* (1939), p. 176, in the Republic clipping file of the Margaret Herrick Library of the Academy of Motion Picture Arts and Sciences, Los Angeles, California.

54. Whalen, "Republic," p. 179.

55. Whalen, "Republic," p. 179.

56. Whalen, "Republic," p. 181.

57. David Hanna in the *New York Times*, February 2, 1941.

58. *New York Times*, February 2, 1941.

59. *Variety*, Ninth Anniversary Edition, October 29, 1942, p. 271.

60. *Variety*, October 29, 1942, p. 271.

61. *Variety*, October 29, 1942, p. 271.

62. *Variety*, Tenth Anniversary Edition, October 29, 1943, p. 455.

63. Vern Haugland, "Don Barry Is Western Star No. 5 after Short, Swift Rise in Films," November 8, [1942]. Unidentified newspaper clipping in the Donald Barry clipping file of the Theatrical Division of the New York Public Library at Lincoln Center.

64. *New York Daily Mirror*, June 4, 1942.

65. Haugland, "Don Barry," November 8, [1942].

66. Interview with Donald Barry, Hollywood, California, May 6, 1976.

67. Telephone interview with Sol C. Siegel, Los Angeles, California, May 5, 1976.

68. Interview with Albert S. Rogell, Los Angeles, California, May 5, 1976.

69. Telephone interview with Bruce Bennett, Los Angeles, California, May 7, 1976.

70. Telephone interview with Robert Livingston, Los Angeles, California, May 8, 1976.

71. Telephone interview with Vera H. Ralston, Santa Barbara, California, May 10, 1976.

72. Interview with Barry Shipman, San Bernardino, California, May 11, 1976.

73. Interview with Rowland "Dick" Hills, Los Angeles, California, May 13, 1976.

74. Interview with Morris R. Abrams, Los Angeles, California, May 17, 1976.

75. Interview with Peggy Stewart, North Hollywood, California, May 18, 1976.

76. "Republic Pictures Celebrates its Tenth Anniversary," *The Independent*, CXXXVIH (June 23, 1945), p. 30.

CHAPTER FOUR

~

The Sound Serial and Republic's Golden Age

Republic did not invent the serial format—the company simply developed it to its highest form in the sound era through judicious application of talent, care, and technical knowledge. The serial, early in its development in the silent period, was locked into the cliffhanger format. In some respects this was a mixed blessing in that it proved detrimental to plot and character development but, because the development necessitated a "thrill" ending to each chapter, it did result in an emphasis on action and violence. By the time that the first tentative completely sound serial, *The Indians Are Coming* (Universal, 1930), was produced, the action-escapist entertainment format was assured.

Thomas Wood, entertainment feature writer for the *New York Times*, summarized the format near the beginning of the sound serial's decline. "The first episode establishes the characters and the goal that is to be achieved. The rest of the chapters try to keep the audience in a state of nervous exhaustion until the star accomplishes the appointed task. The goal, of course, is of earthshaking importance, like a new formula for cracking the atom."[1] This rigid formula based on physical conflict meant that there was a minimum of dialogue. As William Roberts in a feature story entitled "Cliffhanger" put it:

Even the advent of the talkies had little effect on the serials. They contain an absolute minimum of dialogue, for the essence of good serial-making is action. Ron Davidson [Republic director, writer] sets his writers a standard of no more than 700 words per episode, which makes for a pretty tight-lipped 15 minutes.[2]

All of which meant that the serial genre is dependent upon getting its entertainment values, minimum plot, and message to the audience by the simple technique of pacing and action. While not sophisticated, this is not necessarily bad. As Roberts commented: "Many a director and writer learned his trade grinding out serials, and might do a better job today if he went back and rediscovered how to maintain pace and suspense."[3] In any case, the action-oriented "cliffhanging" trademark to grasp and hold on to the audience was irreversibly linked to the sound serial.

Prior to the end of the motion picture serial in 1956, 231 sound productions were released. Universal produced 69; Republic, 66; Columbia, 57; Mascot, 24; and 15 came from independents. Universal depended mainly upon relatively more plot with adequate action, effects, and sets; Republic, and its predecessor Mascot to a degree, relied heavily on outstanding action, special effects, and pacing with secondary consideration upon plot; and Columbia with a few notable exceptions was concerned with short-cut production to maximize profits after the first few years so that the plot and the action, which was usually frenetic if nothing else, suffered accordingly. The quality and value of the independent productions varied greatly.

The serials tended to fall conveniently into several categories although there were, of course, some productions such as *Phantom Empire* (Mascot, 1934) which defied classification—i.e., it had elements of science fiction, the Western, and even musical comedy. Nonetheless, a quick survey of the important categories with an outstanding example from each include:

1. Mad Scientists—*SOS Coast Guard* (Republic, 1937);
2. The Western—*The Lone Ranger* (Republic, 1938);
3. Aviation—*Tailspin Tommy in the Great Air Mystery* (Universal, 1935);
4. Jungle Adventures—*Jungle Girl* (Republic, 1941);
5. Detectives—*Dick Tracy* (Republic, 1937);
6. Costumed Heroes—*Adventures of Captain Marvel* (Republic, 1941);
7. Outer Space Science Fiction—*Flash Gordon* (Universal, 1936);
8. Straight Adventure—*Daredevils of the Red Circle* (Republic, 1939).

The sound serials were generally considered to be in their Golden Age, due mainly to the Republic contributions, from approximately 1938 to 1944 and after the war began to decline.[4] The last really unique serial in the author's opinion was *King of the Rocket Men* from Republic in 1949 and that production, although worthy, was a flawed production showing the pressures of grim economic reality. More will be said of this serial below. Movie serial production ceased in 1956 due predominantly to the competition of television and to an increasing sophistication in the audience. Would that it could be reported that they maintained quality up to the end. However, the last years were quite abysmal with increasing reliance on stock footage and routine action sequences.[5]

In order to understand the serials, their potential influence, and the reaction of their audience to them, it is important to be familiar with the basic value system upon which they were predicated and a simple requirement for absorbing them. The importance of conflict has been established but, more importantly, it was always virtuous conflict. The basic value system of the serial is represented in a plot formula which is a simplistic representation of good versus evil in black and white terms with evil temporarily winning each round but with good ultimately triumphing. The audience comprised of children, the uneducated, and those desiring a temporary escape into a more simple approach to life accepted and understood this basic rule. The concept of good ultimately triumphant over evil resulted in a firm moral and ethical basis for all sound serial production, the foundation of which was a naive idealism. In many respects this simple foundation was beneficial in that the serial audiences seemed to have resulted in relatively stable individuals whereas more recent generations which have been exposed to "gray" interpretations of life, "realistically" portrayed—to more complex moral and ethical issues in their entertainment—seem to be far more unreliable, confused, and unstable in the area of determining right from wrong.[6] This is admittedly a sweeping generalization but the point which resulted in this controversial observation remains fact. The serials had a solid idealistic ethical foundation—at least on the surface.

The requirement for absorbing and enjoying the serial was also a simple one—easily understood by the generations of the 1930s and 1940s but a bit more difficult for the later sophisticated television era. The requirement was simply that the viewer accept a willing suspension of disbelief. No serial would stand up under stern, critical, realistic analysis. It was necessary to accept the spirit of the concept—that villains were maniacal with no redeeming social qualities, that they could have vast networks of henchmen, that heroes were dedicated, compulsive, and believed in direct action, and finally that both sides would clash violently on a regular basis until good won out. These confrontations rarely involved anyone outside the combatants except abstractly in that society as a whole was theoretically a gigantic pawn which represented the final prize in the contest. Oh yes, either side was frequently conveniently identified by a costumed mystery leader. This was a standard gimmick, "the wienie" as it was called, and together with the outlandish situations and basic conflict kept the audience coming back.

It might be pointed out that both the value system and the requirement for accepting the serials has continued in different, somewhat more "sophisticated," and sometimes less identifiable forms in the entertainment media to the present day. A ready example is that of James Bond of the cinema.[7] Times and tastes may change but seemingly the needs and weaknesses which attract the audience remain somewhat constant.

The concept of a willing suspension of disbelief is not only basic, it is perhaps the most important aspect of the serial form's success and the key to whatever influence the genre may have had. Although his interpretation is a bit strained in reaching for grandeur and importance, Jon Tuska touches on it in commenting on the significance of Nat Levine who, as it has been pointed out, headed Mascot and supervised the early Republic serials.

> As a producer, Nat Levine sought neither prestige nor profundity. He loved the serial as a very special medium and assembled on his rented sets and leased lots a dedicated group of professionals that, very often, made the budgets of his pictures a secondary consideration. Mascot story-lines were invariably fantastic, highly original, but visually powerful, even unforgettable. The serials were mostly intended for youngsters and so stressed images and settings and situations that appealed instinctively and indelibly to youthful imaginations. In fact, one of the strongest and most notable aspects of the Mascot serials is this importance of make-believe. It served not only Levine, but many film-makers in the late 'Twenties and early 'Thirties, creating pictures often compromised by the test of time and the increased cynicism of modern audiences.[8]

Because Levine was such a master of make-believe and utilized the suspension of disbelief so well even with inexpensive budgets and extremely limited schedules, Tuska attributes an influence to Levine's serials, particularly the Mascots, which he finds almost mystical. While this interpretation of such significance is perhaps overblown and certainly diverges sharply with the hypothesis of a simple straightforward message of good versus evil, Tuska's viewpoint does indicate that the serial form had an influence and, by implication, that it supported the traditional morality.

> The viewer believes because the characters themselves believe, so caught up in the basic premises of the far-fetched and imaginative plot that, for the moment at any rate, all critical faculties are suspended before the somewhat awesome spectacle. The overwhelming visual impact of Levine's images—and they must be attributed to him, and not to others, because they appear in all his serials to a greater or lesser extent—have an existence of their own and generate a psychic excitement rarely to be found in waking life, a dream-like quality which is vivid and unassailable.[9]

Tuska is speaking of a specific serial but the generalization is that with serials the audience accepted the premise wholeheartedly, and were extremely receptive because they were so involved. As a result, the serials became a learning process for a value system.

The genre might also contribute to learning in yet another way. P. E. Emery, an Australian behavioral psychologist, has studied the potential learning processes in the Western film and discusses the relationship of the learning effect to the completion of the goals of the story or, to put it another way, the attention of the audience and thus its receptivity to learning is held to the climax. To illustrate, he uses the serial as an example.

> In the sense that there may be goal regions in the programmes it is more reasonable to identify them with the climax or series of climaxes that occur within the story. Serial programmes throw some light on this problem. They are usually organized so that the end of each part corresponds with incomplete climax. The resultant tensions toward completion are resolved by further viewing—in other words, even in this case, it makes no sense to regard the finish of viewing as a goal.[10]

Once again, a rather sophisticated and technical study has been utilized to reinforce a simple truth. To make profits and to entertain, the serials continually ended in tension to keep the viewer coming back. This fact also results in holding that same viewer's attention which leads to a potential learning effect. So, while the serial was not created as a learning device, it did so function.

Even the Payne Fund studies single out the serial genre as being an effective learning force, although in keeping with the tone of the series, he uses serials as a negative illustration.

> And a college girl, early fed upon serials with Pearl White and Warner Oland in them, writes: "He, Warner Oland, was always wicked in the canny, cunning, heartless mandarin who pursued Pearl White through so many serials. I carried over this impression to all Asiatics. . . . *I have not been able to this day to erase that apprehensive feeling whenever I see a Chinese person, so deep and strong were those early impressions.*"
>
> In italicizing the last lines of this statement, we wish to point to the fact that . . . her attitude, notwithstanding her greater knowledge, is permanently qualified by the ideas of the movies she had seen in childhood. . . .[11]

Hollywood accepted both the idea that the serials were influential and that, without proper controls, they would be a negative force. Thomas Wood, writer for the *New York Times*, notes this fact rather critically in an unpublished manuscript. "Probably nowhere else in the world does Crime pay less than in the moving picture serial. Because its sub-teen admirers are felt to be in the 'impressionable' state, the serial is considered as harmless as a time bomb. Every episode, before its public release, is subjected to a scrutiny that could do credit to the Gestapo. Not only must the chapter pass the officious Hays organization, but it must also satisfy the delegates of a dozen women's clubs in the vicinity."[12] Wood obviously feels this situation is unnecessary and goes on to point out that in actuality it represents a double standard.

> The fact that the Hays office cracks down on them much harder than on the units engaged in making feature pictures obviously distresses the serial producers. "Raft and Cagney can slug women all over the screen" one observed recently, "but we're ham-strung the minute we make a pass at the girl, even when it's plot. We can't muss her up at all. If she's to be tied and gagged, it must be done off scene. And when we move in on her with the camera, her hair must be just so. As if she's got a date for dinner at Ciro's."
>
> Unfair as it apparently all is, there is no higher court to which the serial maker can appeal his case. Not one theater in the country would even dream of exhibiting a serial that cannot show a clean bill of health from the Hays office. Plus merit badges from the Parent-Teachers Association, the Women's Auxiliary, the Church and Civic groups and the various State Censorship boards. Just about everyone, in fact, except the members of the local Bund.[13]

All of this of course contributed to the moral emphasis of the serials—action, conflict, yes, glorification of evil, no. As previously covered, the outlook of the times and the attitude of Herbert Yates were also involved where Republic was concerned. As a result, the serials were blatantly patriotic. William K. Everson comments on this regarding the Second World War period. "World War II induced a change in serial plots. The intrepid heroes were diverted to blocking espionage and sabotage by Nazi and Japanese villains. Since these enemy agents often operated in African jungles and on Western ranges, there was no great change in serial locations."[14] While he implies that the shift came after December 7, 1941, there were several previous serials at Republic which were either service oriented or, as the war approached, had the home front fending off nefarious schemes by thinly disguised Axis agents as shall be seen.

The patriotic heroics during the early to mid-1940s were generally cheered or at least accepted by moviegoers and critics alike. With the coming of the Cold War, the situation changed. It was almost imperceptible at the time but attitudes alter and in hindsight the anticommunist propaganda, while no worse than the antifascist themes of the wartime period, has been highly criticized. Still, at the time the audiences accepted it, in the McCarthy era the critics could do no more than look down their noses at it disdainfully, and in the context of the times it was understandable. However, the audience was changing and the attitudes varied. On the subject of the Cold War, Everson states:

> The anti-Communist feeling also got into serials, and not a few were utilized for crude propaganda. Nationalities were rarely mentioned, but since the villains were named Ivan and Boris, and spoke about the "unimportance of the individual" and "the leader's liberation of the people," it was fairly obvious that peace wasn't being threatened by the Samoans!
>
> At Republic the slickness and speed of the serials compensated to some extent for their tired subject matter. . . .[15]

What seems a diatribe now, was, at least to some, influential patriotism then.

A related and applicable point to the political implications of the serials lies in a consideration of where its audience was—not only here in the United States but worldwide. Their appeal in the States has already been documented and it was considerable. The serial had pulling power beyond the features in some areas. As William Roberts noted in the *Los Angeles Times*, "At present, serials are slanted at special types of audiences. First in importance is the Saturday-afternoon kiddie trade. Then comes the rural audience. It is a familiar practice to offer serials and westerns to country theater owners as an inducement to take the high-budget A pictures which in the big cities, sell like nylons."[16]

But, at the same time, the serial had vast appeal beyond our borders where the political implications and patriotism also served as effective propaganda. However, since action predominated, too much should not be made of this point. The basic theme of good versus evil regardless of the political climate of the moment prevailed.

> It is precisely this simplicity that makes for the world-wide popularity of serials. All you need are a few subtitles and the picture is ready to be shown anywhere. Whether you are an Incan, Arab or Mongolian, it requires no elaborate explanation to realize that Jack Armstrong is in trouble when the steel walls of his cell start to close in and crush him to pulp.[17]

For example, it was common practice in the 1940s to show serials complete in one sitting in Latin America and the audiences were extremely enthusiastic. In fact the popular wrestling/horror series of films often starring Santos owe a great debt to the American serial.

Thus, the serial genre far from being moribund in the sound era did indeed exert an influence, sometimes political in tone but always basically moral. Despite strenuous efforts to control and water down the content, the serial remained a popular international commodity until its demise and even continues in limited distribution on television, in rural areas, and in foreign markets to the present.[18] What was Republic's contribution to this phenomenon?

With its attention to detail and spirit of teamwork, Republic quickly evolved their serial production work into a science. Republic decided what serials it would schedule each year from the suggestions of their exhibitors and the studio's own ideas of what would be profitable. The final decision rested with the front office. In the spring of each year, four titles for the next season would be announced, the first to be released in the fall and the last the following summer. The four projected serials were then budgeted and divided into two groups—twelve chapter "streamline" serials or fifteen chapter "super" serials.[19]

The producer then met with the writers who worked on schedules of three months for each serial. The writers, totaling up to seven, then developed the plot to go with the title, keeping an eye out for the use of possible stock footage from other films, the use of existing sets, and determining possible location sites available for their use. Each writer then developed several individual chapters and finally as a group they integrated their efforts into a complete script.[20] The first chapter developed the plot, the gimmicks, and laid out the basic cast of characters. Each following chapter began with a brief synopsis of plot, an "overlap" of previous footage reviewing the cliffhanger, and the actual escape. The plot then moved along including an obligatory action sequence midchapter. The cliffhanger was then set up and abruptly upon its occurrence, usually with a great deal of action and/or suspense, the chapter concluded.

Upon approval of the preliminary submission the writers wrote an "estimating" script which was used to determine probable shooting costs. At Republic, these budgets ran from $81,924 to $193,878 over a period of twenty years.[21] This same "estimating" script was used to check any legal problems, was submitted to the review board for censorship, and was the basis for the pressbook publicity campaign even though there might be, and usually were, some rewrites. The polished rewrite became the shooting script which occasionally underwent some alteration during the actual production.

Preproduction was the next step and included casting of leads, costume design, set construction, location contracts, and the lining up of props and equipment. A daily breakdown of set-ups was normally created to permit all scenes on one location or set to be filmed together and re-edited into plot sequence later. This was an ingenious time and money saving device necessary due to the large number of setups used in a shooting schedule that ranged from a minimum of eighteen to forty-eight days.[22]

Production normally began on location with interiors shot later and two crews were often used—the first shooting dialogue and plot and the second unit crew shooting chases and stunt action. The special effects were shot last because they took more time and care and because the miniatures had to match the previously shot footage utilizing full size action. At Republic, after the first few serials, separate music was also composed for the serials which undoubtedly contributed to their slickness. During production, assistant editors daily organized the finished footage by scenes.

Next came the post-production phase in which the visuals for each episode were put together at the rate of one a week. To this was added the music, sound effects, and any rerecorded dialogue, all of which was finally rerecorded by sound-mixers into the sound track. Finally Republic's parent laboratory Consolidated Film Industries processed the results adding titles, opticals, and other finishing touches to produce what the viewer saw on his movie screen. The completed serials of Republic ran from 166 minutes and 40 seconds to 289 minutes and 54 seconds and the final negative costs ranged from $87,655 to $222,906 minus distribution and print costs.[23] Republic began releasing each serial when about half of its episodes were in the can and it generally took between a year and eighteen months to complete each serial's run in original release.

The Republic team with a strong assist from Nat Levine, whose experience and talent with the serials has been documented, recognized the potential of serials and quickly mastered the guidelines set forth in the preceding section through a process of trial and error. Because of the combination of good people and fine facilities, Republic serials gained recognition from the beginning. According to one historian, of all the serial companies, including those of the silent era, only Republic succeeded in making their product "socially acceptable."[24] Not every serial from Republic emphasized the virtues of patriotism, fair play, individualism, leadership, upright living, and other middle American values, but they were present whenever possible and frequently prevalent.

The first serial made under the Republic banner was *Darkest Africa*, released in February 1936, and directed by B. Reeves Eason, noted action director and film second unit man, and Joseph Kane, who graduated to Republic feature director. A jungle adventure with fantasy overtones, the story centered on the Lost City of Joba hidden in the African jungle where a white girl named Valerie was kept prisoner and worshiped as a goddess. Her brother, Baru, escapes from the city and seeks help. Clyde Beatty playing himself returns with Baru to the Lost City. They are secretly followed by two greedy animal traders, rivals of Beatty, who have reason to believe there are emerald deposits in the Lost City. Thus, Clyde and Baru have to contend with the machinations of these villains, plus those of Dagna, high priest of Joba. To keep things active they also are menaced periodically by wild animals as well as an array of flying Bat-men who guard the Lost City. After fifteen chapters of confrontations, they eventually rescued Valerie.[25] Rugged individualism and fairness versus greed and cheating were a prominent motif but the message was subdued.

Since the Republic staff was feeling its way, the serial suffers from padding—a result of Republic's well intentioned decision to make first chapters of their serials a hefty one-half hour and subsequent chapters approximately twenty minutes—and from some rather poor acting throughout. However, the special effects were well done, especially those of the flying Bat-men in flight. They are a worthy predecessor to the flying figures in *Captain Marvel* (1941) and *King of the Rocket Men* (1949), and were an early indication of the studio's striving for quality. All in all the serial was a good, if not outstanding, beginning.

Since the element of fantasy had worked in their first serial, Republic continued it in its second effort, *Undersea Kingdom*, again directed by Eason and Kane and released the same year. This was the first of the service-oriented serials, but since the Navy was in prominence only in Chapters One and Twelve, its patriotic theme was limited. The plot concerns a young Naval officer Ray "Crash" Corrigan, a girl reporter, a scientist, and his twelve-year-old son who dive to the ocean floor in a rocket propelled submarine to investigate the source of extensive earthquakes. They find the Lost City of Atlantis on the ocean floor where two factions were in constant combat. The white robes are under the benign high priest Sharad, and the black robes are ruled by the tyrannical Unga Khan who intends to rule not only Atlantis but the upper world as well. The newcomers soon find themselves allied with the white robes obviously.[26]

Battle scenes between the two factions in Chapter Four, repeated in Chapter Ten, were considered superb and on a par with the battle sequences in *Intolerance*. They were directed by Eason who also specialized in doing massive second unit direction for the majors, including the burning of Atlanta in *Gone with the Wind* and the crowd sequences in *Duel in the Sun*[27]—again showing the expertise of Republic personnel. The serial made use of a curious mixture of ancient paraphernalia such as chariots, catapults, and swords and futuristic weapons such as superplanes, bombs, flame throwers, and atom guns. It also utilized robots, television, an impressive anti-aircraft gun, and a machine which turned men into mindless slaves.[28] The influence of the comic strip *Flash Gordon* and its Universal serial adaptation was undeniable.

The message to the audience was fairly clear. The hero was a clean-cut, handsome, athletic American youth and a pride of Annapolis. His heroism and leadership abilities are heavily stressed although the heroics sometimes approached the foolhardy. For example, at the end of Chapter Eight, he is captured and bound to the front of the futuristic tank utilized by the villains. When the action heavy threatens to run the tank through the fortress gates using Corrigan as a battering ram unless he cooperates, the hero's brave reply is snarling bravado, "Go ahead and ram!" It was a moment of hero-worship for the youth in the audience and led to an exciting chapter ending but one which is known as a "cheat." In Chapter Eight, the tank obviously smashed with great force into the recessed fortress gates. In Chapter Nine, however, the gates were opened at the last second and the tank stops quietly in the courtyard. Such "cheat" endings were relatively infrequent at Republic, incidentally.

Republic's third serial was *The Vigilantes Are Coming*, and was the first of Republic's eighteen Western serials. It was directed by Mack V. Wright and Ray Taylor, both veteran serial directors. The story had a Zorro-like masked man called "The Eagle" organizing vigilante opposition to a would-be dictator in California in the 1840s. It also bore some resemblance to Rudolph Valentino's feature *The Eagle* (United Artists, 1925) which was set in Russia. Released in 1936, it was somewhat slower than the first two Republic serials, but did serve to introduce to Republic Robert Livingston, who was to become a Republic stalwart, in the lead. While Livingston was not enthusiastic about doing serials, he told the author that Republic certainly knew what they were doing with the serials. While not unique or imaginative, the serial was an acceptable Western effort. It was loosely based on factual incidents in California's early history in the 1840s involving attempted Russian colonization and stressed the bravery and scruples of the vigilantes especially in Chapters Five to Seven in a lengthy battle with the Cossacks.[29]

Republic's fourth and last serial for 1936 was entitled *Robinson Crusoe of Clipper Island* directed by Wright and Taylor. It was an adventure serial about a Polynesian member of the United States Intelligence Service who was sent to a small Pacific island to investigate a dirigible crash. He finds an international spy ring operating on the island headed by the first of Republic's many mystery villains. Throughout fourteen chapters, the hero has to contend with both the spy ring and a tribe of unfriendly natives before he is able to defeat and unmask the mystery man. While this was a good straight action serial with some fine special effects involving aircraft and volcanoes, about the only really notable thing concerning it is the unusual number of chapters—fourteen as opposed to the normal twelve or fifteen. That and the fact that William Witney, of whom more will be heard, served as a film editor.[30]

Republic began 1937 by producing the first of their comic strip heroes in serial format. *Dick Tracy* as portrayed by Ralph Byrd was an unqualified success and eventually led to three sequels. In the first Tracy outing, he was directed by Ray Taylor and Alan James, and was opposing a gang of criminals headed by a mastermind known alternately as the Spider and the Lame One. This colorful evildoer utilized a flying wing and Tracy's own brother as a member of his forces. This serial included an economy chapter which was a money-saving device that Republic and other studios utilized in order to save money. In Chapter Thirteen of *Dick Tracy*, various members of the cast sat around and discussed what had happened up to that point using flashbacks from earlier episodes before bringing the episode to a conclusion with a new cliffhanger ending.[31] Despite this factor and some questionable comic padding, *Dick Tracy* is considered to be a fine example of the detective serial although its action and pacing were not on a par with its three follow-ups.

Since Republic was in only its second year of serial production, the serial unit was still finding its way but was convinced that the use of comic characters and specifically Dick Tracy would be a successful venture. To this end, Republic was extremely competitive with both Universal and Columbia to obtain rights to this property.[32] Of course, the success of not one but four Tracy serials was to vindicate Levine's confidence. However, he and others at Republic did have one reservation about Tracy and it was concerned with influence and censorship. Tracy symbolized hard line law and order but with massive doses of explicit violence. "This violent means of self-preservation and approach to eradicating crime—upon which both Gould [Tracy's creator/author] and Patterson [*Chicago Tribune-New York Times* syndicate] bestowed their blessing—evinced Republic's only cause for concern. . . . Levine, although admitting the strip's 'blood and thunder' would have to be toned down to circumvent unfavorable reaction from women's clubs and churches . . . contacted . . . [the syndicate] which represented Gould."[33]

The Los Angeles office of the FBI cooperated in the production of this serial and the result was an action coated paean to the forces of law and order. So effective was the figure of Dick Tracy as the archetypal representation of law enforcement that the identity of the lead actor was submerged to that of the hero which he played. As Thomas Wood noted at the time of Tracy's greatest popularity, "On a recent personal appearance tour Ralph Byrd, who plays 'Dick Tracy,' was billed as 'Dick Tracy in person.' 'The name Ralph Byrd wouldn't have meant a thing,' one theater exhibitor said."[34]

Republic's next release in 1937 was *The Painted Stallion*, and it was directed by Ray Taylor, Alan James, and William Witney—the third of whom took over this production in progress and went on to become one of the greatest of the Republic action directors. The straightforward Western plot was set in the early nineteenth century when Mexico had just broken ties with Spain and wished to establish trade relations with the United States. Clark Stewart, portrayed by Ray Corrigan, represents the United States and is traveling with a wagon train to Santa Fe to sign a pact with the new Mexican governor. Opposing the wagon train was the about-to-be-ousted Lieutenant Governor of Santa Fe who moonlighted as the head of a gang of outlaws which preyed on wagon trains. This serial introduced another favorite Republic gimmick—the mysterious helper. An unknown Indian girl called the Rider, who rides a painted stallion and accurately dispatches whistling arrows, appears to help the heroes frequently. The serial also utilized actual historical figures but little history and was well paced although stock footage and some padding was included.

Despite the fact that it was bogus history, this serial did maintain a historical flavor and somewhat paralleled the westward movement in the 1820s. The prologue set the tone. "Westward! The Trail to Empire! From Independence, Missouri to Santa Fe, New Mexico, dogged pioneers fought to penetrate a wilderness of savage Indians . . . massacres and death. To the heroes of yesterday!—Those pioneers who braved the perilous trek westward, defeated a hostile wilderness, and blazed a glorious trail across the pages of American history."[35] Stirring words which in emphasizing our historical heritage perhaps made history classes a little more palatable and maybe even interesting to the Saturday matinee audiences.

Republic's third serial of 1937 was *SOS Coast Guard* and had Ralph Byrd as Terry Kent of the Coast Guard opposing a mad inventor portrayed by horror star Bela Lugosi. The villain has invented a disintegrating gas and plans to sell it abroad. The Coast Guard foils him in twelve chapters. Although not especially outstanding, the serial was later edited into a movie version and has interesting special effects. Republic was beginning to hit its stride as a purveyor of action. William Witney and Alan James directed this serial which was Republic's annual honor to a branch of the military service complete with patriotic prologue. The preceding year, it was the Navy. In 1937 it was the Coast Guard. The next year it was to be the Marines. After the third year the policy was dropped.[36] The patriotism of the war years was to more than make up for the omission.

For the last serial of 1937, Republic turned to the pulp character Zorro. *Zorro Rides Again* concerns the exploits of the great-grandson of the original Zorro, James Vega, as portrayed by John Carroll, in his fight to save the California Yucatan railroad from a crooked American entrepreneur trying to seize it with the help of an outlaw gang headed by El Lobo. Like the original Zorro, Vega masquerades as a fop to conceal the fact that he is the masked hero. Rather than relying heavily on strained comedy relief for padding as had been done in the previous serials, the studio decided to use musical numbers to fill in. There was a song sung by the hero in nearly every chapter and it was a questionable improvement indeed. Also, due to a change in the script, the fate of the main villain is unresolved—an odd slip to be sure.[37] However, this serial is a landmark in that it was directed by William Witney and John English. With this serial the Witney-English team was formed. Together, they proved to be perhaps the best sound serial directors of all time. The Witney-English professionalism, pacing, and technical knowledge was evident in *Zorro Rides Again* and in sixteen serials that followed. It was this directorial team which was responsible for a large portion of the "Golden Age" serials.

There have been many tributes to the Witney-English team but one of the most interesting appeared in the French movie journal *Positif*. A liberal translation includes the statement, "The serials directed by William Witney and John English . . . are as a group among the most lively and intense expression of art from the American cinema of the period. These films present the spectator with the sense of suspense and danger . . . of camaraderie. . . . In these films Witney and English are mirroring the life of the present. . . . Frontiers of violence, cooperation, destiny, scientific inquiry . . . this is the purpose of the cinema."[38] Allowing for the French propensity for overstatement concerning the art of the film, it is still clear that the serials of Witney and English did indeed have some impact on more than just American children.

Consciously or unconsciously, Republic Studios had utilized its first eight serials as a continuing experiment to determine the best format for this type of production. While these first eight serials varied from good to fine, they were merely a prelude to what followed. As Ed Connor stated in *Screen Facts*: "At the end of their first eight serials, Republic had 'found' themselves. Having ironed out the kinks in their serial armor, they now set out to apply a high polish, and in the next six years they would produce the finest talking serials ever made."[39] The Golden Age of Republic serials lasted roughly from the beginning of 1938 until the end of 1944.

Before discussing the Golden Age, a slight digression is in order concerning the Republic brand of action as analyzed by William Witney, one of the men who brought it to near perfection. Just as Republic conceivably had a positive effect upon their audience with their action laden serials and B movies, so might these same films be criticized for their potential negative influence of the violent aspects of such action sequences. Witney has spoken to this point. In an interview published in a major serial journal, he recounts that they had a sign on the wall at Republic which read "A pair of wet panties for every little kiddie."[40] Although the story of the sign might be apocryphal, it illustrates that the goal of the sound serials was to excite, to thrill, and sometimes to slightly frighten (although through apprehension and excitement rather than shock) the children at which they were aimed. To re-emphasize the point made by Witney (endnote 40), this was not realistic, sadistic, or gory violence. If someone was struck with a gun or club it was never shown in close-up. No wounds were shown. In fact blood was a rarity even in small amounts. It was "clean" violence and the thrills came from the gimmicks, the stunts, and the special effects as opposed to brutality, gore, or sadism.[41] Of course, "clean" violence is also controversial but that controversy is beyond the scope of the present study.

The first serial in 1938 was *The Lone Ranger* based on the well known radio show and directed by the Witney-English team. Set in Texas in the Reconstruction era, the story opens with the leader of a band of outlaws capturing and killing a professional investigator from Washington. Using his name, credentials, and position, the villain sets out to make himself dictator of Texas. He orders the destruction of a group of Texas Rangers who are on their way to see him. However, one, whose face is not seen by the audience, is found by an Indian named Tonto and recovers. Calling himself the Lone Ranger and wearing a mask, he sets out to oppose the dictator and is so successful that his capture becomes the main concern of the villain and his henchmen.

It was determined by the heavy that one of five men in the town which he uses as headquarters was indeed the Lone Ranger. In the course of fifteen chapters the quintette of Ranger suspects is gradually lessened, one after the other being killed off every three or four chapters, until in Chapter Fifteen only two remained. One was shot and killed, but his identity was not yet disclosed to the audience. After a service for the four dead Rangers in the last chapter, the Lone Ranger, portrayed by Lee Powell, identifies himself to the heroine before making the traditional exit so familiar to the radio audience.[42] *The Lone Ranger* is considered to be one of the best Western serials ever made by many serial experts although it is rarely seen today and exists only in a bowdlerized version with Spanish subtitles. The mystery hero motif first utilized by Republic in this serial proved highly effective.

And the serial was quite successful at the time of its initial circulation and gave the genre in general and especially the Republic product a noticeable boost. Thomas Wood summarizes it.

> The best record hung up in recent years is that of the "Lone Ranger," a serial which cost $285,000 and eventually grossed $1,250,000. Based on a radio program emanating from Station WXYZ in Detroit, the film played 7,500 houses in Canada and this country, including some of the swank Loew's theaters in New York City, and was ultimately translated into ten different languages: French, Dutch, Belgian, German, Spanish, Italian, Swedish, Turkish, Portuguese and Chinese. The only country which didn't go for it was Great Britain, which has always been a blind spot for serials. In 1940, however, the "Lone Ranger" was telescoped into a feature picture and re-released under the title, "Hi-Yo Silver." The British liked it fine in the abridged form.
>
> The popularity of the "Lone Ranger" reversed a serial trend. It inspired King Features, the newspaper syndicate, to release a cartoon strip based upon his activities.[43]

The Lone Ranger as presented by Republic was a classic good guy. This was partially due to contractual demands by the character's official creator, George Trendle. "Trendle envisioned his creation in real-life form as following the mold of such contemporary western stars as Tom Mix, William S. Hart, and Richard Dix. Specified to be a clean-shaven, rugged outdoors type of a height not less than 5-foot-11 and a weight of approximately 170 pounds, the white-stetsoned, boot-shod, but chap-less Lone Ranger was not to swear or drink and could only smoke if the plot demanded. . . ."[44]

Not only did the Ranger behave with heroic selfless qualities, his four helpers emulated him admirably, each eventually dying heroically. For example, in Chapter One all five suspects are imprisoned in jail whereupon the real Lone Ranger identifies himself and states, "I didn't tell Jefferies [the villain] because I wanted to speak with you men first. There is a lot to be accomplished. Texas needs loyal fighters." One of the heroes replied, "Jefferies won't keep his word anyway. We're in this thing together and we'll stick together." The Lone Ranger points out, "I can't let you die on my account." To which a spokesman for all the heroes replies, "If we die, it will be together and for Texas." The Ranger concludes, "You men have the spirit of Rangers. I am glad."[45] The ideals of loyalty, honor, and dedication to a just cause were thus impressed on a youthful audience. Nonetheless, owner George Trendle was not enthusiastic about the liberties taken with the Lone Ranger.

Republic utilized two of the stars of *The Lone Ranger*, Lee Powell and Herman Brix, in its next serial, *The Fighting Devil Dogs*, again from the Witney-

English team. This is an excellent serial which oddly enough was produced with a great deal of economy. The serial made numerous use of newsreel clips, stock footage, and included not one but two economy chapters, Chapters Seven and Eleven, made up entirely of flashbacks as the characters discuss earlier events.[46] Nonetheless due to good direction, pacing, effects, and a strong villain figure, the serial worked. The plot basically concerns the exciting, non-stop, action-packed events surrounding the attempts of two marines to stop the campaign of a mad scientist who, in an especially arresting secret identity as "the Lightning," is well on his way to taking over the world. Armed with serial torpedoes which he calls electrical thunderbolts, and other electrical devices of a destructive nature, "the Lightning" is indeed a magnificent and colorful antagonist. The identity of the "the Lightning" is the major mystery element and audience attraction until the final chapter of the serial. The Lightning is generally considered to be the direct inspiration for *Star Wars'* Darth Vader.

Despite the emphasis on the powerful mystery villain, this serial was the third and last service oriented chapterplay and the Marines were spotlighted accordingly. Not only was there the traditional patriotic credit in the prologue—"To the United States Marines—vigilant guardians of our flag at home and abroad"—Chapter One opened with a thinly disguised real marine assignment in China in 1937, thus giving a good excuse to include actual newsreel film.[47] Whatever the reason, the flagwaving scenes and patriotic dialogue were obvious but still subdued to the action themes and worked very well in the context of the story.

Republic's third serial for 1938 was the first sequel to the successful *Dick Tracy*. It was entitled *Dick Tracy Returns* with Ralph Byrd again repeating the title role, although the supporting cast was new. The story centers around Tracy's battles against notorious West Coast criminal Pa Stark and his five sons in their imaginative criminal activities. While it was a more straightforward detective story than any of the other Tracy vehicles, excitement was not lacking in this entry. The Stark gang were enmeshed in plots involving an armored truck, attempting to steal army and navy secret weapons, extorting money by threatening to wreck a two hundred inch lens of a giant telescope, and other nefarious plans. The resemblance to Ma Barker was intentional and the serial lacked the science fiction elements of the first and later Tracy entries. Although intentional, this un-gimmicked crime drama approach possibly strengthened the law and order message of the serial. Despite the somewhat rambling plot and the presence of two economy chapters, the second Tracy serial was still well made and was saved by rapid pacing. It was the fourth success in a row for the team of Witney and English.

That both Republic and the censors were aware of the impact that serials might have is shown in this case. *Dick Tracy Returns* received some sixteen separate cuts in the first chapter following its initial release. These were categorized as "details of crime" and "scenes of gruesomeness" and included a brutal killing of a wounded FBI man and the graphic suffering of a victim writhing in an iron lung.[48] Republic of course made the required cuts in the questionable scenes which in no way detracted from Tracy's image as the guardian of the law.

The final serial release of 1938 was *Hawk of the Wilderness* loosely based upon a novel of the same name. The rather complex story line (for a serial) has the hero, Kioga, a white boy raised by Indians on an island near the Alaskan coast, rescuing and defending a shipwrecked scientific expedition from both pirates and hostile Indians. In Chapter Twelve the group finally escapes the island in an abandoned plane. The outdoor adventure serial was highlighted by the usual Republic quality and several special effects—engineered volcanic eruptions as well as extensive location shooting. It was again competently directed by Witney and English, and starred Herman Brix (Bruce Bennett) as Kioga.

Although this serial has no outstanding positive message other than the reoccurring theme of rugged individualism—the hero is an Indian version of Tarzan and acts accordingly—it does have two incidents of racism, an unconscious and unintended negative factor. In Chapter Two the Indian chief doesn't comprehend the black skin of the comic relief Negro and screams when threatened with the same fate. Although done for humor, the poor taste is blatant in retrospect. Also in the final chapter, one character calls the hero an "imitation white man." The "insult" clearly puts the character in an unsympathetic light. He is subsequently killed and by dying helps the hero's party to escape the island and thus resolve the plot.[49]

The Lone Ranger Rides Again was Republic's first release of 1939, and was a sequel to the earlier *Lone Ranger*, although no closer to the radio origin than was the first serial. This time the Lone Ranger was portrayed by Robert Livingston and was identified as Bill Andrews, a completely different character from that of the Lone Ranger in the original serial. He was a scout for a wagon train of homesteaders and went into action as the Lone Ranger when the homesteaders were threatened by villainous ranchers, again accompanied by Tonto. It was a standard Western plot of ranchers versus settlers and showed little imagination. "It was unfortunate that four writers in developing a sequel, should offer the Lone Ranger nothing more than a range war to cope with—a plot used over and over again in other western productions."[50] The serial is considered to be notably weaker than the original but has the usual good stunt work and chapter endings. Nonetheless, it is often felt to be a lesser Witney-English effort.[51] The problem may have been related to a change in lead actors as well as a weaker plot structure. "Kids are very fierce in their loyalties. Two years ago Republic switched 'Lone Rangers' on them. From a $1,250,000 gross on the first, the take on the second fell to $500,000," was a contemporary opinion.[52] Whether it was the plot, the casting, or another factor, this sequel was considered to be less than its predecessor. But it is still a good Western serial when not held up to comparison.

These facts in no way detract from the continuing popularity of the main character and the serial was still a success, only relatively less so than its almost archetypal predecessor. Based partially on the widespread popularity of the first serial, the Lone Ranger radio program had increased circulation fourfold, a comic strip version had been created, and various merchandising products had been authorized. The figure was truly an influential force for American youth. And the serial counterpart retained his heroic proportions and virtuous image—although oddly enough he did manage to kill seven heavies, a violation of his "shoot to wound" code.[53]

Perhaps the most obvious example of the Lone Ranger's power as a force for good came in the concluding scenes of the final episode when one of the antagonists, now at peace with a treaty signed and the plot resolved, eulogized, "Lone Ranger . . . New Mexico, as well as your mother state of Texas, owes you an overwhelming debt of gratitude. Owing to your efforts, this is now a peaceful territory. Law and order prevail. This document guarantees that now a man can live with safety, work in the fields, ride the range, or otherwise indulge in the pursuit of happiness."[54] A more succinct statement of the hero's goal and therefore of the message found in this, and many other Republic serials, would be hard to locate. Nonetheless, George Trendle decreed no more sequels and the two original serials were not reissued. The only existing copies come from poor existing Spanish copies.

After a bit of a slip with the Lone Ranger sequel, Witney and English came up with an outstanding serial in the next release, *Daredevils of the Red Circle*. An escaped convict who prefers to call himself by his old prison number has set out to revenge himself upon the industrialist Horace Granville, the man responsible for his imprisonment. He impersonates the real Granville in a basement cell, takes over his identity with the use of makeup, and with the aid of Granville's doctor gradually begins to wreck all of Granville's enterprises. One of these enterprises is an amusement pier where a death defying act is done by the daredevils portrayed by Charles Quigley, Herman Brix, and David Sharpe. It is these three "daredevils of the red circle," who, because of the death of the leader's younger brother, determine to stop the attacks upon Granville enterprises. Following an outstanding first chapter cliffhanger in which an underground highway tunnel is destroyed at its dedication by sabotage which results in flooding from the river above, the daredevils fight schemes in such ideal serial locations as a chemical factory, a gas plant, an oil derrick field, a radium mine, and a power house, until the villain is unmasked in Chapter Ten and the real Granville rescued.

The special effects at the conclusion of Chapter One incidentally match and surpass a similar sequence in the more expensive *Earthquake* from the 1970s. It is again an example of Republic's talent and attention to detail. Chapter Eleven is an economy episode and Chapter Twelve brings the villains to justice. Nonetheless, it was an excellent serial and is often rated as the best single example of the adventure serial in the sound era.[55] It was in this serial that the Witney technique of choreographing fight sequences, famous among fans, first appears—which is to say that the sequences were laid out in advance, filmed in short segments with rest periods or less strenuous shots in between, and expertly edited into a finished flowing action shot later. Witney got the idea from observing Busby Berkley's dance choreography. While this development may not have been directly influential upon the audience, since fight sequences, good and bad, were an integral part of the serial genre, it was certainly a contribution to the technique of stunting and made the final product all the more polished and exciting. Perhaps this fact—i.e., the slickness of production—increased the audience acceptance of the story and therefore did contribute to potential impact upon the viewer. Slickness of production, although sometimes overlooked or downgraded as insignificant, does contribute to audience receptivity of a film and this would include any conscious or unconscious messages the film might contain.

Dick Tracy's G-Men, the third release of 1939 and the third of the Dick Tracy serials, followed. Again Tracy was portrayed by Ralph Byrd, although the supporting cast was once more changed. In this entry, Tracy is up against a master villain named Zarnoff, the head of a vast spy organization, portrayed by Irving Pichel, a sometimes director of interesting films. Although executed in the first chapter, the spy leader is brought back to life and makes attempts on the Great Industrial Canal, the life of a Latin American president, a two and one-half million dollar gold shipment, army and navy secret weapons, and a dirigible called the Pan Pacific (in reality the Hindenburg landing in Lakehurst, New Jersey). As previously noted, Republic always made good use of intercutting newsreel footage with their fictional plots and the dirigible sequence is a magnificent example of this money-saving but successful technique. Witney and English directed.

Here again, Tracy as the master detective represented the theme of law and order. Only this time out, there was a slight variation, one which would become dominant over the next few years. Instead of fighting a science fiction criminal mastermind or the fictional counterparts to a real life criminal family, Tracy was up against an international spy ring. With this type of plot, the themes of patriotism, the FBI as guardian, preparedness, and protection of democracy were prevalent throughout.

In the opening sequence, a pseudo-newsreel report showed Tracy capturing Zarnoff and concludes with an interview of Tracy. He states, "Nicholas Zarnoff was like a rat, gnawing at the foundations of democracy. Like any other rat carrying germs of plague and disease, he had to be exterminated. I sincerely hope his execution . . . will serve as a warning to any other spies or troublemakers who might think America is easy pickings."[56] The effect upon the Saturday matinee crowd was predictable. It still worked fairly well when the serial was re-released sixteen years later in 1955 even though the external enemies and the international situation had altered.

Zorro's Fighting Legion was Republic's final serial for 1939 and was the only one of the five Zorro titles and two imitations in which the original Zorro character actually appeared. Zorro/Vega as portrayed by Reed Hadley, with Yakima Canutt handling all the stunts, is opposed to an activated Indian idol, Don Del Oro, who is in reality a white man attempting to take over Mexico by using the Indians for his own end in 1824. The idol-god rouses the Indians against the whites to wreck the new Republic. A Legion to fight the enemies of the Republic is formed by Vega's uncle and, upon his death, is taken over by Zorro, hence the title of the chapterplay. The Legion is opposed by two groups under Don Del Oro, the aforementioned Indians, and a group of white renegades for good measure. Under the direction of Witney and English, it took Zorro twelve action-packed chapters filled with fine stunt work, chases, bull whip tricks, and even frequent sword fights to discover the true identity of Del Oro from four possible suspects and defeat the villains in the process.[57]

At least one critic feels that *Zorro's Fighting Legion* surpassed *The Lone Ranger* as the best Western sound serial. Francis Nevins states: "A sense of exhilaration, good humor, joy in life, and in fighting the good fight and in making movies, permeates every frame. From *Zorro's Fighting Legion* we learn what the serial at its best can be."[58]

Again, a Republic serial was based loosely upon historic events which served as a springboard for a completely unrelated plot. This time the period was in the 1820s in Mexico. And, also again, censorship came in to play although the end results were a bit different for once. Concern was expressed over the fact that Zorro lightly carves his initial on his opponent's forehead during sword play in Chapter One. Although the event occurs in the original story, it was felt that the scene might have implications of horror for the youthful audience. However, it was allowed to stay but with a minimum of blood. Quickly done, it gave the appearance of a surface scratch. "Exactly one year later the Hays office refused to pass such a scene for the Tyrone Power feature *Mark of Zorro* (Twentieth Century-Fox, 1940). So what was okay for the kiddies was too much for their parents."[59] This amusing anecdote was an exception to the reverse rule in an environment where the effects of serials on the younger audience was a continuing concern as pointed out by Thomas Wood earlier in this chapter.

In 1940 the Golden Age of Republic serials really moved into high gear. Late in 1939 the *Motion Picture Herald* had carried the news item that Republic Studios had paid in excess of one hundred thousand dollars for the screen rights to Sax Rohmer's *Drums of Fu Manchu* to be made into their first serial release in 1940.[60] Oddly enough, after paying this extremely high price for the rights to a serial property, Republic turned the book over to six of their own writers who rewrote the plot utilizing very little except the title. Nonetheless, this Republic serial production was unique in that it relied more on plot than most Republic serials while still retaining a great amount of action for fans.

The basic plot concerns the implementation of a plan by Fu Manchu to have himself declared the messiah who would appear bearing the sceptre of Genghis Khan to unite the Orientals of the world. Fu Manchu, portrayed by Henry Brandon in a bravado performance, and aided by his daughter and the SiFan, a secret organization, plus a small army of dacoits arrives in California to obtain the Dali Plaque, the first in a series of clues which will enable him to find the lost tomb of Khan and the necessary sceptre. Fu and his minions are opposed by six whites including Fu's old adversary Nayland Smith, Doctor Petrie, and the action hero portrayed by Robert Kellard. During the succeeding fourteen chapters following Chapter One, the heroes and the villains follow up various clues in the United States and Asia in order to find the tomb of Genghis Khan. In Chapter Eleven Alan Parker, the action hero, obtains possession of the sceptre. The final four chapters then become a struggle between Fu Manchu and the heroes for control of the sceptre enlivened by uprisings among the hill tribes. Although Fu was defeated in the final chapter, he escapes with his life and swears vengeance.[61]

Obviously a sequel was planned, but for various reasons was never completed. This serial is considered one of Republic's finest chapterplays predominantly due to its emphasis on an ominous mood and Brandon's performance. It used a great deal of stock footage from 1938's *Storm over Bengal* but nonetheless profited from a complex plot, fine acting, and some futuristic sets and weapons. Incidentally, the sequel was never made due to two factors: (1) complaints from the Chinese government due to the touchy international situation in 1940 (apparently the yellow peril motif, blatant as it was, was not appreciated universally), and (2) because of complaints from various parent groups that the serial actually frightened children due to its excellent use of suspense.[62] This second point is ironic indeed because steps had been taken prior to production to remove the fearful aspects of the dacoits. "Perhaps the most gruesome of the entourage was the chief dacoit, Loki. The writers decided to make him a real terrifier and described him in their original script as not having a mouth. Obviously the censor felt this was a little too much, so Loki remained mute, and had a mouth, with two vampire-like fangs protruding from under his upper lip."[63] The censors spotted the horror potential in the obvious visual menace of the dacoits but failed to see the influence that suspense, a much more nebulous but effective force, might have on the audience.

The second serial of 1940 was another Witney-English Western and another winner. *The Adventures of Red Ryder*, adapted from the popular comic strip by Fred Harmon, had a straightforward formulaic plot. It centers on the villainous activities of a banker trying to gain control of the territory needed as a right-of-way by the Santa Fe Railroad and utilizing the services of an outlaw gang headed by Ace Hanlon, portrayed by Noah Berry. After the leaders of an organization organized to fight this gang were killed, Red Ryder takes over—his father having been one of the slain leaders. The outlaws indulge in wholesale murder of the opposition, rob a stage coach, dynamite a dam and a pass, poison a creek, set fire to a reserve water tank, kidnap Little Beaver and Red Ryder so that he cannot take part in a crucial stage coach race and indulge in other nefarious deeds.[64] Of course, Red Ryder, portrayed by Don "Red" Barry, triumphs in Chapter Twelve, but not before many thrilling and well staged stunts were enacted. These sequences were so good in fact that they were much used in later features and serials as stock shots.[65]

Red Ryder, while perhaps not in the same category as the godlike Lone Ranger, also was quite a popular figure and great care was taken that his upstanding good guy image remained untarnished. In Chapter Eleven he was to kill a major villain in a showdown and it was originally planned to have him shoot this unfortunate four times. Joseph Breen of the Motion Picture Producers and Distributors of America cut this down to one shot as the additional three would seem both brutal and revenge motivated—not appropriate reactions on the part of the hero.[66] Oddly enough, although this serial gave Don Barry his nickname and led to a B Western series for him, he did not want the role. He told me that Herb Yates insisted on his casting even though he was physically inappropriate.

The third serial of 1940 was *King of the Royal Mounted* and again was taken from a comic strip character. However, this character had also previously originated in a book by Zane Grey. Since the United States was not yet at war with Germany, although Canada was, the villains were not identified as Germans but the implication was obvious. The writers concocted a plot concerning discovery of a "Compound X" at a Canadian mining spot. The mysterious "Compound X" had both the power to cure infantile paralysis (good) as well as being important in the manufacture of magnetic mines (evil). One villainous mine owner kills his more humanitarian partner and makes a deal with the "foreign power" whose agent arrives via submarine and spends the twelve chapters attempting to obtain "Compound X" and arrange its delivery to his country. He and his gang of outlaws are opposed by the Canadian Mounties led by Sergeant King, portrayed by Allan Lane. During the course of the serial, Sergeant King's father and best friend, both Mounties also, give their lives to save his, and he is ultimately triumphant over powers of evil as represented by Germany. The entry had the usual Witney-English polish and served to introduce Allan Lane to the Republic stable of serial stars.

This serial was the second to emphasize patriotism in relation to contemporary international affairs (the first was *Dick Tracy's G-Men*) and, by setting the action in Canada, the plot was able to get across a message concerning a situation in the offing but not yet upon us. "In the character of Sergeant Dave King, the studio had the perfect hero for a well-made 'preparedness' chapter-play at a time when our country had not entered World War II, but was feeling the tensions the Axis powers were causing."[67]

The theme of self-sacrifice was logically interwoven with the patriotic message. In the final chapter, King's best friend, fellow Mountie, and secondary hero sacrificed himself and saves King by knocking King out, ejecting him from a submarine through a torpedo tube, and destroying the sub, the villains, and himself—an act which King had planned to personally perform before his friend intervened. Later King tells his friend's sister, "Orders are orders Linda. Tom obeyed his, that's why the King presented him with the Victoria Cross. You must be awfully proud of him." She replied, "I am. I don't even think of him as dead. I'll always see him riding as he used to ride . . . happy, free, proud of the uniform he wore . . . proud to serve Canada. I'll see him riding like that as long as I live."[68] This theme and similar dialogue, appropriately rewritten, was to reoccur in other Republic serials and was undoubtedly an effective influence in promoting the romantic concept that submission to the cause of right even to the ultimate sacrifice is worthwhile. It must be remembered too that such scenes did not have to overcome the sophistication, maturity, and cynicism of the modern audience. Its acceptance was assisted by the prevailing ideals of the time and by a more receptive audience. This serial long unavailable was released in 2004 to the general public through the courtesy of Jack Mathis.

Republic's final serial for the year was not based on a book or comic strip character unlike the preceding five entries. However, it is an outstanding example of the serial genre and is a favorite among serial fans and invariably makes various top ten lists. Entitled *Mysterious Doctor Satan*, it has an adventure plot with elements of the costumed hero and science fiction and is strong in the basic dichotomy of good versus evil as outlined in the beginning of this chapter. A superscientist criminal, named appropriately Doctor Satan, portrayed by the well known character actor Eduardo Ciannelli, invents a robot which he intends to be the first in an army of mechanical men to take over the wealth and power of the world. Since the robot can be controlled over a limited area only, Doctor Satan sets out to obtain a remote control cell developed by a Professor Scott. To this end, he kidnaps the Professor, obtains the secret of the cell, and gets the necessary tungite for its construction and operation. Throughout the serial, Doctor Satan is opposed by a colorful masked hero, the Copperhead who wears only a chainmail hood as a disguise in order to vindicate the memory of his father who had used the same identity in the Old West but was identified unjustly as a criminal. Witney and English utilize a variety of sets and situations which made for fifteen well produced chapters without the inclusion of the usual economy chapter. Whereas some entries in the Golden Age of Serials made during the period after which the United States had entered the war in spite of good production values nonetheless still show necessary economic limitations, *Doctor Satan*, made well before the war, not only showed no such limitations, it positively sparkled with variety and unusual sets. A great deal of exterior work and excellent stunts were included to give the serial pacing and movement which was outstanding.

Two outstanding examples of the thrills which were included in this serial are offered as examples—one based in special effects and the other in first class stunt work. At the end of Chapter Eight, the villains release a fuel along a hillside road from a gasoline truck and set fire to the resulting stream. The Copperhead pursuing in a speeding car is engulfed in the flaming gasoline and the car explodes in a spectacular long shot. The miniature work done in this sequence by the famous Lydecker brothers was superior to many major productions of that time and later periods.

Secondly, at the end of Chapter Ten, the Copperhead is again pursuing a villain in a gas works, this time on foot. After a thrilling chase involving climbing over and fighting among the vast storage tanks, the villain crosses over a girder between two tanks and, when the Copperhead attempts to follow, the heavy swings a huge grappling hook suspended from above striking the Copperhead in the chest and throwing him from the beam apparently to his death. The stunt work by David Sharpe and Levon James was excellent and, again, was better than that found in many major productions during this one sequence alone.[69] As an aside, it might be mentioned that the escape was not a standard simple out such as grabbing hold of the girder or of a projection as the hero fell. Rather the Copperhead grabs the rope at the other end of the grappling hook and swings down thus managing to stop his fall when the hook reaches the top of the pulley. He eventually climbs back up the rope to continue the fight until he is victorious over the fleeing villain.

Nevins incidentally cites this serial as exemplifying Witney's "regeneration theme" but this rather mystical interpretation was lost upon contemporary audiences and it is not totally applicable to a study of more immediate forms of influence.[70] However, a more direct effect from this serial is applicable. The Copperhead was originally motivated by a desire for vengeance—a favorite motif but always a touchy problem. Joseph Breen once again interceded, resulting in this motif being toned down in the dialogue and legitimatized by having the hero legally deputized in the first chapter to fight against the evil Satan.[71]

Incidentally, *The Mysterious Doctor Satan* was originally written as a *Superman* vehicle but contractual problems resulted in a dead-end to this project and the script was rewritten extensively to fit the concept of a mortal vulnerable hero. Republic continued in an attempt to obtain the screen rights to the comic strip *Superman* but was again unsuccessful since the publishers wished to have control over the completed script—a situation which Republic rarely allowed as will be seen.[72] Therefore, it turned to *Adventures of Captain Marvel* from Fawcett Publishers and this became the studio's first serial in 1941. In terms of stunt work and special effects, this is considered to be perhaps the best sound serial ever produced. Fans who lean toward "fight and chase" sequences have some objections, but nonetheless most recognize the quality of this serial.

The story, with its inherent strains of white supremacy and racism, centers around a scientific expedition in Siam which discovers in a sealed tomb a Golden Scorpion idol with five lenses in its claws and a scroll with instructions for how the lenses can be arranged to either turn base material into gold or, rearranged into another position, to become a powerful disintegrating ray.

Unknown to the five scientists, Billy Batson, a reporter who has accompanied the expedition but has refused to enter the "cursed" tomb, has been given, in return for his respect for the curse, the power to become Captain Marvel, a nearly invulnerable mortal with powers of flight. The scientists agreed to divide the five lenses among themselves as a safety precaution against greed and to give the scroll with directions and the scorpion idol to Billy for safekeeping. One of the scientists, the prerequisite villain, masquerades as the Scorpion God and arranges for the local natives to attack the expedition in order to obtain the power of the idol solely for himself. Captain Marvel engages the natives in combat in an amazing display of stunt work and special effects techniques. The expedition returns to the United States where it becomes obvious that the mysterious Scorpion villain is either one of the five scientists or their native interpreter. The remaining eleven of the twelve chapters are concerned with the gradual destruction of the scientific group as the Scorpion obtains the lenses and comes closer to his goal of world power. During the last two chapters the expedition returns to Siam, where Captain Marvel unmasks and defeats the villain whereupon the power is removed from Billy Batson.[73]

Because Republic controlled the rights to the character in so far as the serial was concerned, it was able to take certain liberties including the arbitrary removal of superpowers from the main character at the conclusion. However, in this case, these changes did not seriously damage the image of the comic book creation. Tom Tyler portrayed Captain Marvel and Frank Coghlan, Jr., portrayed Billy Batson. Witney and English again directed. The special effects of the Lydeckers were numerous and outstanding and are invariably commented on favorably. Using a wired lightweight dummy slightly larger than life-sized, they gave an extremely effective visual image of Captain Marvel flying through the air from various angles, across a dam pursuing a villain in the same frame, and up to the tops of buildings—the latter sequence being filmed in reverse for a smooth flight.[74] Dave Sharpe provided the close-up stunts of the leaps and the fight sequences for Captain Marvel. Although the superman aspects of the hero decreased the traditional fight and chase action motifs, the serial was indeed a *tour de force*.

Captain Marvel was unquestionably a force for good as shown in his last statement—and one of his longest speeches. The character was not given to words where action would suffice. Upon destroying the Golden Scorpion, he delivered a stirring plea for decency, "This scorpion is a symbol of power that could have helped build a world beyond man's greatest hopes . . . a world of freedom, equality, and justice for all men. But in the greedy hands of men like Bentley it would have become a symbol of death and destruction. Then, until such time when there's a better understanding among men, may the fiery lava of Scorpio burn the memory of this from their minds."[75] Oddly enough, given Marvel's heightened moral image, there were also a few surprising moral lapses in *Adventures of Captain Marvel*—the hero kills some men without justification in two separate encounters and the action heavy escapes unpunished in Chapter Ten (a script error)—but these slips have been treated in detail elsewhere and do not detract from the overall moral tone of the serial. In fact, their existence goes so against the grain of serial morality that they are quite noticeable to most viewers.[76]

Republic's second effort in 1941 was *Jungle Girl*, loosely based on a book by Edgar Rice Burroughs, which is to say Republic used the author's name and title. It was an attempt to revive the era of the silent serial queens—a project which Republic undertook periodically with limited success throughout the 1940s.[77] The plot was a little thin, not especially imaginative, and concerned the exploits of Nyoka, portrayed by Frances Gifford, who assisted by the hero, portrayed by Tom Neal, attempted to block the plans of the villains to obtain the diamond mines of an African tribe—inherent racism again. Nyoka's father was a doctor respected by the tribe who has been killed by his criminal twin brother and replaced by the twin unknown to the heroes. The evil twin brother, his larcenous henchmen, and the witch doctor of the tribe spend fifteen chapters alternately trying to obtain the diamonds or to sacrifice Nyoka to the Lion God. As jungle series go, Witney and English with the aid of fine production values and some entertaining cliffhangers made this a very good if not outstanding one. Gifford was good to look at and a few of the set action pieces were imaginative and pulse pounding. Which is not to say that the serial was unsuccessful. Far from it. Thomas Wood elaborated, "Suppose . . . you stumble in on 'Jungle Girl.' Chances are about three to two that you will. For this super-serial, which tells of a mistress of an empire of savages and beasts in fifteen dragged-out chapters, has been cleaning up all over the country. It was released last May and so far it's hit 6,000 screens, leaving out the prestige places, like the Radio City Music Hall, there's only 4,000 or so left."[78] *Jungle Girl* was pretty much a case of saturation marketing for a serial and it undoubtedly reached a vast number of people. While it had no specific messages such as patriotism or sacrifice, its basic theme of good versus evil was quite prominent as can be seen from the plot synopsis.

The third Republic release of 1941 was to have not only the required message of good prevailing over evil, it was also to have liberal doses of patriotism, preparedness, sacrifice, fair play, and Americanism. It also included an explicit vengeance theme until this aspect was toned down. Why Republic writers continually introduced this plot device knowing full well that it was verboten and would be watered down or removed by the watchdogs of morality is an unresolved mystery.

The serial was entitled *King of the Texas Rangers* and attempts to revive yet another serial tradition of the past, only this time the attempt was a one-shot. The serial starred "Slinging" Sammy Baugh, former All-American quarterback and professional football player with the Washington Redskins, and was a throwback to the utilization of sports stars such as Gene Tunney and Red Grange in serial productions. Tom King as portrayed by Baugh leaves professional football and thus sacrificed a brilliant career to join the Texas Rangers to avenge, through legal means, the death of his Texas Ranger father. He and a Mexican aide battle espionage activities on the border. The fifth column menace was a timely and, in this period, an obvious theme. The villains led by Don Barton, portrayed by ex-motion picture star Neal Hamilton, take their orders from a foreign power whose representative bases his operations in a dirigible cruising over the Texas/Mexican border. Once again the villains were obviously German and Nazi, although not specifically identified as such. The saboteurs are attempting to either obtain control of or destroy the oil fields of a Texas border town but, after twelve well-paced episodes with outstanding miniature explosions by the Lydeckers, are defeated by the cooperative efforts of the Texas Rangers and the Mexican Rurales. This is a good example of a modern Western serial but, while it benefits from the expected Republic quality and touch, it was not exceptional. Witney and English again proved themselves masters of the genre however and the messages were recognizably there.

The vengeance motive did not fit into the traditional idealism of a fairminded, justice oriented hero and brought about some detailed and severe comments from the censors.

In Episode One, "The Fifth Column Strikes," [the hero] learns the whereabouts of his father's murderer, and quite naturally, expresses a desire to even the score. But the Hays office turned on the red light. In a letter to the studio, it wrote:

We have read the estimating script, dated May 14, 1941 of Episode 1, "The Fifth Column Strikes," for your proposed serial KING OF THE TEXAS RANGERS (Production #996), which is not entirely satisfactory in its present form, but which will be approved by us if the suggestions made hereinafter are complied with. At the beginning of this serial we wish to give you the following general cautions which will apply to the whole story:

1. Killings must be held to an absolute minimum.
2. Gruesomeness must be avoided at all times and all horror angles must be handled with great care.

3. Under the provisions of the Production Code, it is unacceptable, in a modern story such as this, to suggest that your hero, King, is motivated by *revenge* at any time. This element of revenge is now present in Episode 1, in the scene where King takes off his badge and goes across the border to get the man who killed his father. This motivation must be changed, and it must be clearly indicated that the reason for King going after this man is to bring him to Justice. We call your attention to the paragraph in the Production Code which states: "Revenge in modern times shall not be justified."

4. Even when acting within his duly constituted authority as a Texas Ranger, it is important that Bob be not shown killing heavies indiscriminately. The action should be modified so that these heavies die as a result of their own actions rather than the actions of your hero.

5. Also have in mind that under the provisions of the Production Code, we cannot approve scenes showing gun battles between criminals and law-enforcing officers. As now written, Episode 1 contains several scenes, to be mentioned below, which violate this provision. It is important that the actual shots fired in these battles be held to two or three. It is also unacceptable to show illegal weapons in the hands of criminals. For your information, an illegal gun is one which fires two or more shots without releasing the trigger.

The letter then takes up specific points in the script in detail. And it is made clear that "(a) Muzzles of guns cannot look straight into the camera, as on Page 13; (b) Heavies cannot be shown in possession of machine guns on board Zeppelins, as on Page 21; (c) References to 'nitro glycerine' and 'nitro' are objectionable and must be deleted although such words as 'soup' or 'explosives' may be substituted, as on Pages 29, 43, 48, 49, 51, and 53; (d) Scenes showing characters being hit on the head with chairs, stools and other implements are not allowed, as on Page 34; and (e) There must be no undue emphasis on the sound track when the King clunk Ross, the heavy, out of frame, as on Page 45."[79]

It is true that the Hays office letter was somewhat inconsistent in that scenes such as (4), (5), (a), (d), and (e) were periodically included in both Republic productions and in films at other studios. Still, the incident shows the concern and care which the serials received and speaks indirectly as a strong argument in favor of their significance.

The final production for 1941 was the fourth of the Dick Tracy quartet and again stressed law and order, honesty, fair play, and other basic values. Entitled *Dick Tracy vs. Crime, Inc.* it again starred Ralph Byrd as Tracy, and concerns his continuing battle against a mysterious masked individual called The Ghost, who through an ingenious invention, was capable of making himself invisible. Tracy doesn't discover this ability until Chapter Fourteen which gives the heavy a definite edge. The Ghost is systematically killing off the "Council of Eight" which had been formed to fight his successful reign of crime. As in past serials, it is obvious that The Ghost is one of the "Council of Eight" but his identity is not absolutely known until Chapter Fifteen. His attempts to gain wealth as well as to decimate the "Council of Eight" are certainly on a grand style as befits a serial villain. At one point he bombs a geographic fault near New York Harbor to flood and destroy New York City when the governing officials refuse his demand for ransom. Stock footage from RKO's *The Deluge* (1933) was used in this sequence as well as in two future serials. In fact, much stock footage was used in this Dick Tracy serial including some of the best sequences from the first three Tracy serials. Nonetheless, a good deal of new footage was shot and shows the usual fine special effects and stunt work on which Republic built its reputation. The final chapter has a concluding confrontation which is invariably commented upon.[80] Tracy has a lamp equipped with an infrared ray which makes the invisible Ghost visible. A violent, surrealistic, weird fight between Tracy and The Ghost follows his discovery and is photographed entirely in negative. Although The Ghost eventually breaks the lamp in the fight and escapes temporarily, he is electrocuted while attempting to cross some high wires. As he dies, his body bursts into flame. Strong stuff but well done.

This entry unfortunately was the last of the seventeen Witney-English serials for Republic, although each director went on to do some very good work on his own. Together they had been responsible for over half the total output of the Golden Age of Republic serials. Had this team continued, perhaps the Golden Age of Republic serials would have extended indefinitely. Nonetheless, it still had two to three years to run before the luster wore off and routine set in.

For their first production of 1942, Republic turned to *Spy Smasher*, another Fawcett publisher's comic book character which they had obtained the rights to at the same time that they contracted for *Captain Marvel*. Alan Armstrong alias Spy Smasher, portrayed by Kane Richmond, is doing battle in a wartime situation against his Nazi enemy, the Mask—a carry over from the comics. Spy Smasher is aided by Admiral Corby and his daughter Eve, as well as a character newly created for the serial, Alan's twin brother, Jack. Jack strengthened the story line and provided a most intriguing cliffhanger in Chapter Eleven. At the cliffhanger, Spy Smasher is obviously killed without a chance of escape even if a "cheat" situation was introduced the following week. In Chapter Twelve it turns out that it was his brother masquerading in his place who heroically met his death, thus enabling Spy Smasher to go forth, "reborn," to defeat the Mask and the Nazi saboteurs in the thrill-packed conclusion which was exhausting even for a serial.[81] This chapterplay was solo directed by William Witney and, since he specialized in action rather than dialogue sequences, is non-stop action whenever conceivable. In fact, Chapters Nine, Ten, and Eleven are one continuous action sequence with only a short break before leading into the final hectic action sequence in the concluding chapter. *Spy Smasher* shows all of Witney's previous experience in that it is crammed with magnificently staged fights and chases, and also includes a group of technically difficult, matched split screen shots involving the star Kane Richmond portraying the identical twin brothers. In spite of the outstanding action and special effects however, the message managed to be delivered.

If the themes of patriotism, sacrifice, and a glorification of Americanism were noticeable in previous serial efforts as they obviously were, then it might be said that in *Spy Smasher* these themes became all pervasive. *Spy Smasher* was especially rich in high moral, middle class American values—the motifs which influenced the American youth of the period. In addition to being a fine action serial, it was a primary example of the serial with a message—and it worked. Since it was the first Republic serial production released during the war and was in the planning stages when war was declared, any flimsy pretense of neutrality which might have watered down the message was unnecessary and so it went all out. As a result, "'Spy Smasher' is still considered to be one of the best comic-strip based spy fighter serials."[82] The serial was "charismatic in its presentation as a prime example of the sound serial's finest hour."[83]

Prior to our actual entry into the war, a prologue to *Spy Smasher* was written to be delivered on film by none other than FBI head J. Edgar Hoover. At this time, he was still held in high esteem. He accepted the offer and was to pontificate:

> Unlike almost every other country in the world, the United States has never resorted to the use of spies except for purely military purposes when we are not actually at war. Unfortunately for the peace of the world there are nations that do not hesitate to use not only spies but their more sinister companions, the propagandist and the saboteur. Today is a time of crisis; a period during which all Americans must be alert to these enemies within our borders as well as the dangers from without. Only by the utmost vigilance can we safeguard our liberty and maintain our national unity. While this picture you are about to see is entirely fictional, its hero Spy Smasher symbolizes American patriotism in action against those subversive forces which may be far from imaginary.[84]

When war was actually declared prior to *Spy Smasher*'s filming, this prologue was dropped as no longer being relevant. But its existence and original acceptance shows the tone of the serial quite well. It also indicates that the FBI felt a serial could deliver a message.

There were of course related themes dear to American audiences. Pierre Durand, the hero's French ally, sacrifices himself for Spy Smasher in a submarine encounter bridging Chapters Two and Three which is very similar to the previous confrontation in *King of the Royal Mounted*. Spy Smasher's brother later comments "This must have been his way of saying 'Go on and win for freedom and democracy.'"[85] Then, the same theme was even more forcefully brought forth when, as mentioned above, Jack substitutes himself for Spy Smasher in Chapter Eleven, walks into a trap, is shot several times, and falls from a high building, thus making the ultimate sacrifice for the American way of life as represented by the godlike hero.

In another vein, that of fairness, Spy Smasher in the comic book has the use of a futuristic aircraft called the gyrosub. In the serial, this is transposed into the Bat plane and was at the service of the villains, though only for one chapter. The reasoning behind this reversal was that should Spy Smasher have this weapon it would give him an edge. In the interest of justice and fair play, it was considered inadmissible for the hero to have the advantage over the villains.[86]

Lest it be considered that all of this interpretation is being read into the serial by outsiders with the advantage of hindsight, it might be well to include the reaction of *Spy Smasher*'s director. At a revival of this serial, William Witney was interviewed and claimed, "'It was an era of ruggedness in America. My generation won a war with them (serials).' 'Although he knows that the serial is gone today, he thinks that the audience for which they were made is still the same. Anyone under 13 today still has the same dreams and hopes that you and I did when we were under 13,' he said."[87]

Republic's second entry in 1942, again directed by Witney alone, was *Perils of Nyoka*. This pseudo-sequel to the previous *Jungle Girl* actually involved a different character with the same first name. This deliberate manipulation was undertaken because Republic owned the rights to the name Nyoka while Burroughs owned the rights to the rest of the material in his book *Jungle Girl*.[88] Thus, in the second serial Nyoka's last name is different, the locale is somewhat changed—partial desert and a whole lot of Republic cave sets— and the plot development is totally unrelated to the first chapterplay. Also this serial was legally available whereas the former was not for many years. In the new version Nyoka is portrayed by Kay Aldridge and assisted by hero

Larry, portrayed by Clayton Moore. These two and their aides are pitted against Vultura portrayed by Lorna Gray (Adrian Booth) and her minions in search of lost mystical tablets called the Golden Tablets of Hypocrites. While the secrets of these tablets were invaluable to medical science (including the cure for cancer), they unfortunately also are the key to lost treasures and therein lies the conflict between good and evil. Nonetheless, far more new thrill footage was shot and some rather unusual sets and stunt work were included. The serial incorporated the expected action and special effects work so well known at Republic and is, in many respects, superior to its predecessor.[89] It is pretty much non-stop, well-paced chases and fights and remains a favorite.

While Nyoka lacked the patriotism and obvious Americanism of those serials directly related to topical events, it nonetheless included many of the standard values of the traditional morality play. And it had something extra. It, like *Jungle Girl* before it and several serials to follow, was ammunition for the women's liberation movement served up in an action package. William Everson notes,

> Another interesting wartime development was a momentary return of the serial queen. Republic, which has been responsible for some of the best quality serials, tried to build Frances Gifford and Kay Aldridge into modern Pearl Whites and Ruth Rolands—with stress on the word 'modern.' The pattern was action with cheesecake, and the girls went through their energetic paces clad in fetching blouses and shorts. To give them their due, they handled their fair share of the action—though doubles took over in the really hectic stunts that Republic writers loved to sit up all night devising.[90]

The aspect of equal rights and justice for women as represented in the self-reliant serial queen was also commented on more directly by the contemporary columnist, Hedda Hopper.

> Back in the dear, dead days when woman's place was in the home and she was plenty burned up about it, we had quite a sizable escape literature in the form of the serial queen . . .
> Last year Republic again decided to take a crack at the serial queen. "Perils of Nyoka" was readied and the hunt was on. . . . [T]he winner emerged in the shape of Kay Aldridge, a former Powers model and Billy Rose's selection for 'most beautiful girl in the world.' . . . [m]uch more important than her beauty is her ability to take it on the chin and elsewhere! These flowers of the Old South may look as if a breath would blow them away but underneath their fragile exteriors they're as tough as whipcord and will tackle their weight in wildcats once their dander's up—as many a man has discovered to his sorrow . . .[91]

Allowing for Hopper's chatty "Hollywoodese," the point is still valid. How effectual the message of the emancipated, self-sufficient woman was is open to debate. For example, Linda Stirling, who portrayed similar roles upon several occasions, feels that female serial fans were and are a rare breed—something like "one out of ten."[92] However, Peggy Stewart, also a serial heroine but not quite so obviously self-sufficient in her roles, says that not only has she been complimented on her toughness by fans (she often played the "tough no nonsense Ella Raines type of heroine") but that she finds female fans quite numerous especially at Western and serial conventions. But whether the viewer bought the message or not, it was present. And, Adrian Booth says Vultura was her favorite role.[93] It certainly shows her off to good advantage. She is devious, ruthless, and attractive. Although not the most positive poster girl for feminism, Vultura still makes a good case for take charge women.

King of the Mounties, a direct sequel to the 1940 *King of the Royal Mounted*, with Allan Lane again portraying Sergeant Dave King, was the final entry in 1942. This time, King's adversaries were clearly identified and their goals clearly specified. The plot was basically a wartime espionage story with some science fiction themes included to increase the excitement. Sergeant King was not only up against the Nazis—to add to the challenge he faced all three enemy nations. Japan, Germany, and Italy were represented by Admiral Yamato portrayed by Abner Biberman, Marshal Van Horst portrayed by William Vaughn, and Count Varoni portrayed by Nester Paiva. The villains were basically out to obtain strategic materials from Canada and to destroy the Canadian war effort utilizing, among other things, a Falcon plane which was a variation on the flying wing and a reworking of the Bat plane in *Spy Smasher*. They were finally destroyed during a spectacular volcanic eruption at their secret base by Sergeant King and his allies in Chapter Twelve. Patriotism was again emphasized with U.S.-Canadian cooperation a strong secondary theme brought home by a stirring speech delivered in Chapter Twelve by the heroine beneath pictures of Franklin Delano Roosevelt and Winston Churchill with appropriate background music.[94]

Again directed by William Witney, the serial makes extensive use of location filming and special effects by Howard Lydecker (and brother Theodore). The small scale planes, boats, trains, buildings, and cars as well as many magnificent pyrotechnic effects were scattered throughout the twelve chapters. Although some stock footage from the earlier serial was of course utilized—stock footage was heavily used even in "Golden Age" serials especially after wartime economies were instituted—more good footage was shot so that it in turn provided stock footage for later serials from Republic in its declining days. In fact every chapter ending in this serial was reused in some form in future releases. This resulted from two factors: (1) the sequences were excellent, and (2) the original serials could not be reissued. Since Republic's rights to the character ran out in 1949, they were contractually obligated to remove both serials from circulation. The rights and prints were purchased by Jack Mathis but this sequel does not have a complete sound track and is being restored by The Serial Squadron, a dedicated group in Pennsylvania.[95]

The first entry for 1943 kept with America's wartime awareness, as did the majority of appropriate contemporary Republic releases in this period—which will bring up a strange situation in the discussion of *Captain America* as will be seen in the next chapter. Entitled *G-Men vs. the Black Dragon*, 1943's first serial starred Rod Cameron in the first of two serials which he would do for Republic portraying secret agent, Rex Bennett, Republic's only non-comic originated continuing hero. In this particular serial he was fighting the Oriental Axis secret society, the Black Dragon of Manzanar. Bennett had assistance from both the British and Chinese Secret Services thus plugging allied cooperation upon every possible occasion. Witney again directed and the Lydecker special effects were again in prominence. The Orientals and their gangster allies under the leadership of the Japanese villain Haruchi, portrayed by Nino Pipitone, engage the hero in the outstanding fistfights which the audience had come to expect from William Witney's direction. It was a fast-paced quality production but was nonetheless basically a standard wartime plot with government agents protecting the country against enemy activities. The social significance of the continuing popularity of this type of story is the basic point in our discussion of Republic's wartime serials.

And it was a popular serial. As Eric Hoffman, movie archivist and serial buff, puts it, "Crammed with action, 'Black Dragon' was one of the many 40's adventures that moved like a runaway express train, with fights, chases and cliff-hangers popping up at the drop of a hat. . . . Here the villains were truly hissable with none of them above shooting, killing, strangling and stabbing anyone in their way."[96]

Specifically, Haruchi stated his goals in Chapter One. "Keep in mind that our aim is to spread terror and confusion . . . to attack industry and leaders of industry . . . to cripple America's war effort and undermine her morale. So we shall speed the day when Japan will completely rule the Pacific and all the lands bordering on the Pacific."[97] By Chapter Fifteen after several dialogue (as well as the expected physical) confrontations spelling out the good versus evil theme, the villains were defeated.

Recalling Albert S. Rogell's claim that, according to Yates' instructions, Republic films would be flagwaving whenever possible, this serial took that suggestion literally. "One bit of amusing patriotism was that a villainous organ grinder used a raven in helping Haruchi. . . . At the fade-out of the last chapter, Rex asks the raven to show his colors and the bird waves a miniature American flag."[98] Corny but effective for the juvenile or unsophisticated audience of the era.

Daredevils of the West was the next Republic production and was an original Western not based on material from another source. It logically avoided topical themes and was a straightforward treatment using the traditional American virtues of individualism, fair play, and justice. It starred Allan Lane and Kay Aldridge who were billed as the "King and Queen of Serials." The not unusual story concerns the attempts of June Foster, portrayed by Aldridge, to retain a Federal Franchise Commission grant for a stage coach line by completing a new road through the lawless Comanche strip. She is aided in this endeavor by Duke Cameron, a calvary officer, portrayed by Lane, and is opposed by cattleman Barton Dexter who wishes to retain the strip for grazing purposes. He therefore does not want the stage line to go through, thus encouraging settlers. Stock footage aside, the crunch of wartime economies had not yet noticeably affected Republic's budgets in choosing locations or constructing sets, and the serial benefited from extensive outdoor shooting as well as two huge interior sets. The giant alcohol distillery used in Chapter Five was the scene of a tremendous fight involving unusual stunt work. Both the elaborate mine tunnel in Chapter Four and the picturesque lava pit in Chapter Eleven are worthy of mention. Republic featured a great many cavern sets in all of their action pictures and serials, utilizing ingenious moveable tunnel sections that, coupled in a variety of ways, produced an infinite variety of cavern or mine settings.

The twelve chapters are perhaps even more pronounced than previous Western serials in their strong slant toward continuous action and were directed by John English in his only solo chapterplay outing. This observation establishes a bit of a paradox in that English had always specialized in dialogue direction and left the action sequences to Witney as his specialty.[99] However, Bill Witney had gone off to the real war and English had returned to serials for a short time. He was to prove himself quite adept at handling non-stop action as shall be seen. In their individual serial productions, both men used the plot mainly as an excuse for the action generally speaking. *Daredevils of the West* is considered to be an outstanding Western serial, but is somewhat of a rarity in that, unlike most Republic serials, it was never re-released theatrically, sold to television, edited into movie form, or made available through film rental libraries. This is not because of any legal restrictions but was due to the odd reasoning on the part of the Republic distribution office that it was just another Western.[100] This decision served to make it into a "cult" Western serial.[101] For years, it was rumored to exist only in a visual print but at least four complete chapters can currently be obtained and a complete visual/sound version of the whole serial might soon be located.

This production was followed by the second of the Rex Bennett serials starring Rod Cameron with the intrepid secret agent this time going abroad to defend his country against the evils of Fascism. This one was entitled *Secret Service in Darkest Africa* and basically has federal agent Rex Bennett doing battle against the Nazis and Arabs in Northern Africa. Directed by silent serial ace Spencer Gordon Bennet, it is an elaborate production again with the emphasis on action. Bennet had a lifetime of experience in this field and was second only to Witney in the direction of action fare although his later Columbia efforts were hurt by the studio's poor quality.

The hero, now in the military, is opposed by Nazi villain Baron Von Rommler who has a hideout in Casablanca. The fights are unusually well paced—Spencer Bennet was an expert at this given the proper production values—and include one in Chapter One in which the hero is discovered in Gestapo headquarters and duels furiously with a German officer instructed to take him prisoner. With time at a minimum and a plane waiting nearby, the hero disarms the Nazi and then flips his sword back to him so that the duel can continue. After disposing of his opponent, the hero hurls his sword into a portrait of Adolf Hitler in a perfect imitation of Errol Flynn. It might sound a bit overdone but the fifteen chapter serial was an extremely satisfying product and dealt with the headlines of the day. "Almost every chapter had two or three super-brawls interspersed in the action while the screenplay provided audiences additional ideas as to what kind of s.o.b.'s the Nazi spies were."[102]

The serial once again concludes on a patriotic note. The hero frees the imprisoned leader of the African sheiks who is friendly to the allied cause and this sultan addresses his peers, "Ours is the cause of freedom, of justice, and of truth. The mission of the United States is a crusade against tyranny, intolerance, and oppression. Our banners will never be lowered until the light of freedom shines not only over the peoples of North Africa but the entire world."[103]

A little background on Spencer Bennet and his reaction to Republic is in order since he specialized in the serial and to a lesser degree the B Western genre.

Early in 1956 the last studio to make serials—Columbia—made its last one: *Blazing the Overland Trail*. It was directed by Spencer Gordon Bennet, who had been connected with serials since 1912, the year the Edison company made the prototype of the serial—*What Happened to Mary?*

Bennet had learned how a serial should be made from the man who had directed the great ones in the serial's heyday—George B. Seitz, . . . Bennet was Seitz's all round utility man and took command when Seitz retired from serials in 1925.

In the 31 years since then Bennet directed 52 serials, and 54 features which contained the same kind of action and melodrama serials did. Physical action is natural to Bennet. He has been an athlete all his life.[104]

Bennet was quite appreciative of the quality he found in the Republic serial unit. "Spence thoroughly enjoyed his period with Republic and states that Republic was extremely well organized and the budgets for their features and serials were always adequate to make a good picture. One problem which affected all of the outdoor scenes, shot in the Los Angeles area, was the continual noise of airplanes flying overhead. Republic solved this problem. If a plane was flying over, the direction was to stop action for one minute and resume shooting. If there was background noise on the film, this portion was taken out and dubbed in, thus saving hours of retakes."[105] Bennet expanded on his comments concerning Republic to this author. He felt that "Republic was geared to the action picture." They had "better equipment," the "technical know how," and a group of workers "who knew their jobs." As an example he relates how Republic had rheostats on their cameras which enabled him to shoot chase sequences without interruption and increased his efficiency. "We didn't have those things at Columbia. Republic gave us what we needed to do a good job."[106]

Spencer Bennet's second Republic serial also had a patriotic motif and proved to be a favorite—which is to say, that even non-serial buffs recall it if only title. The title has in fact become a cliché but this does not detract from the quality of the original serial—*The Masked Marvel*. The last entry in 1943, it utilized the same theme of the earlier Lone Ranger serial transposed to modern World War II espionage backgrounds. The Masked Marvel, in reality portrayed by veteran stuntman Tom Steele, who is on screen more than any other character in the film although he received no official credit through a billing oversight, is one of four insurance investigators who have joined ranks to fight the espionage activities of Japanese villain Sakima, portrayed by silent film comic Johnny Arthur. Gradually the four are decimated strategically throughout the serial until only two remain. In the closing scenes of Chapter Twelve the true Masked Marvel reveals himself to the heroine and to the audience but requests that his identity remain unknown in case he is needed to fight America's enemies in the future.[107] Unfortunately, the implied sequel was never forthcoming—at least not as a Masked Marvel adventure. The serial fairly boiled over with furious action, chases, and stunt work. The Masked Marvel, dressed in a nondescript gray business suit, wide brimmed white hat, and a black mask molded to tightly cover the entire upper portion of his face, was indeed an awe inspiring, if somewhat simply garbed, hero. Both loyal Americans and the insidious villains recognized him as a hero of the first order throughout the serial. The Japanese spies and their gangster allies never stood a chance!

The Masked Marvel proved to be the last Republic entry with a wartime patriotic background. Nonetheless, the advertising campaign made extensive use of the theme. "Who is this fearless man who risks his life at every turn to thwart Jap attempts at sabotage?" asked the newspaper ads. Another proclaimed, "SENSATIONAL SABOTAGE UNCOVERED! . . . A fast, exciting surprise-studded serial showing the Jap menace crawling underground in an attempt to destroy the American war effort!"[108] And wartime activities, events, and paraphernalia—air raid alerts, posters, ration stamps—were liberally scattered throughout the serial and sometimes used in the plot development.

The serial includes large doses of dialogue illustrating the baseness of the villains as opposed to the essential honesty, decency, and justice of the heroes as was normal for this type of product. However, the concluding confrontation was somewhat different, slightly more realistic, and subtly amusing, although still obvious propaganda. "In the last chapter Sakima and the Marvel engage in a gunfight in the former's hideout. After the Marvel fires six bullets, Sakima emerges from his hiding place to announce: 'Your bullets are gone, but I still have one left.' He is felled by another bullet, then the Marvel asks: 'Didn't it occur to your Oriental mind that I might reload.'"[109] In other words, yellow peril deviousness is no match for American pragmatism!

It is the author's contention that the Republic serials reinforced Middle American values and that in so doing they influenced predominantly the youthful audience and inculcated these virtues into their lifestyle. Patriotism was a basic among these values, and the serials of the late 1930s and early 1940s which emphasize this theme were among the most successful examples of the serial's impact. When Republic dropped this theme in relation to the war it lost one of its most effective forms. The message of patriotism continued although in a diluted form but the war effort serials were discontinued following *The Masked Marvel*. Of course, by force of circumstances, they could have lasted more than two additional years in any case. Possibly, Republic felt that the public was tiring of war themes or felt that they had done all they could with the subject. But it is interesting that they were dropped so early and also coincidentally and ironically the Golden Age began to taper off at approximately the same time and drew to a close within a year or two at the outside.

> With the end of the war, B-pictures and serials lost probably the best real-life heavies they could ever hope to find in the Axis forces. Incidental adventures with Axis heavies popped up for a year or two, but new menaces had to be found. Enemies from mythical foreign powers, visitors from space and gangsters seemed to take over. The next batch of spy-villains would come when everyone was seeing Red under their bedsheets. Their villainy was fairly nasty as well on the screen, but somehow, it was a pale shadow compared to the all-out ruthlessness of the World War II heavies. They provided the basis for some of the best action-packed chapter-plays to come out of film studios in a time when a true-life horror made the menace on the screen look tame by comparison.[110]

The first production of 1944 was *Captain America* which will be discussed in detail as a case study in Chapter 5. The second 1944 release was *The Tiger Woman*, directed by Spencer Bennet, and starring Allan Lane and Linda Stirling in her first movie and serial role. This twelve chapter serial centered around oil deposits and a missing heiress who had become an exotic jungle queen. Right eventually triumphs but it's not for lack of opposition in the form of greedy villains and their violent henchmen.

Linda Stirling, who was soon to be known as queen of the serials, has fond memories of her years at Republic.

> But despite everything, those years were wonderful fun. Everyone was congenial; we managed to find time to laugh a lot, play practical jokes, and kid around. And I couldn't have had a better training ground for learning how to work in front of a camera. All the actors were pros—temperamental actors didn't last long on our serial sets—and I learned how to work fast and well. . . . Yet when the old serials are shown today, audiences marvel at the production and quality they had. That's because everyone did his best to make the serials good.[111]

Despite this tribute, Stirling in all honesty had serious reservations concerning her career, the Republic product, and its potential value and influence.[112] She more valued her career as a college teacher. But the fact remains, she made a superb jungle goddess and also did well in her remaining serial appearances. The ending to Chapter One of *The Tiger Woman* was adapted on a much grander scale in Steven Spielberg's second Indiana Jones adventure incidentally.

Following *The Tiger Woman* came *Haunted Harbor* starring Kane Richmond and Kay Aldridge. The plot was basically an adventure and detective mystery and concerns the attempts of the hero to prove his innocence of a murder charge. The value of justice was obviously a theme. It is based on a novel by Dayle Douglas and was directed by Spencer Bennet. The fifteen chapters include some elements of science fiction and the action is quite well handled. The plot was a direct example of the Wolfenstein-Leites theme of a wrongly accused hero.

Finally, 1944 saw *Zorro's Black Whip*, a Western starring George J. Lewis in a heroic role for a change as well as the legitimate and now acknowledged queen of the serials, Linda Stirling. Directed by Spencer Bennet, this twelve chapter effort is unique in that Zorro is never mentioned by name aside from the title and the black-masked mysterious Zorro-like figure was a female— none other than the heroine.

In fact this change in gender was a major selling point in convincing Republic producer William J. O'Sullivan to accept the property. After noting that the story was a standard plot, he states in a studio memo, "However, the character of a masked girl lead has never been used in a Republic serial and has definite possibilities."[113]

The serial was quite strong in its espousal of law and order as the prologue shows: "IDAHO—1889. Law abiding citizens call for a vote to bring their territory into the Union. But sinister forces, opposed to the coming of law and order, instigated a reign of terror against the lives and property of all who favored statehood."[114] Secondary themes included freedom of the press—the heroine's murdered brother was an editor and she takes over for him both as editor and as masked hero with appropriate dialogue and patriotism—a patriotic speech by the heroine in Chapter Five was interrupted by the villain with, "Never mind the Fourth 'uh July Speech."[115] The undisguised patriotism was expected and the mysterious female lead was an unexpected and different reward.

Some might argue that the serials which were produced by Republic after 1944 were equally as good as those heretofore mentioned, especially those directed by Spencer Bennet before he switched to Columbia. However, it is generally conceded that, although the action, special effects, and pacing continued unabated at Republic through at least 1949, the plots and the general care which were lavished upon earlier productions gradually fell off after 1944. Also, with the exception of some anti-Communist themes, the messages and morals of the later productions remained fairly consistent and predictable. Therefore, after a detailed examination of *Captain America* in Chapter 5, the declining years of Republic serials will be surveyed generally for the sake of completeness since their production values, influence, and significance were admittedly in a state of deterioration.

However, before leaving the Golden Age, an important, upbeat point should be made. It is often implied that serials had little impact on the moviegoing public. Did the serials have a market? Did the serials have popularity? Did the serials have an effect and an influence on the general moviegoing audience? The answer is definitely YES. In 1946, the movie industry's best year, although the quality of the serials was beginning to go down, the product was still much in demand. That year Universal and Republic each produced their normal quota of four serials, and Columbia produced their usual three serials. In that year it is interesting to note that *Film Daily Yearbook* reported that out of the 18,765 theaters operating, approximately 8,000 houses regularly showed serials, not including 2,000 more which utilized serials periodically but not fifty-two weeks out of the year. Furthermore, the average serial played to an estimated audience of four to five million people according to the *Yearbook*.[116] Thus it can be seen that the serial phenomenon in the mid-1940s was an important aspect of the motion picture audience's diet and that, as a popular culture phenomenon, it is not to be underestimated or overlooked.

Notes

1. *New York Times*, December 22, 1946.

2. *Los Angeles Times*, November 20, 1946.

3. *Los Angeles Times*, November 20, 1946.

4. Robert Malcomson, "The Sound Serials of Yesteryear," *Yesteryear* (1971), No. 1, pp. 2–5.

5. For annotated bibliographic reference to the sound serial, see Richard M. Hurst. "Violence in the Popular Entertainment Forms," Seminar paper at the State University of New York at Buffalo, 1974, footnote 75, p. 47. This lengthy paper was published as a continuing column of essays in the *Western New York Popular Culture Society Newsletter* beginning with issue number 7 (October, 1976). The appropriate section appeared in November 1977.

6. For an elaboration on this point, see Hurst, 77 ff. in the *Western New York Popular Culture Society Newsletter*. The appropriate section appeared in December 1977.

7. John Brosnan, *James Bond in the Cinema* (New York: St. Martins, 1971), Chapter 1.

8. Jon Tuska, "From the 100 Finest Westerns: The Lightning Warrior," *Views and Reviews*, II (Spring, 1971), 4, p. 50.

9. Tuska, p. 55.

10. P. E. Emery, "Psychological Effects of the Western Film: A Study in Television Viewing," *Human Relations*, XII (1959), 3, p. 201.

11. Forman, p. 162.

12. Thomas Wood, "Corn in the Can," Unpublished manuscript, dated 1941, in the Serials clipping file of the Margaret Herrick Library of the Academy of Motion Picture Arts and Sciences, pp. 4–5.

13. Thomas Wood, p. 7.

14. William K. Everson, "Serials with Sound," *Films in Review*, IV (June–July, 1953), 6, p. 271.

15. Everson, "Serial," p. 273.

16. *Los Angeles Times*, November 20, 1946.

17. *Los Angeles Times*, November 20, 1946.

18. Interview with Rex Waggoner, National Telefilms Associates Publicity Director, and Ernie Kirkpatrick, National Telefilms Associates Technical Services, Los Angeles, May 12, 1976.

19. Mathis, p. vii.

20. Interview with Barry Shipman, Republic writer, San Bernardino, California, May 1, 1976.

21. Mathis, p. vii.

22. Mathis, p. viii.

23. Mathis, p. viii.

24. Lahue, *Bound and Gagged*, p. 23.

25. Edward Connor, "The First Eight Serials of Republic," *Screen Facts*, II (1964), 7, p. 52. Also, for the record, I have seen all of Republic's serials recently. The one exception, *Daredevils of the West*, I saw in 1943 during its initial release.

26. This, and other Republic serials, have been shown at meetings of the Western New York Popular Culture Society and have been viewed again recently by the author. Additional information was obtained from Eric Hoffman, "Undersea Kingdom," *Those Enduring Matinee Idols*, I (December 1970–January 1971), 8, p. 90.

27. Rudy Behlmer, ed., *Memo from David O. Selznick* (New York: Viking Press, 1972), p. 369.

28. Connor, "First Eight," p. 57.

29. Mathis, p. 21.

30. Eric Hoffman, "Robinson Crusoe of Clipper Island," *Those Enduring Matinee Idols*, I (February–March, 1971), 9, p. 110.

31. Connor, "First Eight," p. 57.

32. Mathis, p. 35.

33. Mathis, p. 36.

34. Thomas Wood, p. 20.

35. "The Painted Stallion," *Those Enduring Matinee Idols*, I (April–May, 1971), 10, p. 122.

36. Mathis, p. 79.

37. Letter from Francis Nevins, May 1, 1975. Corroborated in Mathis, pp. 60–61. It was recently determined that this problem was caused by a script change during shooting.

38. Letter from Ulrich Von Thuna, quoted in *Films in Review*, XXVI (November, 1975), 9, p. 574.

39. Connor, "First Eight," p. 60.

40. "Serial Panel Discussion," *Those Enduring Matinee Idols*, III (n.d.) 4, p. 351. In the transcript of the Serial Panel Discussion at the Houstoncon '73, Witney elaborates: "I'll tell you something about the violence in serials. We felt that it was all play acting. You never saw any blood, you never saw a bullet go into a man and blood spurt out fourteen feet. You never saw anybody's teeth get kicked out, and never in any serial saw a man get hit over the head with actual contact. You never saw a man get physically beaten up, where somebody holds him and just beats him to death as we see now. Sure, it was play acting violence. The Hays Office had certain codes and they would look at these things. Sometimes there were arguments and you'd have to cut something out, but you'd ALWAYS argue about them. They had a lot of backup—they could ban your pictures. We weren't as afraid of the Hays Office on the serials as we were of the Church groups—the Catholic League. We never had a serial put on the list, as far as I know. They were made for children and we always had in the back of our mind that while the slogan on the wall said, 'A pair of wet panties for every little kiddie,' we really didn't mean it."

41. Francis M. Nevins, Jr., "Ballet of Violence: The Films of William Witney," *Films in Review*, XXV (November, 1974), 9, p. 525, makes the following point about Witney which can be generalized to most action films of the 1930s to the 1940s: "Violence, of course, is a key element in his films; few minutes go by in a Witney serial without a chase or fight. But as Witney points out, violence is an ambiguous term. The new breed of Peckinpah films is not Witney's brand (although by his own account his recent film *I Escaped from Devil's Island* is more in that style). Witney's serials depict something completely different, an unrealistic, ritualized imitation of combat, which by its unrealism would seem to purge viewer's primitive instincts rather than encourage them to take up weapons." While the cathartic theory is admittedly a moot point, the distinction between the forms of violence is basically what the controversy centers around. The author of the present work had a series of essays appearing as a continuing column in the *Western New York Popular Culture Society Newsletter* beginning in number 7 (October, 1976) which deals in detail with the subject of violence in the media from the earliest time for anyone wishing to pursue the subject. The section in this aspect of serial violence was in the December, 1977 issue.

42. Edward Connor, "The Golden Age of Republic Serials, Part I," *Screen Facts*, III (1968), 5, pp. 48–49.

43. Thomas Wood, p. 18.

44. Mathis, p. 68.

45. Mathis, p. 73.

46. Bob Malcomson and Eric Hoffman, "The Fighting Devil Dogs," *Those Enduring Matinee Idols*, II (October–November, 1971), 3, p. 172.

47. Continuity (estimating) script in the Republic Studios Collection #979 of the Special Collections Library of the University of California at Los Angeles Library.

48. Mathis, p. 90.

49. Ron Stephenson, "Concerning Serials and Trends," *Those Enduring Matinee Idols*, III (n.d.), 9, p. 444.

50. C. M. "Parky" Parkhurst, "The Lone Ranger Rides Again," *Those Enduring Matinee Idols*, II (April–May, 1972), 6, p. 218.

51. Connor, "Golden Age, Part I," pp. 55–56.

52. Thomas Wood, p. 4.

53. Mathis, p. 108.

54. Shooting script in the Duncan Renaldo collection of the University of Wyoming Library.

55. *Daredevils of the Red Circle*, Cliffhanger Ending and Escape Pictorial Series (Chicago: Jack Mathis Advertising, n.d.). This series of privately published pamphlets makes extensive use of pressbooks, Republic data from Mr. Mathis' own collection, and blow ups from the actual film. Next to having the film, these are perhaps the best research tools available concerning film content. Unfortunately, only 11 titles were issued before the series was discontinued.

56. Continuity (estimating) script in the Republic Studios Collection #979 of the Special Collections Library of the University of California at Los Angeles Library.

57. *Zorro's Fighting Legion*, Cliffhanger Ending and Escape Pictorial Series (Chicago: Jack Mathis Advertising, n.d.).

58. Nevins, p. 531.

59. Earl Michaels, "The Serials of Republic," *Screen Facts*, I (1963), 1, p. 56.

60. Edward Connor, "The Golden Age of Republic Serials, Part II," *Screen Facts*, III (1968), 6, p. 20.

61. *Drums of Fu Manchu*, Cliffhanger Ending and Escape Pictorial Series (Chicago: Jack Mathis Advertising, n.d.)

62. Eric Blair, Jr., "Reminising with Henry Brandon," *Those Enduring Matinee Idols*, II (December, 1972–January, 1973), 10, p. 291. Publishing transcript of interview.

63. Eric Hoffman and Bob Malcomson, "Drums of Fu Manchu," *Those Enduring Matinee Idols*, II (December, 1972–January, 1973), 10, p. 284.

64. *The Adventures of Red Ryder*, Cliffhanger Ending and Escape Pictorial Series (Chicago: Jack Mathis Advertising, n.d.).

65. Connor, "Golden Age:, Part II," p. 26.

66. Mathis, p. 149.

67. Bob Malcomson and Eric Hoffman, "King of the Royal Mounted," *Those Enduring Matinee Idols*, III (n.d.), 3, p. 338.

68. Mathis, p. 161.

69. *Mysterious Doctor Satan*, Cliffhanger Ending and Escape Pictorial Series (Chicago: Jack Mathis Advertising, n.d.).

70. Nevins, p. 534.

71. Mathis, p. 165.

72. Connor, "Golden Age, Part II," p. 26.

73. *The Adventures of Captain Marvel*, Cliffhanger Ending and Escape Pictorial Series (Chicago: Jack Mathis Advertising, n.d.).

74. Interview with Theodore Lydecker, Republic special effects expert, West Hollywood, May 17, 1976.

75. Mathis, p. 177.

76. Richard M. Hurst, "Conscious and Unconscious Ethical and Moral Standards in Movie Sound Serials: With an Emphasis on *Captain Marvel* and *Captain America*," delivered at the Fifth Annual Meeting of the Popular Culture Association, St. Louis, Missouri, March 21, 1975, and published in microfilm edition by the Popular Culture Association, Bowling Green State University, Bowling Green, Ohio.

77. Everson, "Serials," p. 271.

78. Thomas Wood, p. 3.

79. The Hays office letter is quoted verbatim in Thomas Wood, pp. 5–6.

80. Connor, "Golden Age, Part II," p. 33, as well as every critical commentary that covers this production of which the author is aware. The use of negative photography is quite striking.

81. *Spy Smasher*, Cliffhanger Ending and Escape Pictorial Series (Chicago: Jack Mathis Advertising, n.d.).

82. Eric Hoffman, "Saturday Matinee Spy Hunters of World War Two," *Serial World* (1974), 1, p. 8.

83. Mathis, p. 199.

84. Mathis, p. 200.

85. Mathis, p. 205.

86. Interview with Theodore Lydecker, Republic special effects expert, West Hollywood, California, May 17, 1976.

87. *Edwardsville* [Indiana] *Intelligencer*, November 29, 1973.

88. Harmon and Glut, p. 12.

89. Harmon and Glut, p. 12.

90. Everson, "Serials," p. 271.

91. *Los Angeles Times*, May 31, 1942.

92. Interview with Linda Stirling, Republic actress, West Hollywood, California, May 13, 1976.

93. Interview with Peggy Stewart, Republic actress, Van Nuys, California, May 18, 1976. Interview with Adrian Booth, Republic actress, Newtown, Pennsylvania, May 20, 2006.

94. *King of the Mounties*. Still Manual. (Hollywood: Republic Pictures, 1942). Still manuals were a series of photographs from the film accompanied by publicity information for use by the theaters. They were created and released by the picture companies

themselves, and, in the case of the serials, were the most extensively used promotional material (along with pressbooks) provided to the theaters. Advertisement copy from pressbooks was also extensively used in small towns but studio written "reviews" which were from pressbooks also were rarely run by the local presses.

95. *King of the Mounties*, Cliffhanger Ending and Escape Pictorial Series (Chicago: Jack Mathis Advertising, n.d.). Also information gathered from Serial Fest, 2006, and the Serial Squadron website.

96. Hoffman, "Spy Hunters," p. 9.

97. Mathis, p. 225.

98. Stephenson, p. 445.

99. Harry Sanford, "An Interview with William (Bill) Witney," *Those Enduring Matinee Idols*, III (February–March, 1973), 1, p. 310.

100. *Daredevils of the West*, Cliffhanger Ending and Escape Pictorial Series (Chicago: Jack Mathis Advertising, n.d.).

101. A deteriorating copy exists at National Telefilms Associated (Ernie Kirk-patrick). Although there are no known collectors copies available, at least one is ru-mored to exist (and possibly four).

102. Hoffman, "Spy Hunters," p. 9.

103. Shooting script in the Duncan Renaldo Collection at the University of Wyoming Library.

104. George Geltzer, "Forty Years of Cliffhanging," *Films in Review*, VIII (February, 1957), 2, p. 60.

105. Glenn Shipley, "King of the Serial Directors: Spencer Gordon Bennet," *Views and Reviews*, I (Fall, 1969), 2, p. 21.

106. Interview with Spencer Bennet, Republic director, Beverly Hills, California, May 10, 1976.

107. Harmon and Glut, pp. 275–282.

108. *Kokomo* [Indiana] *Tribune*, March 30–31, 1944. Kokomo is a small city in northern Indiana, had a population of 40,000 during the 1940s, six theaters, and is representative of a major segment of the Republic market.

109. Stephenson, p. 445. Based on several viewings, the present author is aware that this exchange has been abbreviated by Stephenson but the flavor of the scene and the impression intended by it remains accurate.

110. Hoffman, "Spy Hunters," p. 9.

111. "Linda Stirling's Fond Memories of the Serials," *The New Captain George's Whizzbang*, IV (n.d.), 2, p. 15.

112. Interview with Linda Stirling, Republic actress, West Hollywood, California, May 13, 1976.

113. Mathis, p. 279.

114. Mathis, pp. 279–280.

115. Mathis, p. 280.

116. Quoted in Malcomson, "Sound Serials of Yesteryear," p. 4.

~

Captain America: A Case Study

Captain America, the first Republic serial of 1944, was produced in the last year of the Golden Age of Republic serials and, as will be seen, is in many ways a flawed production. Moreover, while the character was a natural for a patriotic wartime plot and the country was still in the midst of World War II, the seven writers chose to use a more standard "good guys versus bad guys" approach thus weakening the obvious patriotism of Captain America and the logical message. The serial is not one of Republic's strongest serials in terms of heavy handed morality although production values are high. Nonetheless, *Captain America* is a representative sample of the Republic serial product. It is not the best example of the Golden Age but it was of that period. It was not directed by the hallowed teams of Witney and English but one of them is included. It is a comic strip adaptation—a technique extensively used at Republic—which was imperfect as an adaptation but not a failure as a serial. And it was at the turning point in Republic's serial history when the Golden Age was ending and a gradual decline was on the horizon. For all of these reasons, *Captain America* is a good example of the average Republic chapterplay. Nonetheless, *Captain America* as an adaptation has noticeable drawbacks which leave it open to criticism as should any fair example of the serial genre.

Captain America as a character is an excellent example of a popular culture hero who has withstood the test of time. Created in 1941 as a comic book hero by artist Jack Kirby and writer Joe Simon in response to the growing concern of the American people with the imminence of involvement in the European war, the figure immediately caught on, and the hero's battle for the American way of life became representative of the good of democracy against the evil of totalitarianism. At his height of popularity during the Second World War, the figure was purchased by Republic Studios and converted into an excellent 1944 motion picture serial. The term excellent refers to the quality of the serial production and not to its success as an adaptation. As an adaptation of a comic book figure to film, the production was not accurate and resulted in some criticism as will be seen. Nonetheless, the serial stands in its own right as a legitimate addition to the development of the figure's popularity. In many respects it contributed to the reputation of Captain America and certainly broadened his audience. After the war, the attempt was made to convert the comic book figure to a standard crime fighter, a move which proved to be less than wise at that time. In 1949 the comic book was allowed to die a natural death.

However, this was not to be the end of the Gospel according to Captain America. The figure became somewhat of a cult figure in the annals of comic book collections over the years, and in 1961, under the sponsorship of publisher Stan Lee, the figure was revived. He appeared, slightly altered once again, as a member of a comic book team under the Marvel Comic Group banner. With this rebirth, the "messiah" figure—an appropriate designation under the circumstances—proved to be as popular, if not more popular, than during its original run of the 1940s. At least one paperback novel was written concerning Captain America; a series of profitable byproducts such as dolls, lunch boxes, puzzles, and posters, were "endorsed" by Captain America; and he remains a very popular figure in the Marvel Comic lineup, appearing in several titles including his own series up to the present.

Republic's version, as has been implied, relied less on Captain America's patriotic image as a savior of democracy and more on his fame as a comic strip figure of heroic proportions fighting for the cause of right and justice in an era when such figures were not only acceptable but necessary to movie audiences. Steve Kelez, editor of *Amateur Producers Magazine*, defines the attraction in saying, "Looking back on the cinematic year of 1943, one might call it the time of the comic strip hero. Serials were going great guns then and on a Saturday afternoon one could see the Batman foiling the plans of the Japanese spy, Dr. Daka; Tailspin Tommy doing battle in the skyways; or Captain America saving another intended victim from the clutches of the Scarab. Yes, this was the era when entertainment came in the form of action and escapism, not in sex and psychology." [The release date of *Captain America* was 1944 but the point remains the same.][1] The Republic newspaper ads set the tone. One proclaimed: "HE'S HERE! CAPTAIN AMERICA HERO OF MILLIONS! Now on the screen! Adventurous and death-defying, as he pursues a desperate and crafty criminal bent on world destruction!" Another emphasized his comic strip background: "THE NUMBER ONE CHOICE OF YOUNG AND OLD—CAPTAIN AMERICA! . . . The thrilling exploits which have spellbound a nation of comic fans—now catapulted to the screen in a serial packed with action—adventure and excitement!" A third enthused: "NOW—ON THE SCREEN. . . . The country's favorite . . . bold, daring, fearless . . . in a serial packed with action entertainment!"[2] Patriotism and other wartime virtues might be played down but good versus evil was in the forefront nonetheless.

There are several chapter-by-chapter synopses of this serial available. However, for our purposes, a summary synopsis of the entire serial will suffice. It is interesting to note that the plot of this serial utilized none of the tried and true gimmicks developed over the years—no mystery villain or mystery hero. The only gimmick was a presold costumed hero against an uncostumed mad villain with the emphasis on straight action/adventure with a strong overlay of science fiction overtones.

The plot, as usual, is relatively simple but with plenty of twists and turns to keep things moving for fifteen chapters. The Republic Story Department actually pretty well summarizes the story in one line. "Because he feels he has been cheated of the wealth and fame accruing from an expedition he headed, Dr. Maldor secretly starts a campaign to kill and rob every member of the expedition."[3] The strong modern vengeance theme was acceptable to the censors since it involved the villain and his forces of evil. While the Republic story synopsis develops the plot somewhat further, this vengeance theme and the attempts to discover and block the related crimes are basically all there is to the story. Maldor's program of attack is ill defined and, although it is never specified, one assumes that he plans to use the wealth and scientific treasures he obtains from his victims to gain more and more power. An articulated ultimate goal such as world domination would have given the serial needed cohesiveness and a more logical development.

Calling himself the Scarab, Maldor eliminates his enemies by means of a poison known as the Purple Death which is contained in small, scarab-shaped tokens. From his most recent victim the debonair but cruel villain has secured plans for a Dynamic Vibrator, a machine which harnesses light and sound waves into a weapon of massive destructive power. But Captain America who is in reality the district attorney Grant Gardner, portrayed by Dick Purcell, interferes in the middle of Chapter One with no more introduction or explanation concerning his reason to exist than contained in this summary. He succeeds in obtaining from Maldor's henchman Matson, portrayed by George J. Lewis, a specimen of the Purple Death amulet and poison.

From this point forward through fifteen chapters, Captain America/Grant Gardner and his Girl Friday, Gale, portrayed by Lorna Gray, carry on a frequently desperate and hazardous campaign to discover the identity of the Scarab, stop his reign of terror and crime, and apprehend him. During this period they unwittingly take Dr. Maldor into their confidence and he, while posing as a friend, malevolently uses the information they give him to evade detection and foil their plans. At one point, the Scarab gains access to a powerful weapon called the Thunderbolt whose potential is limited by a counterweapon evolved by the benign Professor Dodge which can detect the locale of the Thunderbolt when it is in operation. Because Professor Dodge is to be the recipient of a priceless collection of Mayan jewels, Maldor has a twofold reason to mark him as the Scarab's next victim. The diabolic Maldor plans to kill Dodge by means of an explosive laden truck controlled by a robot device which steers it directly into Dodge's house on a large estate. Captain America intervenes in the nick of time, although the truck and a huge garage on the estate are blown to bits in the process, thus providing a chapter ending and more Lydecker magic.

Shortly thereafter, it appears certain that Maldor will be exposed as the Scarab. One of his murder weapons, a blow gun, has been captured by the district attorney and is to be shown to Mr. Grayson who will be able to identify it and trace it to Dr. Maldor. Maldor and his henchmen make a tremendous convoluted effort to keep this from occurring, and are successful. But the district attorney makes equally involved plans to track down the Scarab. The evidence connecting Maldor and the Scarab continues to mount with each succeeding confrontation. Eventually, Matson, Maldor's action-heavy, is killed, but Maldor forces Dr. Lyman, the inventor of a life restoring machine, to bring his lieutenant back to life. Lyman himself is killed in the following battle, and the machine is smashed. Maldor then cunningly arranges to have one of his many henchmen confess that he was associated with the notorious Scarab who he identifies as Dr. Lyman. The henchman is then killed in a standard double-cross. Maldor hopes to deflect suspicions from himself by means of false identification. Maldor becomes increasingly desperate in his efforts to prevent exposure, to defeat his nemesis Captain America, and to gain his evil ends, varied and hazy though they may sometimes seem to be. Gale is finally captured by Maldor when she stumbles onto his identity, by chance strangely enough. Fortunately, she is able to tip Captain America off in a secret message as to the real identity of the Scarab. Unfortunately, she is apprehended in this valiant act, and is placed in a glass case where Maldor in one of his final maniacal acts of vengeance plans to turn on a supply of gas which will shrivel her body into a mummified corpse.

Needless to say, Captain America arrives and a confrontation follows in which the arch villain knows the secret identity of the hero and the hero knows the secret identity of the villain—a rare situation in a Republic serial. Nonetheless, the conclusion is quite exciting in that Captain America and Dr. Maldor have a no-holds barred fistfight while the gas is seeping into the glass case. Captain America, of course, proves victorious, saves Gale, and Maldor is arrested. He and his major henchman die in the electric chair at the stroke of midnight. The District Attorney and various other officials are listening to the knell of the clock signaling the Scarab's execution in the final scene. Oddly enough, Captain America's secret identity is generally known to the public at the conclusion. However, as previously mentioned, Republic normally retained the right in any contract involving a character from another medium to do whatsoever it wished with the character. This move seems to have destroyed any potential sequel to *Captain America* although by that time undoubtedly none was planned as will be seen.

In the course of this monumental fifteen chapter confrontation between Captain America and the Scarab, the hero and/or heroine are threatened by a multitude of dangers. As a serial fan, I cannot resist the cliffhangers. The chapter cliffhangers in order include:

1. Captain America is trapped on the upper stories of a skyscraper which is being shaken apart by a vibrating machine;
2. A tractor out of control threatens to run over the unconscious form of Captain America;
3. Captain America is battling a thug inside a huge burning crate which is the target of the Thunderbolt ray gun;
4. Captain America attempts to gain control of the robot controlled truck as it smashes into a huge garage and explodes;
5. Gale is tied beneath a huge paper cutter which in guillotine fashion threatens to slice her in half;
6. Captain America is knocked out at the bottom of a mine shaft with a huge ore bucket plunging down upon him;
7. Captain America is fighting two heavies inside of a gas plant where the controls are going wild resulting in the explosion of the entire plant;
8. Gale is flying a plane which has a bomb planted in it while the Captain is kept busy fending off two heavies in the hangar somewhere below;

9. Gale is trapped in an underground compartment in a huge warehouse which explodes during a fistfight between Captain America and the heavies;

10. Gale is searching inside a miner's cabin which is blown apart during a battle between Captain America and more heavies;

11. Captain America is fighting inside of a huge spectacular electric generator with one of the heavies while another heavy turns the generator on creating "a million" volts of electricity in the immediate vicinity;

12. Tires of Grant's car are shot out during a high speed chase which results in the car going over a cliff and exploding;

13. Captain America is knocked from the window of an apartment in a high rise building during a brawl with the heavies;

14. The Captain is fighting inside a ranch house while Maldor and Matson release bombs from a plane flying overhead.[4]

This list includes only the chapter endings, each in a different surrounding with differently choreographed fights. There was also at least one lesser dread or action bit which occurred within each chapter rather than as cliffhanger endings. The serial was obviously furiously paced with good choreography and imaginative situations. As an adaptation though, the serial left much to be desired.

This chapterplay, as several others before it, opens itself to conjecture by the very fact that it was an adaptation of a fictional character from one medium to another. The Republic film version by complete contrast to the comic origins of the Captain as U.S. Army Private Steve Rogers professes Captain America's other self to be Grant Gardner, a crusading District Attorney possessing brains and brawn only somewhat above average. The original Captain is a near superman, although mortal, who is pledged to defeat America's enemies. The plot, about as far removed from a war theme as possible, especially given Republic's heavy utilization of this motif prior to the war and up to the serial immediately preceding *Captain America*, revolves round the tactics of Dr. Maldor/the Scarab, a "master criminal" yes, yet truly in no way really awe-inspiring or war related. Essentially then the only thing that carried over from the comic book to the celluloid was the flamboyant costume. While die-hard critics can undoubtedly fault even this adaptation for lacking the chainmail shirt, winged helmet, pirate boots, and fantastic shield, it was nevertheless a relatively faithful and certainly more functional outfit for the live-action visual medium. The change in emphasis and atmosphere nonetheless resulted in a major weakness in the serial which shall be discussed below. In spite of this reservation, the serial is considered to be one of the best of the adaptations of a comic strip figure to the screen in terms of its effectiveness as an action film. Strangely enough, it was the last such hybrid which Republic utilized.

The special effects supervised by Theodore Lydecker (and brother Howard though uncredited) included a batch of new exploding miniatures plus a host of life-sized dummies that provided what must be some sort of a record for film deaths from defenestration. By actual body count, four people plummeted to their fate from a window not to mention a pair of high falls taken by Captain America—obviously non-fatal—and one by Matson—which was temporarily fatal. Since the majority of scenes were staged within the Republic lot and indoors due to the effects of wartime economies on location shooting, Art Director Fred Ritter and Set Decorator Charles Thompson provided a large assortment of "the expected massive, fastidiously detailed sets." The relatively sparse exterior footage was shot at a private estate in Pasadena, the Beverly Hills Women's Club, Los Novas Apartments in Hollywood, the Republic garage, as well as Mulholland Drive, the Van Nuys Police Station, and Chatsworth.[5] Dale Van Sickel, ramrod of the stunt unit crew on this production, doubled Captain America and Grant Gardner in the fight sequences, and the whole army of Republic stunt men who were not on active duty in wartime service chimed in to provide a serial cram-packed with widely acknowledged, finely choreographed fight sequences. The final negative cost $222,906 and it proved to be Republic's most expensive serial.[6]

Captain America was the final serial for directors John English and Elmer Clifton. English had amassed nineteen chapterplay credits (seventeen with Witney) over a period of seven years at Republic while Clifton had directed four titles at various studios. Stock footage included a car going over a cliff in Chapter One and the destruction of the boiler room in Chapter Seven, both lifted from *G-Men vs. the Black Dragon*. The building collapse in Chapter One was borrowed from a destruction montage and was especially effective, while the chase and resultant car crash at the climax of Chapter Twelve was taken from *Dick Tracy vs. Crime Incorporated*. At a private screening in 1975 for a test audience of potential and avowed fans, several persons commented that the building destruction at the end of Chapter One was as effective and more exciting than anything which was utilized in the then current *Earthquake*. Interestingly enough, the second unit director of *Earthquake*, John Daheim, started out in Republic serials and received most of his second unit and special effects training at Republic Studios.[7] It might also be mentioned that Dick Purcell who portrayed Captain America and was, of necessity, utilized in much close-up stunt action died less than five months later on April 11, 1944, of a heart attack.

Captain America was successful at the time of original release and was re-released theatrically on September 30, 1953, under the title *The Return of Captain America*. The serial did have a far reaching audience. In some cases children and young adults who had not read the *Captain America* comic books discovered a newfound interest in the comics. And others remember the Captain America image as created in the cinema more accurately than they remember the figure as portrayed in its original form.

The reaction to the *Captain America* serial over the years by serial fan writers has been generally favorable. Almost unanimously—with only one exception—they agree that the serial was not the same as the comic strip but that on its own the serial stands as a fine example of the genre. For example, a comprehensive 1964 article on "The Return of Captain America" as a comic book hero includes extensive coverage of the movie serial. The reaction can be summarized by the following: "Captain America's fights however were the *piece de resistance!* The amazing talents of Dale Van Sickel (doubling for Purcell), Tom Steele, Ken Terrell, Fred Graham, and their cohorts were combined to make the fight 'choreography' some of the most frantic ever fashioned for film and all this took place among some of the most imaginative settings ever seen in a chapter play; including a wonderful 'power house' set!"[8]

Chris Steinbrunner, movie historian and serial fan, makes the following comments which shall be elaborated on in due course: ". . . instead of avenging himself against the wartime foes of the nation, the serial's Captain is content merely to go after the Scarab. . . ."[9] Steinbrunner goes on rather astutely to point out another problem which will call for further elaboration:

> There is no attempt to explain Captain America's origin and Grant Gardner's stopping to change into costume seemed at times only to impede the action. . . . The real mystery was left unexplained; why should a crusading district attorney, the one person in our society fully capable of running the machine of justice, step well outside the law for jungle combat with evil forces? It just didn't make sense. Not that *Captain America* wasn't a fast-moving, adventuresome serial, it was . . . but it was also the last serial Republic was to draw from the comics. The studio was to continue to make serials of diminishing quality for some ten years but it would never again invest the comic pages with its own aliveness and magic. In a way, it was the beginning of the end for Republic, and for the serials as well.[10]

In a movie genre where good versus evil was an absolute and where justice unquestionably prevailed, this observation on the compromised identity of the hero will bear further analysis in due course.

Jim Harmon and Don Glut also comment on the change of identity in Captain America's alter ego: "Chaos struck when the heads of Timely Comics learned of the changes in their character that would burst on the screen in the 1944 release of the serial . . . In a letter seen by the present writers, Republic coldly informed Timely that the sample comic book pages sent them by the publishers in no way indicated that Captain America was a soldier named Steve Rogers and that he did not carry a revolver. Furthermore, since the serial was well into production they could not and would not return it to the original concept through costly retakes. . . . Since Republic was under no contractual obligations to do any of these things, the matter was closed."[11]

However, Harmon and Glut also recognize the excellence of the serial as such and the fact that this quality was based upon the Republic production values, i.e., good stunt work and special effects. "Those fight scenes, though repetitious and often predictable as to when they would appear, were the highlights of the film. Directed by John English and Elmer Clifton, but largely staged by the stunt men themselves, these celluloid battles were equal to those in any action film. . . . *Captain America* represented the apex of the traditional action film fight, in the opinion of many cliffhanger enthusiasts, but followed the long-dictated formula."[12] The same writers offer the opinion: "Emphasis was placed on the sheer beauty of the flow of action—primarily due to the extraordinary performance of the stuntmen. . . . In the serials a fight wasn't realism and violence—it was excitement and action."[13] They also comment on three occasions in a rather humorous vein upon the fact that, while Captain America would take on two or three of Maldor's henchmen easily, when he finally had a bruising showdown with the middle-aged, slightly heavy museum curator on a one-to-one basis, it took a great deal of effort to subdue the mad doctor. (I particularly enjoyed this observation, since I spent over forty years as a museum professional and never quite achieved the physical prowess shown by Maldor's museum curator. Of course, I lacked his goals and mindset too.) It should be realized that this observation by Harmon and Glut, while accurate, also depends on adult hindsight, and was undoubtedly unnoticed or unquestioned by contemporary audiences.

Raymond Stedman also comments on the change in identity but gives a rather casual and not particularly valid interpretation to the situation, "The Captain America character was significantly transformed for films, from a GI with a scientifically created super strength to a fighting district attorney possessing somewhat less muscle power. The change was probably for the better. . . . Grant Gardner, the Captain America of filmland, at least did not have to go AWOL constantly. And when an avenger was up against a villain

played by the magnificent Lionel Atwill, the fewer inconveniences the better."[14] Alan Barbour's reaction to the liberal changes is as follows: "*Captain
America* was Republic's final entry in the comic-strip sweepstakes, and it was
superb in all aspects of production. . . . All three studios took liberties in the
scripting of their films based on comic strips. . . . But no one really cared.
Each serial was judged on its own merits, and even though some had *no*
merit, they were enjoyable film fare."[15] While Barbour's position is perhaps
too unconcerned for most comic fans, both he and Stedman were at least
able to view these changes philosophically and to appreciate the serial version of *Captain America* as a magnificent piece of action film. At least one
critic was quite upset by the changes. Chuck McCleary in *Serial World* lists
Captain America as Number Three on his list of Ten Most Disappointing Serials with this comment, "After viewing this mediocre serial, one can only
wonder why the rights to this great comic book character were purchased if
only to be misused in such a manner."[16] McCleary's vehement reaction is
unique among all written criticism that I've researched on this chapterplay.

Obviously, the changes, especially in identity, have caused some discussion among the fans and students of *Captain America*. And, aside from the
considerations that the change in identity was perhaps inconvenient, unnecessary, or even untrue to the original character, this particular change also
has some more far reaching philosophical implications. In order to obtain additional viewpoints on the serial, the author discussed it with several people
familiar with the Captain America mystique. These discussions followed a
private showing of the serial arranged through a collector for a small group
over a period of two evenings in 1975. While the film was never meant to be
shown in such a fashion, and the approach undoubtedly created some artificial responses, the "laboratory subjects/analysts" could not be persuaded to
devote fifteen weeks to the project.

Through no advanced planning, the select audience proved to be an interesting cross section of viewers: three children with little if any previous serial experience, three adults with little interest and no past reference to serials, five adults with little past knowledge but a great curiosity about serials,
and six dyed-in-the-wool serial fans—three who were raised on them and
three who developed a retrospective devotion plus a few curious "drop ins"
who were not surveyed. Reactions were taped and are available as documentation.[17]

The children all seemed to like the serial and two were enthusiastic. The
three neutral adults remained unconverted but were politely complimentary:
"It was better than I thought it would be"—or mildly critical: "It was all right
but a fight every three minutes is pretty hard to swallow." It must be remem-

bered that these viewers were not seeing the serial as it was originally intended—one segment of roughly fifteen minutes each per week. The reactions of the five curious adults were much like the three neutrals except that they were more positive: "It was good!" "Not what I expected but very interesting." "I liked it and would like to see more." All five indicated they would be interested in viewing other serials. Incidentally, all seventeen viewers of the first evening indicated they planned to attend the second half of *Captain America* on the following night and even the neutrals expressed some enthusiasm about seeing his adventures through to completion. Only two of the seventeen surveyed failed to return and one new viewer came the second evening. Of course, this sampling is not representative in that no anti-serial representation—i.e., neither the antiviolence fanatics or the "juvenile antiquarianism is beneath contempt" elements—was specifically sought out.

The most interesting aspect of the survey was that the six serial fans proved to be the most critical and volunteered additional interpretations. The consensus seems to be aptly summarized in the statement, "It was a good serial but it wasn't Captain America." The fans could understand the dropping of the comic book sidekick Bucky ("not really necessary . . . a junior district attorney?"), the Captain's all purpose shield ("Too difficult to translate to the screen"), or even his near-Herculean strength (". . . would take some of the conflict and suspense out of the serial"). It is interesting to note, however, that Republic had successfully adapted a comic figure of even greater strength and invulnerability to the screen in *Adventures of Captain Marvel* with relative accuracy and without losing the basic element of excitement. Still, Republic usually specialized in fistfights and a hero of superstrength does limit fisticuffs. There were three such fights in twelve chapters of *Adventures of Captain Marvel* and none involved the Captain.

In any case, the fans did feel that the major flaw in Captain America, which detracted from the character without harming the impact of the serial as such, was the dropping of the wartime motif and the patriotic theme. It was felt that this was the element which made the Captain America figure unique and that without it, the serial could have been about any comic character or about any hero, original or adapted. Oddly enough, Republic had adapted a similar figure, *Spy Smasher*, and made full use of the wartime environment and fifth column activities as has been discussed. But, as has been hypothesized, Republic possibly chose to adapt *Captain America* to an existing script rather than adapt a script to the character. They had the contractual rights to do this. It is theorized that the script was originally for a Copperhead sequel (*Mysterious Doctor Satan*, 1940). The plot was also a likely candidate to have been a sequel to *The Masked Marvel* (1943). All of this is not to say that the element of patriotism was totally absent. It was impossible for some of the comic's image not to carry over. It is just that the theme was gone and the tone subdued. Good versus evil replaced patriotism and even here some potential problems are observable in retrospect.

An additional, and perhaps subtly more far-reaching, effect of this decision to have Captain America fighting a master criminal rather than the enemies of his country results in an unconscious hint of fascism. Here is a district attorney, sworn to uphold the law, donning a masked outfit and, with the blessing of the authorities, using violent extra-legal means including murder to overcome the criminal element which the district attorney and the legal system cannot control through normal channels. This "escapism" is a basic element of attraction in serials and youth-oriented entertainment of the period as has been previously implied. However, in Captain America the incongruity becomes blatant. By making the character a major representative of the legal system fighting domestic criminals with the cover of an unknown identity, the aspect of vigilante violence with the tacit approval of the system is undeniable.

One example will suffice. In Chapter One, Captain America calls the Police Commissioner after first confronting the master criminal's henchmen and discovers that he was too late in his immediate objective: to save a minor figure's life. Somewhat disgruntled, he philosophically reports that he has, as least, killed one of the villains in a fight. Whereupon the Commissioner calls the district attorney's secretary and asks her to inform the district attorney that: "Captain America is on the job!" Actually, this simplistic black and white approach did little, if any, harm and may have had some beneficial effects in graphically portraying good versus evil in terms understandable to young and unsophisticated audiences, but it is nonetheless an interesting comment on the underlying ethics and morals of the serial. Clarence Kelley, a prior Director of the FBI, stated in 1975: "The paranoid person feels constantly outraged, treated unfairly, and will often seek remedy outside the law."[18] The paranoid would undoubtedly feel right at home with Captain America as treated in the serial.

Another point brought out by the round robin interviews which is worthy of comment concerns the slightly different plotting utilized in Captain America. As has been discussed in Chapter 4, the standard serial plotting device normally involves a "wienie"—that is one clearly defined objective, often world conquest or control of a super weapon, which can be accomplished only by achieving a series of lesser objectives, such as obtaining the component parts of the weapon or fulfilling lesser tasks preliminary to a final thrust toward world conquest. The lesser objectives form the individual chapters with the hero consistently losing or receiving setbacks until in the final chapter, with the villain on the verge of success, the hero through brain, brawn, or luck, overturns all of the villain's successes and totally defeats him in the process. Another "wienie"—often secondary—which was heavily used at Republic is the mystery hero or mystery villain. There were exceptions, to be sure, but it was a rare serial which did not incorporate at least one of these motifs as a device to strengthen or unify the plot.

However, in *Captain America* the plotting device is much less clearly defined. Whether this was done through hesitation, chance, or, less likely, a deliberate attempt to alter the standard approach matters little. The presence of seven writers undoubtedly contributed to the problems.[19] Both hero and villain are identified, though not well explained, to the audience from the beginning. The villain is alternately motivated by the goals of (1) revenge against his peers who he feels maligned him, (2) control of the new "super" weapons for illegal use, (3) the possession of great art and historical treasures for apparently spiteful purposes only, and (4) the general harassment of society and accumulation of ill-gotten wealth. As a result, when he is defeated in Chapter Fifteen, it is almost an arbitrary cutting off of the story and not one which had built up to a grand conclusion. He has this magnificent far-flung criminal organization but he is never sure what he wants to do with it. The only potential "excuse" for this undecisiveness is that he is identified as a "homicidal maniac" thus perhaps explaining his erratic behavior.

Nonetheless, the feeling of the audience interviewed seemed to be that this loose plot structure detracted from the impact of the serial and that a more readily identifiable "wienie" or greater goal would have made for a more effective and gripping serial. The reason may have been a poorly developed original script, a script created as the writers went along, a script altered from another character, or the fact that it became apparent during production that no sequel was intended or possible since the studio had so "misused" the character from Timely Comics' viewpoint. Therefore proper thought was not expended on the basic reason for the overall conflict. In any case, the response of the modern adult viewers who were involved enough to analyze the situation was that the magnificence of the villain, the acceptability of a rather high casualty list of subsidiary henchmen, and the grandeur of Captain America and his hero image were all substantially weakened by an insufficiently developed source of contention resulting from a weak plot. A strong plot building to an ultimate confrontation might have helped to mask some specific weaknesses in *Captain America*—many of which have been discussed.

In this case the value system as discussed in Chapter Four was damaged by not justifying the basic conflict in strong enough terms. In other words, the value system of the serial genre seems to require a final goal of sufficient power to justify the multi-chapter carnage inherent in serials building up to the ultimate showdown of the major antagonists. Without it, the value system loses some of its attraction and the basic requirement—i.e., suspension of disbelief—is curtailed.

What then is the status of this serial both as a serial and as a representation of a popular culture hero from another media? Based upon conversations with both serial fans and Republic personnel, upon various published analyses of the serial, and upon several viewings, at the age of seven and some thirty years and then sixty years later, the following conclusion can be summarized. As an adaptation of the original comic book character, the serial was admittedly less than successful and relatively dishonest. However, this was not a great drawback in the overview since many in the serial audience were not that familiar with the comic book, and most of those who were *Captain America* readers were able to accept even the unnecessary changes readily. And, as a representative of the serial genre, particularly of the Golden Age of Republic Serials, *Captain America* was indeed a success, again when considered as a whole. The serial benefited from the expected high quality, and a much higher quantity, of well-staged fight sequences than many serial efforts, from an outstanding performance by Lionel Atwill as the manical curator/mad scientist, and from rapid pacing, all of which resulted in top-grade escapist entertainment which successfully appealed to all aspects of the audience at which it was aimed.

Surprisingly enough, while the much vaunted well-staged fight choreography was extremely good, previous Republic efforts had numerous better staged individual fights than *Captain America*. *Captain America* had a high quantity of fisticuff stunt work, and several individual sequences were extremely imaginative. Nonetheless, it must be admitted that there were individual fight sequences in such prior serials as *Daredevils of the Red Circle*, *Mysterious Doctor Satan*, and *Spy Smasher* which were actually as effective as, if not more so than, any single sequence in *Captain America*. David Sharpe was off to war and perhaps his gymnastic prowess was missed in the fight sequences. Taken as a whole, *Captain America*'s stunt work is outstanding and is justly recognized. However, individual sequences are only on a par with most previous Republic productions from 1939 forward as previously covered.

In spite of these qualifications, the Republic serial version of *Captain America* is a worthy addition to the Golden Age of Serials. *Captain America* achieved its goal and is a credit to its directors, its stunt men, its special effects men, and all others connected with it. In retrospect, the serial did little harm to the image of Captain America; it added a different facet to the character's image, and as a serial it was an outstanding success. Therefore, the movie version has lasting importance in both the serial and the costumed hero comic book genres. The character of Captain America has staying power because it fulfills basic needs on five levels. The first is the patriotic appeal and its reverse image chauvinism.[20] The second is the figure's mythological, god-like attributes.[21] Thirdly, Captain America is a costumed masked hero righting the wrongs of the world—a well documented psychological attraction especially for children and the unsophisticated but also a fantasy to which normal adults were susceptible.[22] Fourthly, Captain America has always been fortunate in receiving good production values in the various formats to which he has been adapted. Finally, the adventures of Captain America have always been action oriented escapist fare wherein the hero aggressively moves forward confidently.[23] The serial version strongly reinforced the last four of these five factors.

Captain America is a member of the pantheon of authentic popular culture heroes created by the mass media. As such, the figure is of interest not only in its own right as a contribution to the growing historical study of popular culture manifestations; the character also tells us something about the America of the Second World War period and about the continuing needs of humanity to find larger than life heroes who offer comfort, security, stability, and, most of all, a positive physical response to the challenges of life and a society where harsh reality frequently interferes with these goals. Captain America fulfills a basic fantasy need and therein lies the explanation for his success.[24] The 1944 Republic serial version was a contribution to the heroic image of Captain America and is a specific, if flawed, example of the attraction of Republic serials. The other Golden Age serials contributed to similar needs in the audiences and successfully delivered related forthright messages in different formats and with varying emphases.

What then is the status of Captain America both as a serial and as a representation of a popular culture hero from another medium? As an adaptation of the original comic book character, the serial was admittedly less than successful and relatively dishonest. However, this was not a great drawback in the overview since many in the serial audience were not familiar with the comic book, and most of those who were *Captain America* readers were able to accept even the unnecessary changes readily. And, as a representative of the serial genre *Captain America* was indeed a success, again when considered as a whole. To the audiences in 1944 and even in

1953 when the serial was re-released, the American faith in basic good winning out over evil with justice (questionable only upon reflection) and honesty rewarded stood out as the message in *Captain America*. The subtleties of analytic criticism were not for serial audiences.

It is generally conceded that, although the action, special effects, and frenetic pacing in chapterplays continued unabated at Republic through at least 1949, the plots and the general care which were lavished upon earlier productions gradually fell off after 1944.[25] Also, with the exception of some anti-communist themes, the messages and morals of the later productions remained fairly consistent. From 1945 on, a gradual decline set in which is not to say that good serials were not released but rather indicates that the general average and overall quality lessened noticeably for reasons which will be seen.

Notes

1. "Captain America," *Film Fan Monthly* (July–August, 1966), 61–62, pp. 25–26.

2. Reprinted in Alan G. Barbour, *Days of Thrills and Adventure, Volume Two* (Kew Gardens, New York: Screen Facts Press, 1969).

3. "Republic Productions, Inc. Produced Properties, 1935–1951," unpublished manuscript from the Republic Studios Story Department, January 1, 1951, in the Theatre Arts Library of the University of California at Los Angeles, p. 21.

4. Personal viewing. Endings verified and collated from Alan G. Barbour, *The Serial, Volume Two* (Kew Gardens, New York: Screen Facts Press, 1969), pp. 35–46 and *Captain America*, Cliffhanger Ending and Escape Pictorial Series (Chicago: Jack Mathis Advertising, n.d.).

5. *Captain America*, Cliffhanger Ending and Escape Pictorial Series.

6. Mathis, p. 255.

7. Harry Sanford, "Men of Action, Interview with John Daheim," *Those Enduring Matinee Idols*, III (n.d.), 9, p. 443.

8. "The Return of Captain America," *Screen Thrills Illustrated*, II (February, 1964), 3, p. 24.

9. "The Four Paneled, Sock-Bang-Powie Saturday Afternoon Screen," in Dick Lupoff and Don Thompson, ed., *All in Color for a Dime* (New Rochelle, New York: Arlington House, 1970), p. 211.

10. Steinbrunner, pp. 211–212.

11. Harmon and Glut, pp. 259–260.

12. Harmon and Glut, p. 263.

13. Harmon and Glut, pp. 264–265.

14. Stedman, p. 131.

15. *Days of Thrills and Adventure* (New York: Macmillan, 1970), pp. 28–29.

16. "How the Serials Rate," *Serial World* (1975), 3, pp. 6–7.

17. Richard M. Hurst, interviewer, "Captain America Interviews," March 4 and 5, 1975, ninety minute cassette. In the Manuscript Department of the Buffalo and Erie County Historical Society.

18. "Does TV Start Crime Trends," *TV Guide*, XIII (March 8, 1975), 10, p. 8.

19. Interview with Barry Shipman, Republic writer, San Bernardino, California, May 11, 1976. Although he didn't work on *Captain America*, Mr. Shipman states that multiple writers on serials sometimes resulted in weakened continuity and that they sometimes had problems in determining the proper plot direction when strong opinions were held and the writers were uncompromising.

20. James Steranko, *The Steranko History of the Comics, Volume One* (Reading, Pennsylvania: Supergraphics, 1970), pp. 52–53.

21. Stan Lee, the comic book publisher who revived Captain America, quoted in George Perry and Alan Aldridge, *The Penguin Book of Comics* (Baltimore: Penguin, 1967), p. 171.

22. For three different approaches to heroes and the roles they play in our society, see Otto Rank, *The Myth of the Birth of the Hero: A Psychological Interpretation of Mythology* (New York: Vintage, 1959); Lord Raglan, *The Hero: A Study in Tradition, Myth and Drama* (New York: Vintage, 1956), and Marya Mannes, "What Your Choice of Heroes Reveals About You," *Today's Health*, LI (September, 1973), 9, pp. 16–20, 69–72.

23. "Captain America Interviews," see footnote 17. Each of the seventeen interviewees acknowledged this factor.

24. Richard M. Hurst, "The Evolution of Captain America as a Popular Culture Hero," unpublished seminar paper at the State University of New York at Buffalo, April, 1975, pp. 65–66. In the Manuscript Department at the Buffalo and Erie County Historical Society.

25. Earl Michaels, "The Serials of Republic," *Screen Facts*, I (1963), p. 54. Most students of the genre concur.

~

CHAPTER SIX

The Serial: Beyond the Golden Age

The first release of 1945 was *Manhunt of Mystery Island* directed by Spencer Bennet, Wallace Grissell, and Yakima Canutt and was basically a science fiction mystery with the heroine searching for her inventor father and assisted by the criminologist hero. The mystery villain, who alters his identity via a transformation machine, is evil personified and wishes to use the inventor's radium power transmitter for world conquest whereas the heroine's side has humanitarian goals. Roy Barcroft, Republic's resident bad guy, had a field day as the archvillain Captain Mephisto. The serial's ads tell the whole story, "Weird happenings on an uncivilized island that hold the secret to a mysterious power that could rule the world!"[1] Still the transformation machine was intriguing and the serial maintained a high level of quality. It could well be considered a Golden Age entry.

The same could not be said of the next serial *Federal Operator 99* directed by the same threesome. It was standard cops and robbers fare with each chapter forming a separate case until ultimately the hero and his secretary defeat the three leaders of the criminal organization. Like all law and order entries, it included a plug for honesty. In Chapter Twelve, the hero concludes, "In the final analysis, even Jim Belmont wasn't so smart. He could've been a leader among men if he'd picked an honest profession. Instead of that, all he gets is a police burial."[2]

The final entry for 1945 despite its rather camp title and a noticeable routineness (same fights, same situations, all done before) has a bit more interest. *The Purple Monster Strikes* directed by Spencer Bennet and Fred Brannon utilized a villain which, while from outer space, foretold of Republic's coming emphasis on anticommunist themes. "The Purple Monster, a man from Mars, murders scientist Dr. Layton, inventor of a plane capable of interplanetary travels. The Monster assumed Layton's identity, stealing plans, and prepares for an invasion of this planet by the Martian Army."[3] He is of course defeated and destroyed by a special detective/attorney hero and Layton's niece.

During the initial, and for Layton only, confrontation, the Monster declares, "My people have planned for a long time to invade the earth and enslave its inhabitants, destroying all those who resist us. . . ." The good doctor replies, "Then you landed in the wrong country, my friend. Do you think the American people will sit by doing nothing while you build a jet plane for the purpose of bringing in an army of conquest?"[4] The patriotism as well as the forecast of the somewhat paranoiac mood of the United States concerning totalitarian governments within two years is obvious and remarkable. Even the ad campaign played on this theme. "Invasion of America from 50,000,000 miles away!" "America Meets Unknown in War of Worlds: Secret Agent from Mars in first war move!"[5] Needless to say, America as represented by the hero and heroine eventually triumph over Roy Barcroft's monster from Mars.

The first chapterplay of 1946 was *The Phantom Rider* directed by Bennet and Brannon. Despite the presence of a masked hero, the story was a routine Western concerning the establishment of the Indian Police Force. Perhaps because of the hero's awkward masked costume (he wore a full face mask which limited vision), the action was noticeably subdued. Beginning with this serial, chapter lengths were shortened by several minutes—a procedure which became standard. The second entry in 1946 was *King of the Forest Rangers* and the tribute to this public service organization revolved around a mystery plot in which a supposedly honorable archeologist is in reality attempting to gain control of platinum deposits known only to him. He is thwarted by the heroic forest ranger, Steve King. This serial was the last to make extensive use of location shooting of any distance from the studio— another economy measure.[6] It was directed by Bennet and Brannon.

Daughter of Don Q was directed by the same team and had a little more realistic basis than many serials. The avaricious villain has discovered an ancient land grant which gave his ancestor land now in downtown Los Angeles and which is worth millions. He systematically begins to kill off the other descendants but is eventually discovered and stopped by the heroine, who is also a descendant, and the reporter hero. The very self-sufficient heroine, jiujitsu expert and archery champion, then unselfishly destroys the land grant since so many innocent people would suffer. Adrian Booth who portrayed the athletic heroine says she enjoyed it very much but didn't enjoy the bruises which came with the role.

While a good enough serial, *Daughter* shows the various economy moves which were coming into play at Republic and lacks the spontaneity of prior efforts. The stunt work remained high quality however. Kirk Alyn says, "'Daughter of Don Q' was the first serial I ever made and I believe it was a good beginning for me because it included so many fight scenes—so essential to the making of serials at that time. While shooting these free-for-alls I formed lasting friendships with some of the guys who were the very tops in the fight business, and I learned from them . . . how to create an illusion of tremendous violence without sending the whole crew to the hospital."[7]

The *Crimson Ghost* was the last release of 1946. Directed by William Witney, recently returned from the war, and Fred Brannon, it features a high quota of action, a mystery villain, and a topical science fiction plot. A counter-atomic device called the Cyclotrode has been developed and the story concerns the battle between the forces of evil led by the hooded, skull-faced Ghost (otherwise a respected scientist until unmasked) and the forces of good represented by the criminologist hero to control the machine. The topicality was stressed in the serial ads which proclaimed, "For THE FIRST TIME an amazing answer to the atomic bomb explodes in a blaze of serial super-action."[8] The Crimson Ghost was a skull-faced, red-caped homicidal maniac who probably gave some of the kids nightmares.

The next Republic serial was the fourth of the Zorro entries. A standard version, *Son of Zorro* concerns the conflict between crooked politicians and a returning officer following the Civil War. The latter assumed the identity and operating procedure of his illustrious ancestor and cleans up the county making it safe for the honest people. It was directed by Bennet and Brannon and was of average quality.

The next entry *Jesse James Rides Again*, a 1947 release, marks the point at which Republic downshifted from four original productions per season to three with one re-release.[9] This again illustrates the economic problems which the serial genre and the movie industry were facing. Directed by Fred Brannon and Thomas Carr, the plot had Jesse, in an attempt to redeem himself, aiding frontier settlers against vicious oil interests who want their land and who conduct a reign of terror to get the valuable land. Jesse blocks the evildoers and saves the day. Republic seemed self-conscious of the fact that an acknowledged outlaw famous in American history was representing the side of the law and order and the ad campaign stressed Jesse's reformed role. "JESSE JAMES. . . . The dreaded name that haunted a thousand lawmen . . .

NOW . . . strikes terror into the hearts of the lawless!" "The Fabulous Pirate of the Prairies Turns Lawman! Thrill to Jesse James pitting his wits and bullets against a ruthless band . . . THE HOODED BLACK RAIDERS."[10] Jesse was portrayed by future Lone Ranger Clayton Moore who was good in the heroic roles. The serial was a success and was to lead to sequels.

The last release of 1947 was *The Black Widow*. Directed by Bennet and Brannon, it concerns the efforts of a power mad Asian dictator working through his daughter known as the Black Widow to obtain American atomic secrets in order to take over the world. They are opposed by a mystery writer hero and a reporter heroine. Bruce Edwards as the hero was unprepossessing (but did share stuntman Tom Steele's size and build—image that!). Although adequate the serial lacked originality.

G-Men Never Forget was also standard fare in that it concerns a gangster look-alike taking over for a police commissioner to carry on his gang's criminal activities. His clever plan is eventually blocked by a federal agent. Roy Barcroft had a good double role and Clayton Moore was once again heroic. Despite the fact that the ad campaign was very complimentary to the forces of law and order—"Criminals Wanted for Murder . . . Arson . . . Robbery! A fast-moving serial paced to the tempo of the most efficient organization ever to blast a criminal!"[11]—the actual FBI protested the use of their name, implied and otherwise, without official clearance. While they had previously cooperated with Republic in such matters, the FBI continued to protest in this instance. Eventually a letter from J. Edgar Hoover himself resulted in an apology from Yates in which he said in part, "All good Americans are aware of the great and perplexing tasks that confront you and your Bureau. In the future, you can certainly rely upon the writer and the entire Republic staff to cooperate with you at all times."[12] Yates' Americanism continued unabated. The serial was directed by Brannon and Canutt.

Dangers of the Canadian Mounted revolves around a group of outlaws who attempt to stop road builders on the Alaskan–Canadian border from opening the territory to settlers. The Mounties of course bring the outlaws to justice. Directed by Brannon and Canutt, this chapterplay utilized stock footage from the previous Mountie efforts for practically every cliffhanger and lacked spirit. It was very ordinary. However, it did have a spirited plea for international cooperation to maintain peace, friendship, and trust in the prologue and the ads emphasized the traditions of the famous Canadian law enforcement agency.[13]

The final release of 1948 brought back Jesse James. In the *Adventures of Frank and Jesse James*, directed by Brannon and Canutt, the brothers again attempt to go straight. In order to pay off their debts, they attempt to reopen a silver mine which they own. The villains want the silver themselves. "Thwarted at every turn by their adversaries, they [the James brothers] manage to live through hazardous and terrifying experiences before they are finally able to quell the enemy and successfully reopen the silver mine, which proves to be rich enough to pay off the people who were allegedly robbed by the James Gang."[14] Obviously the Republic decision makers were still concerned about the James' unavoidable reputation. This story line maintains a continuity with the previous serial while whitewashing the heroes to fit the prevailing morality. Otherwise there was little of note to the serial and stock footage was much in evidence.

Federal Agents vs. Underworld, Inc. opened the 1949 season and had the forces of justice attempting to obtain the Golden Hands of Kurigal, key to a hidden fortune. The law and order elements were opposed by a criminal gang, Underworld, Inc. It was directed by Brannon in his first solo flight, and he directed the next twelve chapterplays. It was straight cops and robbers with an exotic locale and a little archeology mixed in. There was practically no originality and most of the confrontations were recycled from earlier plots.

Ghost of Zorro was yet another Zorro Western. This time out, the hero dons the costume of Zorro when the telegraph company for which he works is blocked by a criminal gang masterminded by a blacksmith who secretly has a private empire and fears the coming of the telegraph with its civilizing influence. Clayton Moore plays the masked do-gooder. This role led to him becoming the Lone Ranger on television according to Moore. It was Zorro's fifth appearance for Republic and stressed comradeship, loyalty, and the fighting of injustice in the obligatory scenes establishing the hero's relationship to the original crimefighter in Chapter One.

The last entry for the 1949 season was *King of the Rocket Men*, considered by many to be the last of the really original serial heroes. The Republic Story Department inventory catches the flavor of this last important serial innovation in its synopsis.

> Jeff King, idealistic young member of Science Associates, a privately operated desert research project, in the guise of the Rocket Man, frustrates countless attempts of the cruel Dr. Vulcan to get control of the project's devices, which if ever secured by the wrong parties, could easily wreak world disaster.[15]

Vulcan was another mystery villain and in their final verbal confrontation, the position of the protagonists was further illuminated. His identity discovered, Vulcan says, "A bizarre name, but it's what I stand for: power! The power of steel forged into what I believe is right!" To which the Rocket Man replies, "Sure . . . the right of a criminal to steal . . . the right of a criminal to betray his country . . . the right of a warped mind that works toward the destruction of peace."[16]

The implied presence of an outside hostile force or nation is very much a part of this serial. In keeping with the headlines of the period, national security is prevalent in the story line. The ad campaign implied this theme in proclaiming: "Top Secret! The brains and brawn of America combine to hold off the madmen who would rock the world in disaster!"[17]

King of the Rocket Men benefited from the expected top notch stunt work and special effects which recalled the Golden Age. In fact Theodore Lydecker points out that the Rocket Man flying sequences used the same techniques and the identical model in a different costume that were used in creating *Captain Marvel*.[18] The success of this serial was to result in two pseudo-sequel chapterplays and a spin-off television series, none of which came close to the original in terms of either excitement or basic undisguised morality. Nonetheless, *King of the Rocket Men*, even with its cost cutting shortcuts, represents Republic's last true Golden Age serial in the author's opinion. It was however preceded by several non–Golden Age efforts as we have seen.

The first serial of the 1950 season was *The James Brothers of Missouri*—the third in the unplanned series on the James epic. Because of the touchy subject matter, no further adventures had been scheduled following the first two serials despite their success but Yates authorized a third installment due to distributor demand.[19] These outlaws as heroes were especially popular in the Midwestern and Western markets. In a continuing attempt to purify the contradictions between serial morality and historic fact, the prologue included the statement, "The exploits charged to Frank and Jesse James were so daring in nature that they overshadowed their efforts to establish themselves as law-abiding citizens under the aliases John Howard and Bob Carroll. This is the story of their attempt to live within the law."[20] What's a little whitewash job between friends given the characters' popularity?

All attempts at continuity with the first two entries were discontinued as the serial deals with the outlaw brothers loyally helping a former gang member run an honest freight line against a lawless competitor. They are successful and eventually exonerated, totally ignoring their similar exoneration in the second serial. The story was routine and the best action was taken from stock. The ads once again stressed the brothers as heroes. "BRANDED FUGITIVES . . . but they fight on for justice! Two Brothers, Hounded By The Law . . . Hated By The Lawless . . . In the Days Of The Wild, Colorful West!"[21]

Ironically, this emphasis on their honesty and legality, while understandable from both the studio's point of view and the desires of contemporary audiences, resulted in a finish to the series. Republic legal counsel pointed out that such inaccurate use of actual historical figures while not grounds for a defamation suit could be construed as legal misrepresentation and brought before the Federal Trade Commission.[22] So even the whitewash might have legal ramifications. While this strange turn of events was considered a remote possibility, it ended the James brothers' serial career.

Radar Patrol vs. Spy King faced none of these thorny schizophrenic problems nor was it particularly remarkable in other ways. In keeping with the growing fear of the Communist threat and the topicality of radar, the plot has an unnamed country headed by warlords engage the services of the sinister Spy King, who leads a group of mercenary saboteurs, to destroy America's radar defense system. The hero (Kirk Alyn, sleepwalking through the role), an operative of the Radar Defense Bureau, smashes the insidious plot by engaging in the standard heroics, routinely presented.

The Invisible Monster has even less to recommend it. It was not even particularly topical and concerns the attempts of a big-time criminal organizer to create an empire using smuggled aliens. He is foiled by an insurance investigator and his heroine assistant with the usual cops and robbers action. The title derives from the archvillain's ability to induce temporary invisibility by scientific means. Unfortunately, even this gimmick is unimaginatively handled and the possibility of special effects redeeming the chapterplay was lost.

Desperadoes of the West was an unusual serial in that it was a completely ungimmicked straightforward Western plot much as was *Daredevils of the West* seven years before. However it lacked both the production values and the interest of the earlier entry. It is the story of a ranchers' cooperative attempting to bring in an oil well against the vicious opposition of an Eastern company. Perhaps the only remarkable occurrence was when the head villain makes the ranchers an aboveboard offer to buy in on the project before embarking on his campaign of terror and violence in Chapter One. Such honest dealings, even if unsuccessful, were rare among serial heavies.

The first entry of the 1951 season was *Flying Disc Man from Mars* and, while nominally concerned with a science fiction menace much in the same category as its predecessor *The Purple Monster Strikes* from which it took copious stock footage, this serial was obviously tied in with the current anticommunist concern in the United States. Ron Stephenson notes this as he summarizes the relationship, "Sometimes even invaders from outer space were pseudo-Communists. In the . . . FLYING DISC MAN FROM MARS, the martian invader attempts to steal atomic weapons in which to enslave the planet Earth. The hero guessed that a foreign power was to blame."[23]

The Martian scientist teams up with a turncoat American scientist and is actually offering him the secrets of advanced atomic weapons to take over the earth and make it a satellite of the Martian dictator. They are eventually defeated by an upstanding American veteran/aviator who stumbles gradually onto their plot. However, in the opening sequence, the Martian villain argues forcefully for the Levanthian theory of Thomas Hobbes. After stating that Mars has been observing earth for years and realizes that we are now on the verge of becoming a major atomic power, he offers the following rationalization, "With unlimited atomic weapons, your people might easily end by destroying this world, which would be fatal to the whole solar system . . . including our own planet. So I am here to see that your world is put under the control of a supreme dictator of the universe. . . . How would you like to rule this planet earth under our guidance, Dr. Bryant?"[24] Not only was the villain thus shown to be antidemocratic and against the American tradition, he was also made to play upon our fears of unleashed atomic power. The contemporary interest in and concern with Unidentified Flying Objects was also worked into this serial and the ad campaigns. Scenes of the UFO in flight were actually stock footage of the miniature Falcon flying wing from *King of the Mounties* (1942).

Don Daredevil Rides Again was the first of two pseudo-Zorro's and was created to economically utilize existing Zorro footage but with a new character. The plot has the lawyer hero becoming a masked mystery avenger to defend homesteaders against dishonest politicians who attempt a violent land grab when the original titles are negated. Ken Curtis (later of *Gunsmoke* on television) was the masked avenger.

The final entry for 1951, *Government Agents vs. Phantom Legion*, was basically a simple cops and robbers tale of the government hero against an organized truck highjacking ring. As had now become the norm, extensive stock footage was incorporated not only from previous serials but also from various Republic features. This chapterplay had two things going for it: (1) a mystery villain know as The Voice and (2) topicality in that the heavy made it clear that he was selling strategic materials to foreign governments. This plot was also clear from the ads. "Danger-filled, Thrill-packed Adventure With the Daring Undercover Men Who Guard America's Secrets!"[25]

With the coming of the 1952 season, the gradual decline picked up speed. Only two productions were forthcoming that year and both were pale imitations of *King of the Rocket Men*. Interestingly enough, Spencer Bennet who had moved to Columbia was quoted at about this time saying, "Heroes follow the trend of the times but the plot remains the same in serials . . . only two studios make them now, and there are only five serial directors left. We seem to be dying out as a breed."[26] He might also have been speaking of the genre unfortunately.

Rocket Man now became Commando Cody and in *Radar Men from the Moon* he headed up a scientific organization which combated a proposed invasion by moon men both here on earth and on the moon which Cody and his allies reached via their own spaceship. The lead heavy was played by Roy Barcroft who had portrayed the Purple Monster some seven years earlier thus leading to yet more stock footage. Following this serial, Commando Cody was turned into a short lived, each episode complete but all interrelated, television series.

Zombies of the Stratosphere, the other Republic theater serial for the year, was produced during the filming of the television series but Cody became Larry Martin, super scientist for reasons never fully explained.[27] Using basically the same equipment as Cody, this hero battled a Martian plot to blow the earth out of orbit using a hydrogen bomb and to replace it with the planet Mars! Stock footage was abundant, the morality was lost in the lackluster action, and even the science fiction was difficult to accept. The ads seemed to be frantically grasping for support. "You'll say . . . AMAZING! STARTLING! UNBELIEVABLE! Yet How Far is it From the Truth?"[28] Unfortunately, even the youth in 1952 were becoming science wise and more sophisticated. Perhaps they did find it unbelievable. It proved to be Republic's last space science fiction serial.

The 1953 season opened with *Jungle Drums of Africa*, the last serial directed by Fred Brannon. A routine jungle adventure, it centered around the conflict between the American heroes and a particularly vicious representative—he kills two of his henchmen in cold blood upon different occasions—of an unnamed power for uranium rights in Africa. *Jungle Drums* just didn't catch fire. Even Clayton Moore as the colorless hero said this serial just didn't click.

The second serial of 1953 was *Canadian Mounties vs. Atomic Invaders* directed by Franklin Adreon as were all the remaining Republic efforts. An agent of an unnamed totalitarian government was attempting to build missile launching bases in Canada to invade both Canada and the United States. He and his gang are defeated by the ever vigilant Royal Canadian Mounted Police. The ads trumpeted, "SPIES AT WORK IN THE FROZEN WILDERNESS!! What secrets are they after? What diabolic plot are they hatching? The Mounties know . . . and they're *ready!!!*"[29] Despite the return of a patriotic motif with appropriate dialogue and the topical subject matter, the serial used more stock footage in the action sequences than new footage and was a pale copy of earlier Mountie chapterplays.

Trader Tom of the China Sea began 1954 and dealt with the efforts of an undercover United Nations agent to keep the peace in a South Sea nation whose rebel forces were inspired by foreign agents. Again, aside from the tie-in with a real international agency properly identified, there was nothing unique. This spy/exotic action entry was followed by *Man with the Steel Whip*, the second pseudo-Zorro serial with a standard Western plot involving the villain attempting to gain control of Indian lands, and later white settlers' lands, because of gold deposits. He is opposed and defeated by El Latigo, an Indian legend brought to life by the rancher hero as a masked dispenser of justice. He was portrayed by Richard Simmons, who was television's *Sergeant Preston*. This was the last of Republic's Western serials (which made up to 25 percent of their total output) and it was an uninspired farewell to the American West.

Republic's last year of serial production was 1955. It lead off with *Panther Girl of the Kongo* which has the last of the jungle heroines, assisted by a white hunter hero, up against a mad scientist chemist who, to obtain illegal control of diamond deposits, created giant crayfish to frighten off intruders. The plot was lackluster and even the special effects were disappointing. The monsters were obviously poorly photographed "crawdads" which frightened no one. Action sequences from the two superior Nyoka efforts were recycled but the overall results were disappointing.

Republic's final serial was yet another anticommunist effort. Given a circus background, *King of the Carnival* had a group of counterfeiters using the big top as a front to ruin the credit of the United States. Their avowed aim was verbalized by one villain when he stated, "Then the countries of the world will do business with my country."[30] The villains were brought to justice by Treasury men represented by the trapeze artists/veteran undercover agent.

The later Republic serials frequently had topical references by tying in with the 1950's news stories, but, as ever, they were always presented in black and white terms. As has been discussed, the antifascist serial propaganda of the Second World War worked during the war and even had a positive effect on the audience but the anticommunist propaganda of the 1950s seemed relatively ineffectual at best. Perhaps the solution partially lies in the approach taken in each era. Ron Stephenson sees a difference. "One main difference between the propaganda of World War II and of the fifties was that the former was more interested in exploiting the potential menace of the individual German and Japanese spy and the latter the menace of Communism itself."[31] It almost seemed an afterthought in the 1950s.

Regardless of the reason for changing attitudes and the success of the serials in either second guessing or influencing them, the fact remains that there was a relationship. It may have been represented by patriotism, antitotalitarism, or simple good versus evil, but it was there. As Bob Malcolmson astutely pointed out:

> Production of new serials ceased almost twenty years ago. When they were popular during the '30s, '40s and early '50s, no doubt they did reflect the general public's attitude of the day.
>
> Today some of these serials are still shown in theatres and on TV—and we (as adults) laugh at the exaggerated stereotyped images. We may think that this is all a thing of the past. But is it? Frankly, no. As the Legionnaires so rousingly sang in *Zorro's Fighting Legion*: "We ride with the wind. . . ."[32]

And so the Republic serial era came to an end. From the end of World War Two, the old magic was missing more and more often. Rising production costs, the problem of a loss of market, and the failure of the studio to adapt to changing times and tastes all contributed to the decline. Serial production had to be inexpensive with a minimum of frill in that a serial averaged four hours in length, far longer than the most expensive epics yet the serial budgets were perhaps five to ten percent of the blockbuster's budget. When costs went up in the postwar period, Republic opted for economy in a system already based on economical production methods.

Scriptwriters dropped from a high of seven to one in the final thirteen Republic chapterplays. Plots became listless and repetitive. Whereas first chapters ran to thirty minutes for plot development in the Golden Age, they ran less than twenty minutes after the war. Later chapters dropped from near twenty minutes to under fifteen. The plot resume and footage overlap so important in keeping things straight were cut to practically nothing. Location shots and ingenious sets were gradually phased out except through stock footage. Moreover, stock shots from Golden Age serials and feature films became prevalent and, even worse, were often the best sections of the "new" releases. Reissues became standard in the late 1940s and equaled new releases the last four years. When Republic ceased serial production in 1955, it was a different time and a sorry product which bore little relationship to the genre and the era which had flourished in the late 1930s and well into the 1940s. But to end this section on the serials of Republic on such a negative, if accurate, note is to do an injustice to a film format which exhibited a great deal of life and interest in the sound period.

There is no denying that the sound serial, even in its most highly developed phase at Republic, eventually came to its final chapter, ended by the competition of television and changing patterns of living. However, at the time of its greatest strength, the 1940s, its fate was unforeseen. Thomas Wood, in 1941, pointed out its pervasiveness:

> With its individual annual output of fifty-four episodes, each producing studio is able to assure its subscribing theaters of an unending dose of action every week in the year. The combined supply is barely sufficient to meet the needs. A Mexican church in San Pedro, California, which holds a theater license, shows three serials every Sunday. Third-run houses in the larger cities, especially in the South, often run two serials at a time. Bill Saal, Republic's exploitation chief, feels there are 5,000 theaters in this country which will always play Westerns and serials. Most of these houses are located in the small towns of the Solid South. A good many of the cities, like Dallas and Memphis, have first-run houses which show serials, however. The next best domestic serial markets are the Middle West, the East, the West Coast and New England, in that order. As is the case in the South, the small towns in the other sections are the serial's front line trenches.[33]

While Saal's optimism proved unjustifiable in the following decade, the serial did have its heyday and indeed experienced periodic revivals prior to its actual demise in 1956. The first such boost was in 1936 with Universal's *Flash Gordon*. Then came the Golden Age of Republic covered in the preceding chapters. Wood describes it:

> Now the serial has come back. With plenty of bang, too. It's the life blood of the matinee business. Ordinarily, theater operators go out of their minds trying to lure people up to the box office. They organize bank nights and cash clubs. . . . It's a different story on Saturday afternoon. No problem then in filling the house. Tough part is getting the kids to get out. Here again the managers resort to give-aways. But this time it's on the positive side of the ledger. And they're mighty glad to give "Lone Ranger" hats to the first ten kids on the sidewalk.[34]

In an article discussing the withdrawal of Universal Studios from the serial field in a reorganization some five years later, the *New York Times* accepts the genre's importance:

> Unless something happens pretty soon to correct it, theatres will be showing fewer serial pictures than ever before in history. While this piece of intelligence probably will be taken calmly along Broadway, it will cause some murmuring in the suburbs, for serials are the life-blood of nearly half of this coun-

try's approximately 21,000 theatres. Quality films with Bette Davis and Greer Garson may be fine for the big cities, but it's the serials, like "Hop Harrigan," "G-Men Never Forget" and "Jesse James Rides Again" that keep the small town operators in business.[35]

In fact, 1946 was the movie industry's best year and although the quality of serials was beginning to go down, the product was still much in demand. In that year it is interesting to note that *Film Daily Yearbook* reported that out of the 18,765 theaters operating, approximately 8,000 houses regularly showed serials, not including 2,000 more which utilized serials periodically but not fifty-two weeks out of the year. Furthermore, the average serial played to an estimated audience of four to five million people according to the *Yearbook*.[36] One source even stated that serials were used in the rural areas to sell A pictures which were less desirable to the unsophisticated, action-oriented audiences.[37]

Then, in 1950, while serials were beginning to decline, *Variety* featured an article on the use of serials to combat the inroads of television which seemed to harken a revival:

> Video's boxoffice inroads are providing a modest upbeat for film serials, as an increasing number of exhibs are starting to book cliff-hangers as a means of again attracting the moppet trade—which has been particularly attentive to tele and consequently frequenting theatres less often.
>
> Columbia and Republic, the only two companies remaining in serial production, hope the currently gentle upbeat trend will grow, and are having salesmen plug the chapterplays as valuable aids to exhibs in counteracting TV inroads.
>
> If the serial trade should materialize, it would be a paradoxical reversal of the situation of the past half-dozen years. During the period, many exhibitors cut out Saturday matinee serials for the express purpose of discouraging kid biz. . . .
>
> Tendency of vandalism has subsided lately, it seems, and, with the general b.d. decline, many theatre operators' minds are changing. Added factor in desirability of juve trade is the tremendous hypo to the concession take.
>
> Serials are a source of modest income to Columbia and Republic at this time.[38]

The final sentence in the quotation is the kernel of true prophecy in the hopeful report. The economics of the serial was against it in an era of declining box office.

It did not seem so at the time however. Three years later William K. Everson was pointing out the profit potential of the serial market.

Income from current serials is hard to estimate, but with low budgets, receipts from abroad, and subsequent feature-versions taken into consideration, serials would seem to be still reasonably profitable. The highest price paid by theatres is $50 per episode, and a fairly well situated theatre will pay $25—or $1500 per year for four complete serials. In due time serials reach cheap tenth run houses where for a one-day spot they earn a few dollars per episode.[39]

Actually his figures are somewhat high—*Variety* reports the average rental to be closer to $5 per episode[40]—and Everson himself puts his finger on the unsurmountable problems of the serial in the early 1950s.

Not only have the old vigor and quality of the serials gone, but there has been a drastic reduction in their quantity. . . .

Rising production costs and television are the usual reasons given for the serial's decline. These reasons are inter-related. Television has created its own equivalent of the serial—short, punchy, half-hour series—films. Though each film is complete in itself and is not continued in the subsequent one in the series, and finishes off without a melodramatic climax, nevertheless the series follows the quick action and violence patterns of the movie serials through 13 or 26 self-contained episodes. Some even utilize the film serials' heroes—Dick Tracy, the Lone Ranger, Wild Bill Hickok, Kit Carson, and others. TV has also revived dozens of the top serials of the talkie serials' peak period (the mid-thirties). These elaborate mounted affairs, the TV's own expensive series-films, put the contemporary cheaply made movie serials very much to shame.[41]

He also expressed the opinion that perhaps television would adapt and revive the serial genre "to vigorous and melodramatic life."[42] Such a hope was not to be—the attempt was not to come until the late 1960s television version of *Batman* and then in an outrageously campy format which was highly successful but equally shortlived.

Even after the official dismissal of the serial genre from the ranks of the moviemaker's options, it continued to be a popular seller in retrospect. *Variety* headlined in 1964, "Theatrical Cliffhanger Serials of Yesteryear Still Sell Far Out'" and reported:

Best market, according to Republic Pictures sales manager Robert Warsaw, is the smaller, far-eastern countries where constant action remains leading requirement and children haven't been TV sophisticated to expect more in the way of story and dialog subtleties.

Harvey Appelbaum, film booker for Favorite Films, distributor for Republic product in California, Arizona and Nevada, however, reports that he still gets a "tremendous amount" of calls for the serials, especially for screenings on

Army, Navy and Marine bases where they continue a staple in the Saturday morning popcorn orgies.[43]

And in 1968, Ben Shylen in *Box Office* was calling on the motion picture industry to consider the serial format to revitalize the moviegoing habit—perhaps not realizing that a similar experiment was conducted in the 1950s. He told of pleas from the exhibitors for assistance. "One of these exhibitors suggested, 'We need something like the serials that, certainly pleased the kids—and a fair portion of the adults—such as we had back in the old days. Don't magazines and newspaper still run serials? And what about the series programs on TV?'"

Shylen quotes extensively from an address by Detroit attorney and author Raymond J. Meurer before the National Association of Theatre Owners. Meurer claims that the youth are returning to the old values and recommends the serial. Pointing out that American youth is not entranced by sex, sadism, and lust on the screen, Mr. Meurer said, "they are rejecting these false values and, at the same time, they are searching around, not for new values, but for a return to the old ones." As one means of reaching and developing the younger patrons, he suggested the basic film serial, "the same format that brought children by the millions into theatres and established viewing patterns that lasted for ten years or more." Meurer argues that the serial could be updated and modernized and "do again what it has done twice before, and that is, re-establish a generation as a movie-going generation."

Shylen concludes that, despite the changing times, the serial might be a viable answer to a declining box office.

> It may not seem feasible, in this sophisticated day and age, for even one of the major companies to undertake the making of serials for theatres. (It doesn't have to be a major.) But aren't virtually all of them making episodic series for television? And haven't the long runs most of them have enjoyed—some for three, four and more years—proven their practicability as "habit builders?"[44]

Of course, with the benefit of hindsight, it can be seen that such hopes and prophecies were just so many dreams.

Republic had produced the best and most technically proficient sound serials and had held the line better than Columbia's cheap productions. But even Republic had failed. As Everson said in 1953, three years before the end of the movie serial, "Republic, by virtue of bigger budgets, slightly better scripts and good library material, has managed to maintain a much higher standard—although the fact that footage from an earlier serial, *King of the Rocket Men*, has formed the basis for three subsequent serials, suggests that even Republic is approaching the end of the serial's tether."[45] He was right. Jack Mathis summarized the Republic serial product:

> Considered the best sound serials ever made, the Republic cliffhanger exhibited that intangible asset of production values which combined with a genius for organization to produce polished products which belied their cost. The array of film-making talent assembled by Republic was unduplicated anywhere in the industry, and the imagination expressed in their writing, direction, regular and process photography, original musical scores, miniatures and special effects, and daredevil stunt work rivaled that of any major studio. [46]

Mathis was not concerned with the influence of Republic but he was knowledgeable on the technical aspects of the studio and his praise is apt.

Is the serial form of the "Golden Age" a thing of nostalgia? Probably. Its influence refuses to die however. The Batman craze of the late 1960s is one example. The continuing James Bond popularity owes much to the influence of the serial cliffhanger. In 1978, NBC actually tried to renew the serial success in the program entitled *Clliffhangers* which utilized loose remakes of three classic serial formats. Lack of ratings caused it to be cancelled after ten weeks—a perhaps hasty decision.[47] *Star Wars* owed a significant debt to serials. And, of course, the popular Indiana Jones movie series is firmly grounded in serial ambiance—a fact acknowledged by Steven Spielberg and George Lucas. A series of Republic ripoffs was found recently in Turkey. England continues to make television serials aimed at the very young. Finally, there is a group of serial fans/historians known as the Serial Squadron releasing old serials and holding an annual Serial Fest Convention located in Pennsylvania. The serial refuses to die a quiet death even if it is a thing of the past.

And, although the movie serial is now a thing of the past, the fact remains that Republic did it well and that it was a factor in the lives of its viewers—sometimes a force for patriotism, sometimes for heroics but always a reinforcement of traditional morality and American value systems.

Notes

1. Reprinted in Alan G. Barbour, *Great Serial Ads* (Kew Gardens, New York: Screen Facts Press, 1965).

2. Mathis, p. 292.

3. "Republic Productions, Inc. Produced Properties," p. 129.

4. Tape transcriptions in possession of author of soundtrack excerpts from *D Day on Mars* (feature version).

5. Reprinted in *The Purple Monster Strikes*, Cliffhanger Ending and Escape Pictorial Series (Chicago: Jack Mathis Advertising, n.d.).

6. Mathis, p. 309.

7. *A Job for Superman!* (Los Angeles: privately printed, 1971), p. 102.

8. Barbour, *Great Serial Ads*.

9. Mathis, p. 336.

10. *Kokomo* [Indiana] *Tribune*, October 9, 1947. The still manual also emphasizes that Jesse is "trying to reform and go straight" and that his new adventure results from his attempts to "prove his innocence."

11. Barbour, *Great Serial Ads*.

12. Mathis, pp. 348–349.

13. Barbour, *Great Serial Ads*.

14. "Republic Productions, Inc., Produced Properties," p. 1.

15. p. 87.

16. Tape transcription in possession of author of soundtrack excerpts from *Lost Planet Airmen* (feature version).

17. Reprinted in Alan G. Barbour, *Serial Showcase* (Kew Gardens, New York: 1968).

18. Interview with Theodore Lydecker, Republic special effects man, West Hollywood, California, May 17, 1976.

19. Mathis, p. 379.

20. Mathis, p. 379.

21. Barbour, *Days of Thrills and Adventure, Volume Two*.

22. Mathis, p. 381.

23. Stephenson, p. 446.

24. Tape transcription in possession of author of soundtrack excerpts from *Missile Monsters* (feature version).

25. Barbour, *Great Serial Ads*.

26. *New York Herald-Tribune*, October 31, 1952.

27. Mathis, p. 413.

28. Barbour, *Great Serial Ads*.

29. Barbour, *Great Serial Ads*.

30. Stephenson, p. 446.

31. Stephenson, p. 446.

32. Robert Malcomson, "Editor's Notes," *Those Enduring Matinee Idols*, III (n.d.), 9, p. 446.

33. Thomas Wood, p. 1.

34. Thomas Wood, p. 18.

35. December 22, 1946.

36. *Film Daily Yearbook of Motion Pictures 1946* (New York; Film Daily Inc., 1947), p. 206.

37. *Los Angeles Times*, November 20, 1946.

38. November 9, 1950.

39. Everson, "Serials," p. 276.

40. November 9, 1950.

41. Everson, "Serials," p. 269.

42. Everson, "Serials," p. 276.

43. February 12, 1964.

44. January 15, 1968.

45. Everson, "Serials," p. 273.

46. Mathis, p. viii.

47. Richard Hurst, "Cliffhangers," *Serial World*, no. 21 (Winter, 1980), pp. 5–8. Takes an in-depth look at this interesting attempt.

CHAPTER SEVEN

~

Republic's Cowboys—The Three Mesquiteers, Gene Autry, and Roy Rogers

Although Republic prestige among action fans and scholars of the B cinema rested with the serial, it was actually the Republic Westerns, the B "cowboy pictures," made in series of six to eight entries, which were the reliable bread-winners for the studio. While many theaters played serials either on a regular schedule or only occasionally, most neighborhood theaters and even the first-run theaters in small towns featured at least one or two Westerns regularly to satisfy the requirements of the Saturday matinee crowd. And the B Western feature frequently came from Republic, since this studio was acknowledged to make the best of that type of product.

As film scholar William K. Everson pointed out, "From the beginning, Republic got more excitement into their chases, more pep into their stunts, and more punch into their fights, than any other studio. Camerawork was always clean, sharp and crystal clear, and locations first-class. . . . Their musical scores were among the best in the business. Few 'B' Westerns could long escape the taint of standardization, and since the key requirement of the 'B' was action, it hardly mattered that Republic's machinery showed. It was exceptionally well-oiled machinery and operated flawlessly."[1] Republic Westerns also stood out from the young audience's point of view. "Republic Pictures was the King of the Cowboy Hero studios. There would not be a single Front Row Kid from 1935 to television whose heart did not beat faster, whose imagination did not catch fire, and whose Saturday afternoons were not made infinitely richer in Cowboy-Hero fantasies by the mere sight of the Republic Pictures Eagle. . . . The Front Row Kids pledged their allegiance to that bold Eagle and to the Republic Pictures for which it stood."[2] On the strength of such a reputation, the studio remained a leader in the genre until the passing of time and changing audience habits spelled an end to the Saturday matinee. In fact, as Republic began to venture into A productions, the program series were actually strong enough to carry the burden of these A ventures which were not always successful until the late 1940s when the market for Bs also began to slip.[3]

What was the message inherent in the B Western? Like all things complex, it cannot be satisfactorily simplified without encountering some contradictions. Even within individual series among the several hundred such films put out by Republic alone, there are many exceptions to the standard concept of what the program Western was about. But, as a starting point, the general themes of the majority of the genre produced from the early 1930s until the mid-1950s was in the form of the traditional morality play or sermon. The standard Western plot even with its variations was much like the Sunday School sermon and the traditional values of the American Bible Belt. Thus, the B Western emphasized again and again the importance of decency, justice, and law and order in the early United States as well as the search for a fundamental dignity for all good people. The genre thereby formed a basic restatement of American idealism and the general optimism which has pervaded the American way of life.[4]

As was indicated in Chapter 2, both the significance and entertainment aspects of the Western film have made it the subject of several studies, dating almost exclusively from the early 1960s. Most of these works have been popular in concept and, until recently, none have given more than a passing mention to the pervasiveness of the B format and formula. Among those books which dwell on the importance of the relatively scarce A productions but do nonetheless acknowledge the contributions of the Bs, one must include the volumes by William K. Everson. The first was an original pioneering work with George N. Fenin and devoted three separate sections to the B form while his second was solo authored.[5] Jon Tuska, editor of *Views and Reviews* and student of the B Western, published a major work aimed at the entire spectrum of the Western film but which devotes a great deal of space to the program Western.[6] Tuska sees the Western as more of an art form than most scholars acknowledge it to be. And there are a few works which emphasize the B Western film; both Alan Barbour's *The Thrill of It All*[7] and Don Miller's *Hollywood Corral*[8] are unabashedly nostalgic.

Just as the message of the "cowboy picture" can be summarized, so too can it be acknowledged that this message had an effect. Specific reactions, of course, varied with the audience, but the broad effect of such films was that the message set in a period piece could be generalized to the realities of every-day living. As one psychological study states:

> In the film world one may in identifying with the hero strongly wish to draw a gun on and kill the villain, but in the real world there is no such villain, no gun, and an absence of the concerns impelling that film hero to violence. It is in the latent content of the film that one finds a certain congruence and hence the greatest chance of carrying over into real life. Although the actions and concrete circumstances of the Western film are markedly different from those of everyday life they still involve basic features such as the general relations of men in their own actions and desires, to other men, and to the social environment at large. It is very likely that it is because of the manifest differences that the film can work out these basic problems and yet retain and entertain its audiences.[9]

In other words, the B Western entertained with its action/fantasy themes set in a prior time period but also affected the viewer's ability to solve basic problems in the real environment.

Since the behavioral patterns presented in the fantasy Westerns can be related to the real world, it is well to examine the message of the B Western film in a little more detail. The Western film in its long history from *The Great Train Robbery* (1903) to the 1970s anti-hero, downbeat film, such as the *Missouri Breaks* (1976), and into the 1990s with films like *Tombstone* (1993), has advanced many viewpoints on man interrelating with man. Will Wright in his structural study of the genre classifies the multitude of Western plots into four basic approaches: 1) the classical plot of the 1930s to the 1950s, 2) a transitional period in the 1950s, 3) a vengeance variation into the 1960s, and 4) a professional emphasis on the present.[10]

In the classical plot, there is a strong hero defending a weak society with its values of family, school, church, and civilization against the selfish villains who wish to control power for themselves. The hero successfully defends society's basic values, gains its respect and honor, and either joins society or rides off voluntarily at the conclusion. In the transitional period, society becomes a threat to the hero and rejects him as in the classic movie *High Noon* (1952) where the sheriff is not supported by the cowardly citizenry when killers seek vengeance against him. Villains become secondary. The vengeance variation has the hero rejecting society to revenge himself on the villains as in *The Searchers* (1956), where the heroes search for a white girl kidnapped by Indians against advice. He does, however, normally return to society. In the last of Wright's classifications, the theme is on the professional hero fighting the villains who are much the same as the hero but with slightly different goals. The emphasis is on the struggle. Society and the traditional values become secondary and even irrelevant to the theme of doing a job. An example is *The Wild Bunch* (1969) with professional gunmen fighting Mexican military men because they refuse to back down. Wright sees these four approaches as a reflection of the prevalent American values and the economic institutions accepted at the time when each approach was the major format used in most Western films. The traditional B Western fits Wright's classical mold closely because it showed Americans that rugged individualism could successfully combine with society's goals of community and equality to defend law and order and to achieve success over the selfish forces of evil.

What do these theories mean in relationship to the specific themes of the B Westerns? An analysis by Frederick Elkin concerned with the program Westerns summarized the many implications in the typical Republic series Western.[11] A lecturer at the Cinema Department of the University of Southern California who was previously a member of the Research Staff of the Motion Picture Association of America, Elkin was familiar with the Hollywood Western from both the viewpoint of the scholar and the industry. In this pioneering study, he analyzed this genre and its specific themes while the format was still an active force in the entertainment world. He stressed the positive aspects of the B Western and included potential educational influences. At the same time, he avoided the symbolic or deeply subconscious aspects and emphasized effects which are either conscious or easily understood unconscious reactions.

Elkin pointed out that the B Western, with few exceptions, was set in the American West in the late nineteenth century. The action often centered around a small town in which law and order was just coming into its own. The characters were ordinary ranchers, miners, and a few town-folk. The basic characteristics of these films were action and simplicity. The standard B Western became a continual series of chases, rescues, gun battles, and fistfights to appeal to the basic unsophisticated audience. Moral values were those of a Judeo-Christian society, and in the conflict between good and evil, good was invariably held up as right. Those on the side of good were honest, loyal, sympathetic to the oppressed, and had a respect for just law. On the other side, the evil were treacherous, callous, ruthless, and had a contempt for the underdog. It was implied without subtlety that justice and morality were worthy of great risk, and those who fight to achieve the worthy goals were honored and respected.[12]

The B Western had additional positive themes. It emphasized the rich and exciting heritage of America. Rugged individualism, frontier equality, and other popularly accepted characteristics of the Western way of life were focused upon. Whether these concepts were based in fact or folklore was immaterial to the viewer of the program Western. Similarly, the B Western also stressed the value of integrity and character in that the particular participants were usually judged by their surface personalities and abilities.[13] Although the action content was usually emphasized in these program pictures, with the coming of the Western musical, leisure time was shown in which men played and sang Western songs. This little-examined emphasis reinforced the American musical heritage and suggested that life in the open spaces of the West could be a peaceful, rewarding one.[14] A positive emphasis on these values, however, implied a devaluation of some others. For example, the stress on rugged individualism devalued strong family themes. The emphasis on action and accomplishment played down intellectuality and contemplation. Finally, the primary emphasis on the struggle between good and evil de-emphasized any aspect of romance.[15]

The heroes of B Westerns invariably had what some feel to be respectable Anglo-Saxon qualities. They were attractive, rarely lost their tempers, and did not smoke, drink, or gamble except when role playing. Normally, they did not express deep emotion. In a fight, they battled fairly. The coming of the Western musical brought a slight change in the hero's qualities. He had the above qualities but, in addition, he sang and was somewhat more friendly and charming. He wore theatrical costumes and became involved more frequently with the heroine, but not on a romantic plane. For their part, the heroines tended to fall into two types. The first was the traditional female who played a secondary role and was normally in a subsidiary position. The second type was a later development and was much more of an independent heroine. She was more likely to have an important job and to participate in an open camaraderie with the hero in bringing the plot to a conclusion. On the other side of the conflict was the villain with obvious disreputable characteristics. The gang leader was frequently a white collar villain and although dishonest, sinister, and ruthless, appeared to be a respectable citizen within the plot. He utilized the services of the "dog heavy" (action heavy) or the brute villain who was crude, menacing, and almost sadistic.[16] The fourth set of characters who were standard in the B Western and who had some degree of importance were the comic sidekicks. They were rarely held up as ideals worthy of emulation, but were sympathetic, basically good, and provided aid to the hero.

Elkin was aware that B Westerns appealed predominantly to children. Although he stated that children comprise less than half of the audience, he felt that they did not just see a Western, but "vividly and emotionally participated in it."[17] The "cowboy picture" thus filled a void in the children's world. In the B Western the child could imagine himself to be in a well ordered setting. There were no unnecessary characters, no intrusions of complex personalities, and the problems were always resolved in a satisfactory manner. The child could identify with the competent hero in the Western story, could be assured that no matter what the odds he would overcome his adversaries, and could thereby affirm his own strength and importance. At the same time, the vigorous aggressive action in which the hero actively participated, and in which the child could vicariously take part, was justified and condoned because he was fighting for the forces of right. "In fighting for justice and in winning moral victories, the child symbolically wins the love and admiration of his parents, teachers, and religious leaders."[18]

Another important segment of the audience for program Westerns was the almost two-thirds which consisted of adults with a rural background.[19] This group was also gratified by the themes, characters, and general format of the Western film. The rural audience at the time the B Westerns were most popular frequently resented urban superiority. When the Western hero with his strong suggestion of country origins defeated the villains who quite frequently had a "citified" background, the rural audience bolstered their own sense of pride by identifying with the cause of "justice."[20]

Of course, not everyone saw the classical theme of the B cowboy films as benign. For example, during the Second World War, the Office of War Information became critical of the cowboy hero's activities as essentially demoralizing. As previously mentioned, the villain of the B film was often cast as a supposedly responsible head of the community. The Office of War Information noted this frequent occurrence and stated, "This plot is becoming a Hollywood habit, the men who should be the town leaders are bandit leaders instead, and some itinerant cowboy has to administer justice for the people."[21] But, of course, the intention of the writers was not that insidious demoralization which so concerned the Office of War Information. It was to please the audience and to identify believable villains. The audience seemed to understand and took it all in stride.

In the category of the B Western program picture, Republic represented quantity as well as quality. The studio released the following B Western films: sixteen with Bob Steele, eight with Johnny Mack Brown, eight with John Wayne, twenty-nine with Don "Red" Barry, twenty-four with Wild Bill Elliott (sixteen Red Ryder), fifty-one with Allan Lane (seven Red Ryder), fifteen Sunset Carsons, nineteen each with Monte Hale and Rex Allen, four "John Paul Revere" movies (two with Bob Livingston and two starring Eddie Dew), four Michael Chapin juvenile Westerns, fifty-one Three Mesquiteers, fifty-six with Gene Autry (and one additional guest appearance), and eighty-one featuring Roy Rogers (with twelve additional guest or supporting appearances). A single Western entitled *Laramie Trail* brought Republic's total B Western output to 386. Each of these series or B Western stars had its fans and its particular attraction, but all followed the basic format of the morality play.

Of the Republic Western series listed above, the final three were the studio's most successful. They also represented three separate subthemes of the genre, and in one case included a major alteration which perhaps saved the genre in a moribund period. The Three Mesquiteers emphasized cooperation, comradeship, and collectivism. These films were the most successful of all B Western "group" series. Gene Autry was the first successful singing cowboy and his movies stressed the theme of a common man as hero which came to be known as the "Autry fantasy." In the third series, Roy Rogers was the clean-cut, fun-loving boy-hero whose films developed into a glamorous musical environment which Republic hoped resembled a stage play on film.

The Three Mesquiteers novels were originally created by William Colt MacDonald, well-known Western story writer, and were a Western takeoff on the famous literary creations of Alexander Dumas. MacDonald named his trio Tucson Smith, Lullaby Joslin, and Stony Brooke and featured them in a series of Western pulp novels. Two of the novels had been adapted to the screen in prior features before Republic began its series based upon the three friends. A brief survey of some highlights with discussion of a few of the more important titles will be beneficial and illustrative of what made the series unique.

The movie series was the first of the trio Westerns—that is Westerns with three stars—and lasted from 1936 until 1943. In spite of a dizzying chronology running from the Civil War to the present, frequent cast changes in the major roles, and a decline in the quality of production especially toward the end of the series, it had a spontaneity and camaraderie which led to several imitations at other studios. The Three Mesquiteers emphasized both friendship and a high priority of law and order in the framework of the classical Western plot.

Alan Eyles, Western film historian, comments on the law and order emphasis and claims that curiously these pictures were generally set in modern times, "seeming to argue in a naive way that traditional virtues and resources are more than enough to cope with complex contemporary situations."[22] As will be seen, although not all entries were modern, where there were contemporary situations the strong theme of traditional values and law and order did occasionally result in some interesting plot dilemmas. Still, the point is that it was the value system with its reliance on tradition which mattered in both period and modern plot lines. And such traditional values as friendship were indeed emphasized. Moreover, with the three main characters interacting, the significance of comradeship could be made quite clear several times in each film. Ernest Corneau, compiler of Western biographies, has noted, "these were the horse-operas that placed the emphasis on three heroes, each possessing his own individual talent and skills. It was a treat to the audience to see their exciting teamwork, providing us with three times as many thrills. In times of danger, their 'one for all, all for one' attitude gave us the message that true friendship was a valuable asset in life. A lesson that too many people in the world tend to forget."[23]

Of course, this emphasis on collectivism was in certain respects tied into the spirit of the times. Both the Depression Era and the Second World War period gave impetus to the idea of working together, to a collective spirit as it were. The trio Westerns consciously and sometimes unconsciously reflected this feeling. "The trio concept of Westerns ran its course and ended shortly after World War II. It symbolized in its way the collectivism and group spirit of the period and managed, incidently, to elevate the status of the sidekick—in the instance of Terhune [Max, well known ventriloquist] and Hatton [Raymond, silent film star and sound era character actor], at least— to more than a buffoon," according to one critic of The Three Mesquiteers.[24] This symbolism became so overpowering in most of The Three Mesquiteers pictures that it even entered into the physical aspects of the heroes' interrelationship. A review of Three Texas Steers notes, for example, "He [George Sherman, the director] even succeeds in imparting a poetry-in-motion effect in his handling of The Three Mesquiteers, achieving this with unified timing of cowboys mounting, riding, wheeling, galloping and dismounting of steeds."[25] While all Western series upheld the concept of cooperation, the first and most successful of the trio Western series perhaps did it best of all.

The theme of law and order was also inherent in all Western films but was especially noticeable in many of the Mesquiteer films. Robert Warshow related the law and order motif to the personal honor of the hero. "What does the Westerner fight for? We know he is on the side of justice and order, and of course it can be said he fights for these things. But such broad aims never correspond exactly to his real motives. . . . If justice and order did not continually demand his protection he would be without a calling. . . . What he defends, at bottom, is the purity of his own image—in fact his honor."[26] Compare Warshow's statement with a review of Rocky Mountain Rangers which implied that the Mesquiteers enjoyed their roles of dispensing justice and brought forth this comment from a contemporary reviewer. "Of course several of the outlaws did end horribly, but that is to be expected. They have lived horribly; let them die horribly. Hurrah for the forces of law and order!"[27] True, the law and order theme could be brutal. Equally true, the New York reviewers could be somewhat less than serious in their comments on the B Western. The point remains that the law and order theme was indeed noticeable by fan and critic alike and that it did indeed have latent implications to the life styles of the audiences watching these films.

There were several valid reasons for the series' popularity in addition to its heavy reliance on the values of friendship and the importance of law and order. Max Terhune, the best known comic member of the team, provided the following observations to author David Zinman. Terhune told Zinman the series offered something for everybody. "For the girls, it had a running gag of rivalry between Stony and Tucson. . . . It had plenty of action and fights, and the boys liked that. I like to believe the kids liked Elmer [the ventriloquist's dummy], too. And the adults, I think, liked the variety of plots and the scenery and beautiful horses."[28]

The first movie in the series was entitled logically, *The Three Mesquiteers*, and was released in 1936. It starred Ray "Crash" Corrigan as Tucson Smith, Robert Livingston as Stony Brooke, and Syd Saylor as Lullaby. The post–World War I story had the three heroes assisting veterans who have settled on land leased to them by the government and who are opposed by cattlemen utilizing that territory. The updated "homesteaders" plot made ample use of the themes of patriotism and veterans' rights.[29]

In the second series entry, *Ghost Town Gold*, Syd Saylor was replaced by Max Terhune, the ventriloquist comic. Terhune, Corrigan, and Livingston were the best remembered of The Three Mesquiteers. Although Tucson Smith was the leader and stabilizing influence of the group in the MacDonald novels, in the movies the leadership soon passed to Stony Brooke who was portrayed as much more individualistic and even hot-headed, thereby leading the group into various difficulties. While Tucson was still solid and secure, Stony became the more attractive character. Nonetheless, a certain romantic competition normally developed between Tucson and Stony. In spite of this theme of rivalry, both handled the heroics with aid from Lullaby at the height of the action. Tucson was the stronger both physically and emotionally of the two and Stony was the more volatile, dashing lead. Lullaby invariably provided the comic relief. The formula was quickly set and the first eight Three Mesquiteers Westerns came across as unpretentious but solid B Westerns. The fifth entry in the first eight was entitled *Hit the Saddle* (1937) and had a strong law and order plot involving the protection of wild horses on a government preserve.[30] The story as developed also brought in heavy overtones of ecology and conservation long before such themes were popular in the mass media. For example, the need for government protection of wilderness lands and endangered species was advocated by the heroes—although not in those terms.[31] It was otherwise noteworthy in that Stony and Tucson are romantic rivals for the heroine who was played by Rita Cansino, later to become the famous star Rita Hayworth.[32]

In the second of the next series of eight entries entitled *Trigger Trio*, Livingston was replaced temporarily by Ralph Byrd, better known as the serial hero Dick Tracy. The plot was a murder mystery built around the dangers of hoof and mouth disease. Livingston returned in the following film, *Wild Horse Rodeo* (1938). *Wild Horse Rodeo* included a plea for freedom for wild horses, had all three heroes romantically involved, and also included a young actor by the name of Dick Weston in a musical number. Weston, of course, soon became Roy Rogers.

One entry that same year, entitled *Call the Mesquiteers*, had a sequence which appeared many times throughout the series and which emphasized the cooperative aspect of the films. The plot had the heroes falsely implicated in a silk robbery and killing.[33] They obviously had to catch the real culprits. The villains in their attempt to escape the heroes, took off in three different directions; the Mesquiteers in pursuit simply divided the trails and each captured his quarry in his own unique way before returning to the collective group and concluding the plot satisfactorily.

At the end of the second season, Robert Livingston was moved into non-Western Republic features and was groomed for potential stardom. John Wayne, who had not been with the studio for two years, returned and took over the role of Stony Brooke for the next series of eight pictures. The first entry in the Wayne series was entitled *Pals of the Saddle* (1938) and like many of the Mesquiteer films was set in modern times. The plot had enemy agents attempting to gain control of a valuable chemical in order to smuggle it into Mexico for resale to foreign interests. The Mesquiteers, needless to say, patriotically defeated the plans of the spies by assisting the secret agent heroine and saving the war gas/explosive for the United States.[34]

With *The Night Riders* (1939), the Mesquiteers took a journey back into time when they battled a villain in the 1880s by donning hoods and capes to fight for the forces of law and order, and defeated a fraudulent Spanish don with a phony ancient deed. Raymond Hatton appeared as Rusty Joslin (replacing Max Terhune as Lullaby Joslin) in *Wyoming Outlaw* released the same year. The plot revolved around a crooked political boss—a favorite villain as has been discussed.

The final entry in the Wayne series was perhaps one of the more interesting of the Three Mesquiteer Westerns. Entitled *New Frontier* (1939), the plot had strong currents of the rural environment versus metropolitan needs as was discussed by Elkin. The Mesquiteers' ranch, located in a valley settled fifty years before, was about to be flooded in order to make way for a reservoir to fill the needs of a nearby city. Although the plight of the settlers was presented sympathetically, the legal confrontation scene wherein the judge found for the urban interests presented the dilemma quite accurately and seemingly insolubly for the rural folk. The judge, emphasizing "the greatest good for the greatest number," decided that the settlers must be removed and the reservoir project continue. The Mesquiteers representing the rural interest accepted the necessity of change based on law and order. The reservoir builders and a crooked politician proved to be in league to cheat the settlers by removing them to alternate land which was unacceptable and which the villains did not plan to improve by irrigation. The Mesquiteers, functioning as the voice of law and order against the hot-headed settlers, discovered that the promised land had not been irrigated and led the settlers in an attack on the dam builders at the conclusion. The settlers were saved, the villains were imprisoned, and the new land was irrigated. Thus, the urban interests had their needed water reservoir while the old settlers had even better lands than they did before. It was a happy ending which neatly avoided the original questions.[35]

Although it turned out to be a strawman conflict with a rather pat ending well masked by the exciting action-packed conclusion, the two messages were still there. Law and order must prevail and when people work together and communicate all can be satisfactorily accommodated.

It was during this period that John Wayne made the movie *Stagecoach* (RKO, 1939). The last four of his Mesquiteer series were made after he had made *Stagecoach* and all were released after he had begun his successful rise to stardom. "He hated Republic for sending out these terrible Mesquiteer pictures, but he couldn't stop them. Wayne's down home fans loved the Mesquiteers and were glad that John Wayne was back in the saddle. . . . They loved him as a good-guy western hero. They even loved his Mesquiteer movies . . . as much or more than they loved his high-class fancy dude westerns directed by John Ford. Republic Pictures knew their audience."[36] Wayne's biographer, although critical, makes some good points about Republic's contributions and Wayne's indebtedness to the studio. Although Wayne may have resented Republic's using his B pictures after he had finally begun to make the big breakthrough, he did remain under contract with the studio in its bigger productions for many years thereafter. And in retrospect, Wayne has fond words for his years at Republic. "I didn't know how good I had it when I was makin' those quick westerns for Republic. April to September—we worked like Hell, makin' our quota of pictures, which were already sold in advance in a package to the exhibitors."[37] Thus, Wayne acknowledged that the B films had been presold and recognized that he received training and exposure in some of the best B Westerns made at Republic.

The Mesquiteers series now underwent some additional cast changes. John Wayne was replaced by Bob Livingston. Wayne was going on to greater things; Livingston had had his chance and was being returned to the B Western field.[38] Corrigan, who had always resented to some degree the fact that he was not the main lead as had originally been planned, decided to depart also. He was replaced by Duncan Renaldo who became Rico, the second-ranked Mesquiteer. Raymond Hatton continued on in his role as the comic relief. Livingston, Hatton, and Renaldo made seven Three Mesquiteer pictures. The first was fairly typical. It had Livingston and Hatton going to a Caribbean island where they assisted insurrectionist Renaldo in defeating the ruthless and corrupt island dictator thus leading to a strong freedom motif in the film. Renaldo, as Rico, then decides to stay on with the Mesquiteers and returns to the American West with them. The film was *Kansas Terrors* (1939).

For the 1940–1941 series Tucson Smith was recalled and was portrayed by Bob Steele, well known Western star. The new Lullaby Joslin was comic Rufe Davis, who bore a resemblance to Terhune. Bob Livingston continued in his role of Stony Brooke. After seven films with this team, Tom Tyler became Stony Brooke for the final thirteen entries while Jimmy Dodd (later Mouseketeer leader) played Lullaby in the last six films. *The Phantom Plainsmen* released in 1942 is perhaps worthy of mention in that the Mesquiteers opposed the Nazis in keeping with the wartime interest.[39] An unscrupulous American is selling horses to the totalitarian interests and the heroes patriotically intervene. Even with the defense theme in this particular entry, the time period in the series remained quite loose in that some of the films were also still placed in the Old West. In their last season the Mesquiteers once again faced the Nazis and saved a secret rubber formula in *Valley of the Hunted Men* (1942).

The fifty-one Three Mesquiteers had been a highly satisfying B Western series. While the quality declined, overall the series was a significant one.[40] When asked about his career at Republic in the series and whether he had thought of any potential impact on audiences, Robert Livingston replied,

"Not really, the studio put out a good product until they lost interest. The enthusiasm of the people was good. Corrigan wanted to be a Western star. I didn't care. . . . The Republic product was hit and miss. . . . I didn't like the heroes to be too corny. Sam Sherman [the movie historian] gave me a great compliment once. He said, 'Bob, your Westerns did things they're doing today before anyone else.' My Mesquiteer films are good for what they are, Westerns."[41]

Just as Republic's Three Mesquiteer series was the best of its kind, so too did Republic lay claim to the first successful musical Western series. Nat Levine brought young country Western singer Gene Autry to Hollywood in 1935 directly from a Chicago radio station where his radio program and record sales were solidly respectable. Levine's Mascot Studio featured him as a singer in the Ken Maynard Western *In Old Santa Fe* (1935), in the Maynard serial, *Mystery Mountain* (1935), and, based upon an acceptable if not exciting reaction in those films, cast the young Gene Autry as the lead in the serial *Phantom Empire* as a replacement for Maynard. The serial was one of Mascot's most successful. On the basis of Autry's success in these three tryout vehicles, Levine decided to put him in a series of musical Westerns for the newly-formed Republic, which had absorbed Mascot. In doing so, he changed the history of the Hollywood Western.[42]

The introduction of Gene Autry revolutionized the B Western cinema and, according to some critics, ultimately destroyed it. His success was to lead to the creation of his most well known competitor, Roy Rogers, also from Republic. Both contributed significantly to the B Western movie and influenced several generations of youthful audiences. Their importance is tinged with a note of irony:

> It seems a bit incongruous that in a genre that depended primarily upon real he-man action and thrills from its start two guitar strumming, warbling, saddle serenaders should become the reigning kings of the Western film empire in the late thirties and forties—but that is exactly what happened. Gene Autry and Roy Rogers both parlayed pleasant singing voices and winning personalities into public popularity unmatched since the early days of Tom Mix's phenomenal mass appeal.[43]

While there were obvious similarities between the two stars and their movie careers, each was unique and made a separate, if similar, contribution to the influence of Republic upon its audiences.

Not all fans or scholars of the Western film consider Autry's influence to be benevolent. In fact, many felt that the beginning of the "singing cowboy pictures" signaled the end of the B Western genre as a viable format because such movies featured musical production numbers and "superfancy clothes" which made a mockery of the true West.[44]

To his critics, Autry's appeal could not be explained.[45] His lack of acting as well as physical ability, his bland movie personality, and the fact that he did indeed change the B Western are all brought up as adverse points especially among hard core action purists. On the other hand, it is generally acknowledged that the success of Autry's features were the salvation of Republic in the early years, enabling the studio to spend more time and money on their other B Western films as well as improving the lot of their entire output. Also, Autry outlasted all of his competitors and imitators although he did not remain at Republic after the war. Other stars such as Roy Rogers and Tex Ritter retained their popularity and audience appeal until the end of the B Western genre, but they were undeniably followers in the footsteps of Gene Autry.

It is quite true that Autry had little acting ability. However, it was rarely necessary because in most instances he portrayed no personality other than his own. Since his singing ability was very real as compared to his status as an action star, his pictures became more successful as he sang more. Added to this development was the fact that while he started out somewhat awkwardly in physical sequences he did improve as time went along to the point where he could ride adequately if not skillfully and to where his fistfighting technique was acceptable.

Autry made a career out of playing the singing "nice guy" and this pleased his fans. Autry and his studio realized this and cultivated his image. As one movie analyst states:

> Gene was good and his opponents were evil, and to kids who were unable to handle the fine shadings between these two, the moral lesson was clear.
>
> While it might seem peculiar to the generation of today, most of us welcomed and accepted the Autry philosophy that it wasn't a bad world after all and could be made better if every man stood up for his beliefs, even if we didn't care for the singing.[46]

As far as the singing was concerned, it obviously appealed to a segment of the audience. It remains that Autry had a workable formula and morality was a mainstay. A critic for *Harper* conceded that his cynical son could reject Autry's music but was captivated by the image of heroism and action.[47] A Western film authority summarized it, "he came along at the right time. . . . Autry was new, and had something different to offer."[48]

Autry himself was to prove to be a businessman of note and contributed to the commodity of his image.[49] Undoubtedly his own instincts served him well in developing his career as the foremost singing cowboy of the 1930s and early 1940s. While there had been a few isolated attempts at "singing cowboys" previously,[50] Autry's Westerns emphasized the music and there is no denying that this caught the audience's attention. But there was more than this to the image. Autry early pushed his vehicles as good family trade. Jon Tuska noted somewhat critically, "Autry was primarily a singer who consistently tried to build his films around hit songs and, almost begrudgingly, incorporated action sequences. . . . He appealed to parents, extolling the virtues of his clean films . . . encouraging the public to believe that Westerns were intended strictly as family pictures."[51]

This emphasis on family entertainment had an interesting corollary. Autry developed an image of himself as a clean-cut, unassuming, average young man, morally on the side of right who was able to overcome great odds with the use of a smile, a song, and a charmed mystique.[52] Again, this "Autry fantasy" has been ascribed to Nat Levine, Director Armand Schaefer, and Autry himself. Autry and his advisors consciously turned his character into a dandified hero charming and singing his way past villains and danger. He was a hero with which the underdog and physically undeveloped could identify.[53]

Whether Autry's phenomenal fame was due to his timing, his music, his morality, his family entertainment emphasis, or because he represented a change from the usual Westerner may never be determined with certainty. However, the fact remains that he was influential within the industry and was a force with his fans. Autry himself recognized this, "I know that I owe about all I have to the devotion and support of the kids . . . to youngsters, Gene Autry is not simply a human being, but a kind of Superman. They accept anything he does or says as the right thing. That's why Gene Autry has to be so careful about the way he handles himself."[54]

Republic was also aware that Autry represented pulling power for the studio and gave out frequent press releases spotlighting and emphasizing his popularity. For example, in covering the Republic program for 1939, the *New York World Telegraph* used Autry's rise as the lead-in headline "GENE AUTRY OF WESTERNS GOES OVER BIG WITH FANS." The article pointed out his appeal to women and his vast popularity in small towns. He headed all the polls, received more mail than superstar Robert Taylor, and outsold Bing Crosby in the record market. Outside of the large cities Autry outdrew major stars, the article concluded.[55]

The claims were not all studio press agent puffery. Statistics showed that Gene Autry was in the top ten Western stars from the first year the polls were taken in 1936 through 1942 when he entered the service and again from 1946 to 1954. Also, he was number one in popularity from 1937 to 1942. Perhaps even more significant in terms of potential influence on general audiences, he was one of the top ten movie moneymakers for the entire industry from 1938 to 1942.[56] For a B Western cowboy star to be in the same league with the Gables and Garbos was success indeed!

Although Herbert Yates probably did not analyze or even appreciate the basis of Autry's popularity, he recognized it as important to the studio. In an interview in the *New York Times* he spoke of the continuing success of B Westerns and in the process gave an indication of the reasons for Republic's success and a hint of why it was to eventually fail. "The public has always liked Westerns—you know, cowboys, horses and fine scenery— hillbilly comedies, and serials. The proof of the pudding is that Gene Autry is one of the best loved stars in pictures today. Sure, the story is pretty much the same. There's the hero and the girl and the heavy who is trying to gyp them out of a mortgage or land or cattle. But you change it around a little, give it new trimmings. You've got a formula that the public likes and it's as standard as granulated sugar. If you like sugar in your coffee why use salt?"[57]

If Yates was content to accept Autry's success for what it was in terms of profit, Autry was not so complacent. For whatever reasons, economic or moral, he built upon his image, molded it, aggressively propagandized it, and in the process became a major influence on his fans. The "Cowboy Code," a public image list of rules for cowboy stars, is attributed to Autry. Interestingly enough, Autry's "Ten Commandments" of the Cowboy also mirrored quite accurately what Yates considered important in films morally and what were normally featured in Republic program films, Western or otherwise. So Yates and Autry, both hard-headed businessmen, had more in common than the mere pursuit of profit. The Code as developed by Autry stated:

1. A cowboy never takes unfair advantage—even of an enemy.
2. A cowboy never betrays a trust.
3. A cowboy always tells the truth.
4. A cowboy is kind to small children, to old folks and to animals.
5. A cowboy is free from racial and religious prejudices.
6. A cowboy is helpful and when anyone is in trouble he lends a hand.
7. A cowboy is a good worker.
8. A cowboy is clean about his person and in thought, word and deed.
9. A cowboy respects womanhood, his parents and the laws of his country.
10. A cowboy is a patriot.[58]

Although these Commandments were not uniformly followed during the twenty to thirty years in which the B Western series films flourished, in general they were adhered to quite closely, especially at Republic.

The final commandment is particularly significant for Autry. Not only were patriotic themes utilized in Autry's pictures extensively, but he also left a thriving career at its height to enter the Second World War. At that time, he gave an interview widely circulated in the newspapers in which he espoused his philosophy:

> Everybody ought to think of winning the war ahead of anything else. This is the most serious time in our history and our country is in more peril than any other time. . . . I think the He-Men in the movies belong in the Army, Marine, Navy or Air Corps. All of these He-Men in the movies realize that right now is the time to get into the service. Every movie cowboy ought to devote time to the Army winning or to helping win until the war is won—the same as any other American citizen. The Army needs every young man it can get, and if I can set a good example for the young men I'll be mighty proud. Seventeen and eighteen [year olds] are needed, and some of those boys are my fans. I say to them and to all you young men, every young man should give everything he can for the war effort. If we train young pilots and the war continues for a long stretch, those boys of seventeen or eighteen will be a protectorate over the whole country. I wanted to join the Air Corps rather than the other branches of the services because I felt I could do more good for the war effort there than any other place—because I have been interested in flying for the past ten years.[59]

Autry's beliefs, his image, and traditional American values were strongly reflected in his films.

The first film in the Autry series was *Tumbling Tumbleweeds* (1935). It was also the first directorial effort for Joseph Kane, who was to become the premier house action director at Republic in future years. The plot had Autry join a medicine show and then return home to uncover his father's killer using a song as a decoy.[60] Music and action were well balanced. Joseph Kane has stated that he was nervous at his first major responsibility but with so much preparatory experience in various assistant positions, the film was successful and he was pleased with the results.[61]

The second in the series of Autry Westerns was entitled *Melody Trail* and continued experimenting with the new formula. Whereas the first movie had tried to balance the music and the action with a slight emphasis on the action, the second entry relied predominantly upon the musical and broad comedy supplied by Smiley Burnette who had come with Autry from

Chicago. The story concerned a rodeo, rustling, and even some romance and was routine.[62] While the studio was definitely experimenting at this point, time was to prove this second format to be the most utilized and therefore, it is to be assumed, the most popular used in the series. While there were several good action entries, especially in the early years, the music was eventually to predominate. The Autry Westerns were, as were the Three Mesquiteers, to vary between the West of the past and contemporary Westerns. However, in the case of the single star with his musical background, the wide variations in time did not seem to be as noticeable and difficult to accept. Also his period pieces tended to group around his early phase while the contemporary backgrounds clustered around the musicals.

The Big Show made in 1936 was the eleventh in the Autry series for Republic and was a landmark in that it benefited from special location shooting. It was filmed at the Texas Centennial in Dallas which gave the production added gloss and values. Another interesting point is that Autry played a double role, that of a cowboy star and his double or stuntman. Since a stuntman doubled Autry in his stuntman's role, the producers had to be all the more careful. The plot had the prima donna star walking out and his he-man double saving the day. This film included a young singer, Leonard Slye, who changed his name to Dick Weston and finally took the movie name Roy Rogers. Rogers was at that time singing with the Sons of the Pioneers who were featured in the film. The group also appeared in Autry's next picture, The Old Corral, and in the course of the plot development, which has Western lawman Autry defeating New York gangsters, Autry and Rogers have a brief fight which Rogers loses.

Although the music was becoming more and more important as these Autry productions progressed, during this early segment of his movie career a respectable action quota did remain. A good example is Boots and Saddles released in 1937. The story was a standard plot concerning rivalry over an army contract for horses which was decided by a horse race. Autry was of course motivated by altruism.[63] However, it included some lively chase sequences—one of which had Autry turning the tables on two villains by means of unusual stuntwork. As the two villains rode by, separating to avoid sagebrush behind which the hero was hidden, he flipped a branch around throwing each of the villains to the ground simultaneously and as smoothly as a gymnastic routine. Such a sequence is indicative that some good, seemingly spontaneous, action remained in the Autrys.[64]

By this time, Autry was securely on top of the Western field. Knowing his own worth and being a good businessman, he demanded more money. When Herbert Yates refused, Autry finished his current picture and left for an unscheduled personal appearance tour throughout the South and Southwest, the areas of his greatest popularity.[65] The studio's process servers could never quite catch up with him because Autry's fans protected him to the point of escorting these servers directly out of town. Such was Autry's popularity.[66] Yates eventually had to give in and come to terms since Autry was still Republic's top star and because he was so popular in the recording field which boosted the success of his movies. It was at this time, however, that Yates began to promote Roy Rogers as the new singing cowboy star. As a result, when Autry returned, Yates had two stars.

Joseph Kane directed the first two Autrys upon the star's victorious return. But then he moved on to the Rogers unit and other directors came in to handle Autry. It was at this time that the Autry films took a more noticeable turn away from an approximate balance of action and music to a definite emphasis on the music. With the increasing emphasis on the latter, Autry's Westerns tended to remain more in the present time rather than in the period era of the traditional B Western film. This combination of musical fantasy and modern contemporary stories in the West was a deliberate Republic effort to make the emphasis on music more acceptable to the Western fan. The earlier Autry historical Westerns were abandoned and the hero became a radio, rodeo, or movie star moving in a world of autos, planes, and even tanks.[67] Moreover, the stories hinged on modern themes such as political corruption, big business expansion, soil erosion, crop destruction, and various social problems.[68]

An example of the new approach was *In Old Monterey* (1939). It was the last Autry feature directed by Joseph Kane and was considered a Special. It was Republic's policy during this era, in the case of both Autry and Rogers, to devote average budgets to six of the eight features per year and put extra money, stars, musical numbers, and other special sequences into the remaining two and sell them as Specials.[69] *In Old Monterey* ran seventy-three minutes, about fifteen minutes longer than the normal B Western. To increase the attraction and variety, some acts which had audience drawing power in the Republic strongholds such as the Hoosier Hot Shots, a well known Midwestern radio group, were also added.[70]

The plot had an army cavalry background and gave Autry a chance to appear in uniform thus giving a preview of his patriotism in the coming years. In fact, at one point, "Stirred by patriotism, Gabby [Hayes, comic character actor] springs to his feet, shouting he owes the country an apology and breaks into the strains of 'Columbia, Gem of the Ocean.' To a man the town hall breaks into the song."[71] Autry also delivered a hard sell patriotic preparedness speech. Not all critics accepted the message however. One stated, "herein is some phoney flag-waving, as scripted" and offered the opinion that the film's goal was for the "Government to preserve America for the Americans."[72] The story also enabled Republic to use some exciting tank action footage which had appeared in a previous film.[73]

Not all of Autry's films proved a proper blend of music, morality, and action even in this period. For example, in 1939 Autry made a film *Rovin' Tumbleweeds* that cast him as a Washington congressman advocating flood control. It was perhaps inspired by Frank Capra's theme of the honest little man against the corrupt system.[74] However, while Autry's image bore some resemblance to that idea, Autry was no James Stewart, and *Rovin' Tumbleweeds* was no *Mr. Smith Goes to Washington*. Nonetheless, the film is representative of the Autry format during this period and with his personality it might have worked. But it was inappropriate to the B Western market. It was mainly music and politics. As one critic commented, "The picture's resemblance to the typical western lies only in the habiliments of the stars and in a scene laid at a rodeo."[75]

Autry's next film, however, was back in stride and proved to be an important landmark in his career. *South of the Border* gave Autry a hit song and had a plot which was very appropriate to the period. It was released around Christmas of 1939, and included submarine bases, counter-spys, foreign agents, and concerned revolutionaries attempting to take over Mexican oil deposits.[76] Ironically, in keeping with the title song, the heroine enters a convent at the movie's conclusion.[77] Confused as it may sound, the film, its title song, and Autry as a Federal agent were a great hit in broader markets and Republic found Autry's pictures playing first-run houses as well as attracting the usual Saturday matinee bookings.[78]

As Autry's general popularity increased, his films received bigger production values and more music, but as has been indicated the action content decreased noticeably. *Variety* noted that in *Gaucho Serenade* (1940), concerning the hero befriending a small English boy whose father is in prison, there were no horseback scenes for the first forty-four minutes, no suggestion of fisticuffs for fifty minutes, and no gunplay for some fifty-six minutes. In a sixty-six minute B Western film, *Variety* and probably the fans felt that this was indicative that the action content was definitely secondary—a situation worthy of criticism.[79]

Following a loan out to Twentieth Century-Fox to star in the film *Shooting High* (1940),[80] Autry went into *Melody Ranch* released the same year. Autry, as a Hollywood radio star returning home for "frontier day," was supported by comedian Jimmy Durante and Vera Vague as well as by tap dancer Ann Miller. Obviously, this Special Premiere release was definitely more musical than Western in the traditional sense of the word, but it was a success and Republic was pleased with its broader markets. The *New York Times* even commented, "Republic apparently intended the film for a wider audience, weighing this super-Western with romance, radio programs, and comedy and the varied talents of . . . eminent non-Westerners. . . ."[81] This format continued until *Bells of Capistrano*, released in 1942. Then Autry joined the Air Force and spent four years in the service of his country. With an eye always on the profits Republic continued to re-release the earlier films of its top Western star during his absence. This was the time during which Roy Rogers was to meet and surpass the popularity of Gene Autry, becoming the "King of the Cowboys."

After the war Autry returned to Republic apparently interested in regaining his title and crown. His first film was *Sioux City Sue* directed by Frank McDonald and released in 1946. The plot relied more on comedy and music than on the Western formula and was a startling example of how much the Autry success had affected the action Westerns of the 1930s. The plot synopsis from Republic's own files shows how unlike the "blood and thunder" B Westerns of the past the Autry vehicles had become. Autry, a rancher, has a chance to become a movie actor but has to sing to a donkey. He returns to his ranch disillusioned and the female talent scout attempts to make amends. She *saves him* from the villain who wants to ruin Gene. In the finale she obtains a real starring role for him in a Hollywood musical Western.[82]

This was a far cry from the image of William S. Hart and Tom Mix. Still, the mild self-effacing hero came through the comedy, the music, and the media trappings a winner and Autry's fans accepted it. Republic continued the Autry series in this vein although Autry was restless. As a sign of the times, Autry's black and white release played in New York on a double bill with the first color Rogers release and significantly was somewhat overshadowed in the joint review.[83]

Autry's final film at the studio was *Robin Hood of Texas* (1947), directed by Lesley Selander. Ironically enough, it was less a musical and more of a mystery than had been true of previous productions both before the war and upon his immediate return. Autry was blamed for a bank robbery and then released as a decoy. Action and doublecrosses prevailed as Autry cleared himself at a dude ranch. It was closer to a traditional B Western than Autry had been in for years.

Because Autry was interested in setting up his own production unit and exercising complete control, in mid-1947 he left Republic for Columbia where he continued his career until the early 1950s. Although he took with him several of his Republic staff including Armand Schaefer, John English, and Frank McDonald, as well as some experienced technical people, his Columbia productions were not that much different. The major change was a de-emphasis of the musical extravaganza and a return to the more balanced Western movie involving both action for the Western enthusiast and music for the traditional Autry radio/recording fan. Autry sensed that his Republic productions had become lop-sided. Moreover, he watched his budgets at Columbia closely and musical spectaculars cost money. So, aside from making him richer, his series of B Westerns at Columbia did little to alter or improve the traditional image of Gene Autry. It can even be argued that they lacked the spontaneity and excitement of the early Republic releases. Autry's contribution to the Western was developed at Republic and benefited from that studio's expertise.

Long before Autry parted company with Republic, the studio had found and developed along the same lines the man who in some respects surpassed him. Roy Rogers came to the movies as Leonard Slye from Duck Run, Ohio, and appeared with the Sons of the Pioneers in a few Columbia and Republic Westerns. As noted, he received encouragement at Republic after Autry and the studio had financial disagreements. Just as in the 1950s Rex Allen, Western singer billed as "The Arizona Cowboy," was to be groomed as a successor to the then top-rated Roy Rogers, so too Rogers was brought in to answer the threat of Gene Autry.[84]

Rogers, like Autry before him, developed into an image greater than the actor and the themes of his films also paralleled Autry's to a degree. As in Autry's case, Rogers started out with action/historical motifs, shifted into a mid-period of glamorous musical extravaganzas, and finally developed into adventuresome outdoor dramas with a degree of realism unusual for B musical Westerns. Autry left Republic before his third phase really developed and his Westerns at Columbia, while having some aspects of realism, never matched the corresponding Rogers period although the later Autry fights were better than his earlier Republic fisticuff efforts. In some respects, Rogers' career was the culmination of what Autry's might have been at Republic had the war not intervened. Only in Rogers' case the action content was never completely submerged as it seemed to be with the Autry films when music predominated. Rogers' third phase—the action period—was far more stark and brutal than any of the Autry Westerns either at Republic or Columbia.

While Rogers and Autry shared and promoted the "good guy" image, there was a slightly different representative of the clean-cut hero. Whereas Autry was the underdog, conquering through righteousness and music, Rogers was a more convincing and virile hero. He came across as the athletic boy next door who could take care of himself and who would always do the right thing. As one critic said in comparing the two, "His [Rogers] voice is 'more romantic,' his smile warmer, his charm 'far more boyish.'"[85] Pete Martin, film star interviewer, said Rogers appealed to children, servicemen, women, and even "to elderly folk, to whom he represents the sterling qualities of a son or grandson they would delight to call their own."[86] And Rogers always looked more convincing in a fight. Even in his early youthful period he never had the awkward look that Autry did, although admittedly the hand-to-hand combat was avoided at first since his slight build was more obvious in close fights. However, Rogers' other physical activities such as stunts and riding were always more impressive.

Even when Rogers' pictures shifted into the more colorful musical phase and he began to wear fancy outfits never imagined in the pre-Hollywood real West, his image remained untarnished to the youthful audience. The mood of his films seemed to vary from those of Autry's made in the phase where music surpassed the action. Not only did Rogers' films retain relatively more action, but the music was segregated and stagelike. In the Rogers' efforts, the music took the form of reviews and deliberate interruptions in the plot and action whereas Autry's music was frequently integrated into the plotline or at least flowed into the picture.

Rogers even told Jon Tuska that he felt Yates based his films directly on the stage play *Oklahoma*. Rogers stated that a memorandum came down to this effect after Yates had made one of his New York trips. On the basis of this, Tuska concludes, "There was no underlying fantasy in the Rogers pictures the way there was in Gene Autry's Westerns, but there was glamour and a dreamlike quality, music, and magic, beautiful men and women singing and flirting in the Golden West."[87] The fact that the Rogers' musicals had bigger budgets than Autry's earlier ones, as well as the conscious attempt on the part of Yates to mimic a successful stage effort, may account for the difference between the musical Westerns of the two stars. The difference, while difficult to articulate outside a movie theater, was significant.

Rogers' popularity was as unquestionable as his style and clothing as his career progressed. He himself questioned the gaudy outfit but came to accept the image. "His studio—still vigorously at work creating a fictive personality . . . demands that he dress as gaudily as possible in order to attract attention to himself in public. At first Roy, the shy country boy, didn't like it. . . . Now he is becoming more accustomed to his job and appears in dazzling regalia."[88] And the ploy worked. The newspaper *PM* acknowledged his attraction and popularity in a slightly condescending article when he entered his "colorful" period:

A Stranger in Pitchman's Gulch: Roy Rogers
The Cowboy Star Gets Not a Tumble Despite Full Regalia.

The New Yorkers who saw Roy Rogers walking through noonday traffic one day last week, and into the West 57th Street office of Republic Pictures, turned around and stared, but not one of them thought enough of the apparition to ask him for his autograph. He was dressed in a green fitted cowboy suit, bound and appliqued in brown, with a tan appliqued shirt, orange tie, ten-gallon Stetson and fancy orange boots, but blase Broadway let him pass like just another sandwich man. Which goes to show that New Yorkers above the age of twelve or thirteen aren't as familiar with Roy Rogers as by rights they should be . . . This a commentary on New York provincialism when you consider that in Roy's three years in pictures he's become the third ranking western star of the U.S.A. . . . and that outside New York he goes over hell-for-leather with the fans.[89]

Like Autry before him Rogers was indeed a ranking star. When Autry moved out of the Number One position as top money-making Western star in the *Motion Picture Herald* poll in 1942, Rogers moved in and held that position from 1943 to 1954, three years after he made his last theatrical B Western.[90] Again like Autry, Rogers also recognized his worth and potential influence, cultivated his image, and developed his popularity to the highest level possible. While he did this admittedly for profit—he was for a period the most merchandised star in the world—he always was cognizant of the power of his influence over his young fans. Art Rush, his longtime manager, claims that both he and Rogers knew for years the impact which his films were having upon youthful audiences and this was one reason they fought Republic so hard on the release of Rogers' pictures to television.[91] In any case, for commercial, moral, or other reasons, Roy Rogers was concerned with the fact that he had a strong following as shown in his frequent personal appearance tours, his top box office ratings, and general popularity.[92]

At the height of his popularity, Rogers received 74,852 letters in one month, far surpassing the previous record holder, Clara Bow.[93] At that time, he acknowledged his influence. "That's just a part of the job. . . . Children pattern themselves after you. It might be that at home a kid's mother is trying to get him to stop smoking. If he sees me smoking on the screen he'd say, 'Gee, Roy Rogers does it—why can't I?'"[94]

Rogers and his wife, Dale Evans, became very active in religious circles in the late 1940s. This fact proved influential when, in the 1970s, he reactivated his career through record releases, television and county and state fair appearances, and new movie productions. One result is that he frequently reflected upon the potential effect of his B Westerns since they were the basis of his original popularity. He recognized that their period of greatest impact was in the 1940s and early 1950s when he switched from movies to an action-oriented Western television series. When asked about his reputation as an All-American, he noted that he "felt like a babysitter to two generations" and replied, "It's thrilling that people have trust in you. It comes from many things—the books Dale's written, the personal appearances. People like Dale and I [sic] together; we just go good."[95]

Rogers was also convinced that the morality of his pictures was a positive factor. In commenting on the use of violence in later films, he emphasized the end result. "Blood, of course, has always been a Wild West requisite, but Roy claims it was hardly ever gratuitous. 'Oh, you were allowed to have a little smeared under your nose or mouth during a fight scene. . . . But we fought clean and what's more, the bad guys *never* won.'"[96] If Rogers was thinking in terms of the conclusion of each of his films he is absolutely right. However, in some Rogers pictures, especially after the Second World War, when William Witney was consistently directing and Sloan Nibley was frequently writing them, Roy Rogers did have some bruising battles within the films which he lost in relatively bloody closeups. Rogers insisted that the violence and the messages in his B Western series were not harmful compared to later Westerns "that could have an adverse effect on some of the children in the audience."[97]

Regardless of variations in their personal beliefs, their financial successes, and slight alterations in their approaches to the program Western, it is undeniable that Roy Rogers followed Gene Autry in terms of studio, type of entertainment, career development, and a serious concern about image. Rogers proved a worthy successor to Gene Autry. He was a variant upon the image, but in terms of the message imparted by the man and his films he was basically the same. It is also important that Roy Rogers was perhaps more effective as an audience influence in that he was a more believable hero.

Rogers was put under contract to Republic in October 1937 and after a few supporting roles was given the star buildup.[98] Yates rushed the newly named Roy Rogers into a Western series and released *Under Western Stars* in April, 1938. It was directed by Autry veteran Joseph Kane and produced by Sol C. Siegel who went on to better things at Republic and in a few short years into independent production where he became a major Hollywood producer.[99]

The plot of this first entry in the new series did contain music since Rogers was being molded in the Autry image. He was after all a singer and a better one than Autry at that. However, it was a contemporary story with Rogers as a young congressman who attempted to obtain water for the Dust Bowl area. The hero won the day by obtaining the passage of a flood control bill but the Western action elements were not sacrificed to the politics. The *New York Times*, after noting that Rogers was a new star, allowed that "the dust-bowl film shown to Washington society by Roy after his election to Congress on a free-water platform is a darn good documentary."[100] While it cannot be said that the film foretold the future immediately, it was a successful B Western and Rogers' career was underway.[101]

The second Rogers entry, *Billy the Kid Returns*, was a period Western in which Rogers played both the original Billy the Kid and a look-alike who takes the Kid's place after the outlaw's death in order to enforce the law in Lincoln County, New Mexico. The film was both directed and produced by Joseph Kane. He was to handle the next forty Roy Rogers Westerns and, as a proven action director, was to keep the Rogers vehicles well paced.

During this phase of Rogers' career, the action was emphasized over the music. For the next three years, he had a series of quite successful B Western films. "As for Rogers himself, he was more assured with each release, and improving with experience," according to one Rogers filmographer.[102] During this period, also, Rogers' Westerns tended more frequently to be historic rather than contemporary, another similarity to Autry's early development. After *Wall Street Cowboy* in 1939, which dealt with Rogers defending himself against New York gangsters on their own ground, he appeared in such period Westerns as *Days of Jesse James* (1939), *Young Buffalo Bill* (1940), *Young Bill Hickok* (1940), and *Jesse James at Bay* (1941). During this sequence, Rogers' vehicles benefited from solid supporting casts including people not normally seen at Republic on a regular basis, while the heroine roles were taken by such rising actresses as Pauline Moore, Jacqueline Welles (Julie Bishop), Marjorie Reynolds, Gale Storm, and Joan Woodbury.

During this introductory phase, Rogers also was given the opportunity to appear in vehicles other than the B Western action format—a career incentive not offered to Autry with the exception of one loan-out. Rogers was featured in two of the Weaver Brothers and Elviry, hillbilly musical comedies, a formula into which he fit easily, as well as some non-Western musical guest roles.[103]

Rogers also was given a strong supporting role in a Republic "A" production of the period. Raoul Walsh's *Dark Command* (1940) starred John Wayne, Claire Trevor, and Walter Pidgeon with a strong supporting cast and was Republic's well received follow-up to Wayne's success in RKO's *Stagecoach*. Rogers was cast as the headstrong younger brother of Trevor in this top budgeted and quite popular period Western based very loosely on the exploits of Quantrill's Raiders.

While Rogers' performance was quite good and showed promise, Republic considered him more valuable in his now clearly successful B Western series and it was many years before he appeared in another A film.[104]

In 1941 with *Red River Valley*, which concerned a gambler's thwarted attempts to sabotage a dam, the Sons of the Pioneers joined Rogers as a supporting musical group. Their addition, of course, signaled more music in the Rogers films. However, the music still remained secondary to the action content but the second phase was gradually becoming noticeable. The musical part of Rogers' films were noticeably increased when, in 1942, Gene Autry entered the service. Within three months Roy Rogers' B Westerns began to receive bigger budgets, a major portion of which went into the musical production numbers.[105]

The first entry in this phase of Roy Rogers' career was *Heart of the Golden West*. It was considered to be a Special and had Rogers defeating a greedy trucking executive who was gouging cattle shippers—a theme near and dear to rural interests.[106] Bigger budgets, better sets, and stronger supporting casts frequently meant more music and dialogue and correspondingly less action on such pictures but in this case the action content remained high and the pacing was very brisk. While the music was indeed more noticeable, the entry was still a more than satisfying B Western with good balance and production values. A trade review summarized, "Joseph Kane creates an entertaining variant on the straight western and manages to collate an amazing total of standard western thrill elements [action] in with the comedy and the music to heap up an hour's diversion."[107]

With the production of *Idaho* (1942) came the era when Roy Rogers began to don grotesque and unbelievable costumes and when his productions relied more on musical extravaganzas than standard B Western action. The change had come gradually but this film signaled the new emphasis. But, the action motifs did remain in segments of most of the Rogers films and the image of Rogers as an honest hero who saves the day for justice and the common man continued, alternating with patriotic themes as the war progressed. *Idaho* concerned the clearing of a framed judge who helped delinquent boys and while the musical emphasis was obvious, the film was a guaranteed success. "While sophisticated movie-goers will probably stay away from 'Idaho' in droves, the film will undoubtedly reach some 7500 theaters—a healthy proportion of the nation's 18,000—and will turn in a profit of $300,000."[108]

In *King of the Cowboys* (1943) Rogers was combating saboteurs who use a tent show as a cover. This fast-paced film concluded with a wounded Rogers disarming a bomb on a railroad trestle to save American troops while under fire from the spy ring.[109] It was an almost serial-like sequence. Reviewers noted the patriotism in addition to the action content and the musical numbers in this picture.[110]

It was at this time that the standard Rogers format was developing for the Rogers films during the second part of his career—the plot and final action sequence ended early and the film would conclude with a musical review to appeal to those people who were interested in the musical content of the film.[111] Actually, this segregation seemed to work out well and the action content was not so obviously sacrificed as had been the case in the Autry series. Both entertainments could co-exist in the same picture, frequently not intruding in any great degree upon one another. With *Hands Across the Border*, the first release of 1944, the concept of separate musical conclusions became standard in Rogers' pictures.[112]

Two important events in the Rogers series occurred the next year. Dale Evans became Roy Rogers' leading lady with *The Cowboy and the Senorita* and with the following film, *Song of Nevada*, Joseph Kane left as director of the series.

Frank MacDonald directed Rogers in *Bells of Rosarita* released in 1945. This film is an important one in B Western filmography in that it was the first time that Republic used the interesting technique of introducing guest stars in the form of other leading Western players from the studio's various series. Rogers summarized the plot. "Republic has got a new idea for the picture I'm working in now. In the picture, I'm playing myself. According to the script, I'm out on location making a picture when I run into a girl who needs help to keep from being gypped out of a ranch her pappy left her. I send out a call for help to Bill Elliott, Don (Red) Barry, Allan Lane, Robert Livingston, and Sunset Carson—all of whom work for Republic and star in Western pictures of their own. Together, we clean up the evildoers and get the ranch back for the girl. It's kind of *Grand Hotel* on saddles. . . . We had to ration the crooks. We were allowed one apiece."[113]

These five guest heroes each had their own action scenes when they assisted Rogers with the Sons of the Pioneers in rounding up the villains in their uniquely individual ways which were readily recognizable to all Western fans. The unique ploy of major Hollywood Western stars doing good deeds and sharing the action in the same picture was emphasized.[114] As one cinema survey states, "Rogers and the stars appear at Dale's circus in order to raise the money to pay off notes against her property. Perhaps *Bells of Rosarita* should have been *Altruism Rides the Range*."[115] In any case, the guest star routine proved to be so successful that Republic utilized it again several times in various series.

Roy Rogers' own favorite movie was *My Pal Trigger* released in 1946 and directed by MacDonald.[116] A somewhat involved episodic piece, the film had Rogers accused of murdering a stallion whose colt he raises. He eventually saved the ranch of Gabby Hayes and discovered the real killer.[117] The film moved Bosley Crowther, the *New York Times* reviewer, to comment, "the theme of this interloping Western is the beautiful love that exists between kind-hearted Mr. Rogers and his remarkably amatory horse."[118] Besides emphasizing horses and horse raising, the film actually had some dramatic moments and gave Rogers a chance to act. In fact, the advertising campaign emphasized the emotional and dramatic content of the film. "So stirring . . . so exciting . . . so intensely real . . . *My Pal Trigger*. This magnificent story of man and horse . . . will touch your heart . . . will fill you with delight!"[119]

With the conclusion of the Second World War, two events occurred which shifted Rogers' career into its third phase. First, Gene Autry returned to Republic and after a brief attempt to regain his stature as the Number One Western film star saw the writing on the wall and left Republic for his own production company at Columbia. The Autry and Rogers vehicles were too similar. Both made alterations in their formulas. Rogers' films received a transfusion of new ideas as movie personnel returning from the service joined the unit. Writer Sloan Nibley and director William Witney were among the most noteworthy. These new men and changing audience tastes resulted in a de-emphasis of the musical extravaganza and more stress on the action and plot lines.[120]

In this third phase, the Rogers' films were more interesting, rapidly paced and were given themes which often bordered on the brutal.[121] While Witney asserted that he was tired of blood and killing, his experience as an action director came to the forefront and during this period the Rogers vehicles reached their highest quality. Witney felt this was the happiest time of his directorial career.[122]

For his part, Sloan Nibley realized the limitations of the B Western formula and that he had to work within a format. Therefore, he and the other writers would spend most of their time inventing new but workable approaches to plot development. There was also some challenge in developing the character of the villains and supporting characters since the characteristics of the hero, heroine, and comic sidekick were rarely allowed to change drastically. Nibley deliberately made Rogers a little more human, however, in that Rogers would occasionally make a wrong calculation, a misjudgment, and occasionally, as a result, would be badly beaten in mid-plot. Of course he emerged victorious at the fadeout.[123] For example, Nibley developed the plot in *Bells of San Angelo* (1947) around silver smuggling on the Mexican border in a contemporary setting. Roy's elaborate costume was played down and in this picture he received the first major beating of his B Western career. It occurred at the hands of David Sharpe in the middle of the film and Rogers triumphed in the fadeout over both Sharpe and the brains heavy so that the morality message was unimpaired. Still, it was a major change in the image.

The next production was *Springtime in the Sierras* also in 1947, and this time Nibley wrote a script around wildlife preservation. Rogers broke up an illegal game slaughtering ring supplying a syndicate with illegal meat. The ecological message and plea for conservation was there strong enough to be perceived even by children and it undoubtedly had some good effect.[124] However, the true surface appeal of the film was in its beautiful and rousing action sequences handled by Witney and in the alluring villainy of the female leader of the evildoers. Roy and Roy Barcroft (a series regular) had a brutal fight in a freezer at one point. In this film Andy Devine became the comic relief and Dale Evans was temporarily replaced by Jane Frazee.[125] Frazee said that when she began to appear in them she knew it was "the beginning of the end" of her career.[126] Actually many of the actors and actresses appearing in the Rogers Western films were distinguished and had respectable careers before and after their appearance. The Rogers vehicles were enhanced at various times by the presence of such well known and versatile character actors as Jack Holt, John Carradine, Jerome Cowan, Milburn Stone, Bob Steele, and Herbert Rawlinson. The use of the well known faces was another testimonial to the high production values that Republic placed in its then Number One Western series.

In 1950 *Trigger Jr.* was released. It was written by Gerald Geraghty, also a frequent Rogers contributor, and has Rogers as a Western star running down a killer stallion used by lawbreakers in a protection racket. Nibley felt that this film was a particularly good example of the ability of the Republic writers to deliver well within the standard format. The writers, he asserted, did have freedom within the format and *Trigger Jr.* showed that freedom carried too far, indicating that the movie represents an interesting failure in that it was not as successful as most Rogers features. He commented that it was an episodic production which did not follow the traditional Rogers plot in any of the three phases of his career. It was Nibley's experience that while the writers could alter the ingenious devices and schemes within the plots to some degree and develop the character of the villains, the Rogers pictures were much more successful as long as they remained within the realm which the audience expected.[127]

In *Spoilers of the Plains* released in 1951, Nibley had Rogers combating international criminals who menaced the United States through a weather prediction device.[128] The film, while somewhat of a throwback to the patriotic pieces of the Second World War, was appropriate to the anticommunist era and made much of national security. It was indicative that patriotism and preparedness were a continuing part of the Rogers and the Autry images.

Although the Rogers films were maintaining their production values, and could compete easily with similar productions from other studios, the decreasing market for the B Western film was becoming apparent. Profits were down, theater demand was declining, reissues were more frequent, and new productions in many series were less and less attractive. With *Pals of the Golden West* (1951), Rogers and Republic parted and the B Western singing cowboy series came to an end at Republic in so far as its two most successful proponents were concerned. Republic still had Rex Allen and Autry lasted two years longer at Columbia, but the decline was clear. Still, Republic did well with the Rogers series up until the conclusion of the series. As Don Miller said, "It may have been consolation that even at the end, when the Western field was swiftly descending in popularity and the fortunes of Republic were far from sanguine, the Roy Rogers Westerns maintained their prestige and their quality."[129]

Why did the era of the B Western series end? Perhaps Albert S. Rogell, who had a long career in many phases of Hollywood production and directorship and who worked extensively at Republic, summarized it most succinctly when he stated that the Rogers format was perhaps the best and most successful for its period but that it outlived its time.[130] Yet there are those who feel that the Rogers formula maintained its success up until the end. If anything, Rogers quit while his films were still successful and transferred to television while Autry followed two years later. Art Rush indicated that both he and Rogers knew that the Republic Western films, and especially his own, were saleable. He and Rogers approached the television networks in the late 1940s about taking over the old films as a major series. They were turned down but in 1951 Rogers switched to a standard half hour B Western television series and the Rogers name became a television standard.[131]

Perhaps the final word concerning the lasting success of the Rogers vehicles as well as many of the Republic Western series lies in the fact that National Telefilm Associates and Telescene, Inc. in 1974 packaged a series of the best of the B Westerns mostly from Republic under the umbrella title *Roy Rogers Presents the Great Movie Cowboys*. These slightly edited B Western features with new introductions filmed by Rogers at his Western museum were very successful throughout the country, even being sold to educational television stations in some areas.[132]

Each of the three major Republic program Western series discussed used variations on the basic message of the morality play and each had their own coterie of fans. But regardless of these variations, the traditional plot of good versus evil in a formula development with the forces of good prevailing was the overriding theme in all three series. This was also true of the other Western series of the studio. Most were a success although perhaps not on the same level of the three which have been discussed.

Historians Arthur F. McClure and Ken D. Jones best summarized the impact of these B Westerns:

> The popularity of the "B" Western was an extension of the cowboy myth in American life. Historian Carl Becker noted that Americans are prone to cling to what he called "useful myths." . . . The emotional conditioning provided by these films, and the durability of that conditioning should never be dismissed by historians of American life . . . [I]t is entirely possible that in the midst of confusion and uncertainty created by the Depression and World War II audiences sustained many of their "faiths" by identifying with some admirable and powerful symbols of straightforward righteousness as seen in the "B" Westerns.[133]

And Republic made the best and most successful B Westerns.

Notes

1. *A Pictorial History of the Western Film* (New York: Citadel, 1969), p. 141.

2. James Horwitz, *They Went Thataway* (New York: E. P. Dutton, 1977), pp. 125–126. Horwitz's book is devoted to attempting to track down the heroes of his youth and to explaining the ideals of his generation.

3. See Chapter 1, pp. 21–23.

4. An expansion on this interpretation of the message of the B Western can be found in Jon Tuska, "In Retrospect: Tim McCoy, Last of Four Parts," *Views and Reviews*, II (Spring, 1971), p. 15.

5. *The Western: From Silents to Cinerama* (New York: Bonanza Books, 1962) and *A Pictorial History of the Western Film* (New York: Citadel, 1969).

6. *The Filming of the West* (New York: Doubleday, 1976).

7. (New York: Collier Books, 1971).

8. (New York: The Popular Library Film Series, 1976).

9. F. E. Emery, "Psychological Effects of the Western Film: A Study in Television Viewing," *Human Relations*, XII (1959), p. 196.

10. *Six Guns and Society: A Structural Study of the Western* (Berkeley, California: University of California Press, 1976), Chapter Three "The Structure of the Western Film," pp. 29–123.

11. "The Psychological Appeal of the Hollywood Western," *The Journal of Educational Sociology*, XXOV (October, 1950), pp. 72–86.

12. Elkin, "Psychological Appeal," p. 73.

13. Elkin, "Psychological Appeal," p. 75. A similar point is made in James & Folsom, "Western Themes and Western Films," *Western American Literature*, II (1967), pp. 195–196.

14. Morris R. Abrams, Republic script supervisor and assistant director, thoughtfully emphasized his belief that Republic musicals made a contact with basic American chords both musically and emotionally through frequent use of folk music. While somewhat critical of the potential influence of the Republic musical, this was one point Abrams felt significant. Interview with Morris Abrams, Hollywood, California, May 17, 1976.

15. Elkin, "Psychological Appeal," p. 76.

16. Elkin, "Psychological Appeal," p. 78.

17. Elkin, "Psychological Appeal," p. 79. The same point is registered with a clinical emphasis in Emery, "Psychological Effects," pp. 194–195.

18. Elkin, "Psychological Appeal," p. 81.

19. Elkin, "Psychological Appeal," p. 84.

20. Elkin, "Psychological Appeal," p. 85.

21. Gregory D. Black and Clayton R. Koppes, "OWI Goes to the Movies: The Bureau of Intelligence's Criticism of Hollywood, 1942–1943," *Prologue: The Journal of the National Archives*, VI (Spring, 1974), p. 50.

22. *John Wayne and the Movies* (Cranbury, New Jersey: A. S. Barnes, 1976), p. 52. Yet this was not always true. The time period in the series varied from post–Civil War to the 1940s.

23. *The Hall of Fame of Western Film Stars* (North Quincy, Massachusetts: Christopher Publishing House, 1969), p. 183.

24. Tuska, *Filming of the West*, p. 339.

25. *Variety*, July 2, 1939.

26. Warshow, *The Immediate Experience*, p. 140.

27. *New York Post*, June 27, 1940.

28. *Saturday Afternoon at the Bijou* (New Rochelle, New York: Arlington House, 1973), p. 179.

29. "Republic Productions, Inc. Produced Properties," p. 173.

30. *Elwood* [Indiana] *Call-Leader*, December 13, 1946. Re-issue booking. Re-issue booking refers to the practice of holding a film after its first run and then re-circulating it several years later.

31. "Republic Productions, Inc. Produced Properties," p. 72.

32. *Variety*, August 4, 1937. The film was also included in the syndicated television package, *Roy Rogers Presents the Great Movie Cowboys*, WNED-TV, Buffalo, New York, Fall 1976 to Spring 1977.

33. *New York Times*, March 19, 1938.

34. "Republic Productions, Inc. Produced Properties," p. 121.

35. This film under its new title *Frontier Horizon* was included in the syndicated package, *Roy Rogers Presents the Great Movie Cowboys*, WNED, Buffalo, New York; Fall 1976 to Spring 1977.

36. Maurice Zolotow, *Shooting Star: A Biography of John Wayne* (New York: Simon and Schuster, 1974), p. 130.

37. Zolotow, p. 112.

38. Interestingly, Vera H. Ralston offers another, less likely, interpretation. She claims that according to her husband, Herbert Yates, the studio was still willing to advance the career of Livingston beyond the B Western field. However, fan mail was so heavily against Wayne in the series and for the return of Livingston that, even before Wayne made his breakthrough, the studio had decided to remove Wayne from the series and return the popular Livingston. She cites this "tremendous amount of fan mail" as indicative of the popularity of the series and the Republic product as well as the seriousness with which the fans viewed their Western movies. Telephone interview with Vera H. Ralston, Santa Barbara, California, May 10, 1976.

39. *Elwood* [Indiana] *Call-Leader*, December 16, 1943.

40. Miller, *Hollywood Corral*, p. 164.

41. Telephone interview with Robert Livingston, Republic Western and feature actor, Los Angeles, California, May 8, 1976.

42. Alva Johnston, "Tenor on Horseback," *Saturday Evening Post*, CCXII (September 2, 1939), pp. 19, 74.

43. Barbour, *The Thrill of It All*, p. 125.

44. Jack Nachbar, ed., *Focus on the Western* (Englewood Cliffs, New Jersey: Prentice-Hall, 1974), p. 4.

45. Jim Kitses, *Horizons West* (Bloomington, Indiana: Indiana University Press, 1969), p. 17.

46. Kalton C. Lahue, *Riders of the Range* (New York: Castle, 1973), p. 35.

47. "Mr. Harper," "After Hours: Fall Idol," *Harpers*, CC (January, 1950), pp. 99–100.

48. Miller, *Hollywood Corral*, p. 108.

49. Percy Knauth, "Gene Autry, Inc.," *Life*, XXIV (January 28, 1948), pp. 88–100.

50. Two of the more notable ones were Ken Maynard who did his own singing and John Wayne as Singing Sandy in *Riders of Destiny* (Monogram, 1933), whose singing was dubbed.

51. *Filming of the West*, p. 303.

52. Johnston, "Tenor on Horseback," p. 18.

53. Tuska, *Filming of the West*, p. 304. Tuska carried his interpretation even further as he continued the discussion. He states, "I sincerely feel that Autry's massive appeal as a modest cowboy troubadour leading a uniquely charmed life, a musical magician who could turn darkness into light, sorrow into happiness, tarnish into splendor, a Pied Piper able to control men and alter the course of world events by means of a song, is the most tremendous single occurrence in the history of the

American Western cinema. Gene Autry in his magnificent outfits, yodeling a pop tune, is an image so remote from the actual man of the frontier to rival any fairy tale," p. 305.

54. Tuska, *Filming of the West*, p. 309.

55. May 14, 1938.

56. Richard Gertner, ed., *1975 International Motion Picture Almanac* (New York: Quigley Publishing Company, 1975), pp. 43A–44A.

57. August 4, 1940.

58. Knauth, "Gene Autry, Inc.," p. 92 and referred to in many other primary sources. Also attributed to Autry in secondary sources as Jenni Calder, *There Must Be A Lone Ranger: The West in Film and Reality* (New York: Taplinger Publishing Company, 1974), p. 185.

59. Article from 1942 entitled "Gene Autry's Advice to Youth in Wartime," from the Chamberlain and Lyman Brown Theatrical Agency Collection in the Theatrical Section of the New York Public Library. Autry was actually the first of the ten biggest box office stars to be accepted into the war effort according to this article. Clark Gable's induction received a premature announcement. Autry had already been called.

60. Johnston, "Tenor on Horseback," p. 74.

61. Harry Sanford, "Joseph Kane: A Director's Story, Part 1," *Views and Reviews*, V (September, 1973), p. 34.

62. *Elwood* [Indiana] *Call-Leader*, August 23, 1945. Re-issue booking.

63. *New York Times*, November 8, 1937.

64. Miller, *Hollywood Corral*, p. 110.

65. *New York Herald-Tribune*, February 4, 1938, headlined "Studio Enjoins Gene Autry: Says 'Horse Opera' Star Ran Away to Go on the Stage."

66. Sanford, "Kane," *Views and Reviews*, p. 35.

67. Everson, *A Pictorial History of the Western Film*, p. 147.

68. Johnston, "Tenor on Horseback," p. 18. It should be pointed out that these themes which had the hero dealing with modern problems undoubtedly contributed to his influence considering his great popularity.

69. See Chapter 1, pp. 3–6 for the economic guidelines on Republic productions.

70. *Elwood* [Indiana] *Call-Leader*, February 4, 1944. Re-issue booking.

71. *In Old Monterey*. Still Manual. (Hollywood, California: Republic Pictures, 1939).

72. *Variety*, August 4, 1939.

73. Bob Thomas, "Hollywood's General of the Armies," *True*, XXX (July, 1966), p. 87 describes how Yakima Canutt went about staging this outstanding footage.

74. *Rovin Tumbleweed*. Sales Manual. (Hollywood, California: Republic Pictures, 1938). Stressed the movie hero being duped by the political machine but ultimately winning out with the help of the masses, in this case migrants, and even converting the main villain.

75. *New York Herald*, November 23, 1939.

76. *South of the Border*. Still Manual. (Hollywood: Republic Pictures, 1939).

77. *New York Herald*, December 16, 1939. The song is a story in which the girl enters a convent when the hero does not return to her as expected.

78. *Elwood* [Indiana] *Call-Leader*, April 21, 1944. Re-issue booking. The film played Sunday through Tuesday at Elwood's "class" theater. These days were the week's A playdates and the theater was not a B Western outlet normally.

79. May 15, 1940.

80. Here Autry received twice his normal Republic fee ($25,000 versus $12,500). "Double Mint Ranch," *Time*, XXXV (January 15, 1940), p. 47.

81. December 26, 1940.

82. "Republic Productions, Inc. Produced Properties," p. 155.

83. *New York Times*, July 23, 1947.

84. Art Rush, Rogers' manager, claims that both he and Rogers saw Allen as a potential talent and encouraged Allen's career. Telephone interview with Art Rush, Los Angeles, California, May 6, 1976.

85. Lucy Greenbaum, "Sinatra in a Sombrero," *New York Times Magazine* (November 4, 1945), p. 42.

86. Pete Martin, "Cincinnati Cowboy," *Saturday Evening Post*, CCXVII (June 9, 1945), p. 80.

87. Tuska, *Filming of the West*, p. 463.

88. H. Allen Smith, "King of the Cowboys," *Life*, XV (July 12, 1943), p. 54.

89. Louise Levitas, May 20, 1941.

90. Gertner, *International Motion Picture Almanac*, p. 44A.

91. Telephone interview with Art Rush, Roy Rogers' business manager, Los Angeles, California, May 6, 1976. See also Chapter 1, pp. 20–21, for additional discussion of the conflict between Rogers and Republic on the use of his films.

92. *New York Times*, February 2, 1941. In 1943, *Newsweek* stated, "Rogers and his Palomino horse, Trigger, make about fifty stage bows a year. In between chores, he appears as a guest star on radio programs, stars in rodeo shows, and makes Decca records that sell at the rate of 6000 per week." "King of the Cowboys," XXI (March 8, 1943), p. 76.

93. Greenbaum, "Sinatra in a Sombrero," p. 42.

94. Greenbaum, "Sinatra in a Sombrero," p. 42.

95. *Los Angeles Times*, Calendar Section, April 21, 1974.

96. *Leisure, The Sunday News* (New York), December 28, 1975.

97. *Los Angeles Times*, January 6, 1975.

98. Ashton Reid, "Hero on Horseback," *Colliers*, CXXII (July 24, 1948), p. 62.

99. Siegel commented that the Rogers Westerns were quite well done and something to be proud of from a studio as small as Republic. Telephone interview with Sol C. Siegel, Los Angeles, California, May 5, 1976.

100. June 25, 1938.

101. Oddly enough, the film had been planned for Autry and in the Republic synopsis the leads are referred to as "Gene and his pal Frog" although it is identified as a Rogers release, "Republic Productions, Inc. Produced Properties," p. 184.

102. Miller, *Hollywood Corral*, p. 113.

103. Greenbaum, "Sinatra in a Sombrero," p. 42. *Lake Placid Serenade, Hollywood Canteel,* and *Brazil.*

104. The film was *Son of Paleface* (Paramount, 1952) with Bob Hope.

105. H. Allen Smith, "King of the Cowboys," p. 48.

106. *Heart of the Golden West.* Sales Manual. (Hollywood, California: Republic Pictures, 1942).

107. *Variety,* November 16, 1942.

108. "King of the Cowboys," *Newsweek,* XXI (March 8, 1943), p. 76.

109. *King of the Cowboys.* Still Manual. (Hollywood, California: Republic Pictures, 1943).

110. *Variety,* April 5, 1943.

111. Miller, *Hollywood Corral*, p. 119.

112. *Elwood* [Indiana] *Call-Leader,* November 9, 1944.

113. Martin, "Cincinnati Cowboy," p. 80.

114. *Elwood* [Indiana] *Call-Leader,* February 14, 1946, ads publicized the guest stars prominently.

115. Rudy Behlmer and Tony Thomas, *Hollywood's Hollywood: The Movies About the Movies* (Secaucus, New Jersey: Citadel Press, 1975), p. 223.

116. Rogers' introduction to *Roy Rogers Presents the Great Movie Cowboys,* WNED-TV, Buffalo, New York, Fall 1976 to Spring 1977.

117. "Republic Productions, Inc. Produced Properties," p. 109.

118. *New York Times,* August 17, 1946.

119. *Kokomo* [Indiana] *Tribune,* June 12, 1947.

120. For example, *Home in Oklahoma* (1946) is a detective story with Rogers as a small town newspaper man who consistently outwits a big city newspaper woman, played by Dale Evans, when she fails to play fair with him in covering a local murder. The blend of action and music was good with action and plot returning to the forefront. An interesting sidelight was the emphasis on how the local clean-cut hero handled, with a combination of humor and firmness, the arrogance and slightly dishonest techniques of the city reporter. Small town and rural audiences invariably appreciated this type of theme, according to Sloan Nibley in interview, Los Angeles, California, May 4, 1976.

121. Everson, *A Pictorial History of the Western Film*, p. 152.

122. Nevins, "William Witney," pp. 535–536.

123. Interview with Sloan Nibley, Los Angeles, California, May 4, 1976.

124. *Springtime in the Sierras.* Still Manual. (Hollywood, California: Republic Pictures, 1947). So strong was the message, the advertising aid even emphasized the problems caused by the illegal game syndicate.

125. *Kokomo* [Indiana] *Tribune*, November 13, 1947.

126. Richard Lamparski, *Whatever Became of . . . ?* The New Fifth Series (New York; Bantam Books, 1976), p. 49.

127. Interview with Sloan Nibley, Los Angeles, California, May 4, 1976.

128. *Spoilers of the Plains*. Still Manual. (Hollywood, California: Republic Pictures, 1951).

129. Miller, *Hollywood Corral*, p. 124.

130. Interview with Albert S. Rogell, Republic director, Los Angeles, California, May 5, 1976.

131. Telephone interview with Art Rush, Los Angeles, California, May 6, 1976.

132. Interview with Rex Waggoner, National Telefilm Associates Publicity Director, Los Angeles, California, May 12, 1976. They ran on educational television in Buffalo, New York, WNED-TV, Fall 1976 to Spring 1977.

133. *Heroes, Heavies, and Sagebrush* (Cranbury, New Jersey: A.S. Barnes, 1972), p. 11.

~

CHAPTER EIGHT

Republic's Other Films:
Series and Non-Series

While the serials and the B Western series were aimed primarily at the youth and young adult audience with a calculated strong secondary attraction to small town and rural audiences, much of the reverse held true with the other area of Republic series strength. The comedy series were meant to appeal to the adult audiences in neighborhood theatres and in urban as well as rural areas. That they should attract the youthful audience was the secondary goal of the studio. A good example of the Republic family comedy product with an urban background and aimed at the neighborhood theatres as well as small towns was the Higgins Family series. The Weaver Brothers and Elviry films were a variation, stressing a rural family in a comedy musical format which appealed first to rural audiences and secondarily to the urban trade. Perhaps the best and most famous of the rural comedy musical type of film at any studio was the Judy Canova series at Republic. The latter was especially successful, was sometimes considered more than a B product, had a little extra message beneath the merriment, and is still remembered.

The Higgins Family series was nothing more or less than Republic's competition for the higher budgeted Hardy and Jones series at Metro Goldwyn Mayer and Twentieth Century-Fox respectively. While the Higgins entries always relied a bit more heavily on physical humor, this was entirely natural in that Republic's advantage lay in action and pacing while the writing department at the studio frequently was a weaker area. Nonetheless, the Higgins Family films like their competitors contained the message, often delivered without subtlety, that family unity was important. In these films, it was a truism that goodness and family loyalty would overcome stupidity and indiscretion on the part of the family or greed and conniving on the part of the adversaries to ultimately deliver justice and satisfaction.

The series was originally directed by Gus Meins, who received comedy training under Hal Roach, and starred real life father, mother, and son, James, Lucille, and Russell Gleason in film portrayals of that same relationship. Well-known character actor Harry Davenport was the grandfather, Tommy Ryan the younger son, while varying actresses played the grown daughter. The formula was quite simple and basically situation comedy. The father usually became involved in an impossible situation through his wife's stupidity and his own ignorance, pride, or lack of caution whereupon the family would rally together, extricate themselves, and save the situation in a finale frequently containing an element of slapstick. The plots were usually improbable and often insane but the entertainment was there. A few examples will suffice.

The first movie, *The Higgins Family*, came in 1938 and had the father after twenty years trying for success in advertising having his ambitions frustrated by family affairs including the inventive projects of his elder son and the romantic problems of his daughter. Of course, it was worked out successfully by the fadeout. In *My Wife's Relatives* (1939) the father was fired from a candy factory when he quarreled with the owner because his daughter was going with the owner's son. Without a job he could not pay for an expensive ring he had purchased for his wife. He went into his own candy business and his wife lost the ring supposedly in the chocolate mixing machine. Here again the plot was impossible but the family managed to pull through. *Photoplay* found the film "acceptable" but did compliment the acting talents of the Gleasons.[1]

Another entry included a similar theme of the dignity of the common man. *Earl of Puddlestone*, a 1940 release, has Grandpa fighting the snobbery of the rich toward Betty, his granddaughter, by creating imaginary royalty. Betty proves herself on her own merits thus delivering a blow for democracy and rugged individualism as well as for family unity.[2] The series proceeded much along the same lines and might have continued but for the death of Gus Meins.[3]

When Meins died in 1940 the series was furloughed briefly and was revamped the following year with Roscoe Karns and Ruth Donnelly replacing the leads. However, it was not particularly noteworthy or profitable at this point and was quietly cancelled. While there were only nine releases, possessing little that was unique, this family situation comedy was pleasant enough and did offer the comforting theme of family support—always a strong middle American ideal but especially attractive during the Depression and war years of the 1930s and early 1940s. As one author put it, "All but forgotten now, the Gleason-Higgins family were nice neighbors to meet at the neighborhood theatre."[4] It was basically a warmth series, not in the sense of the Hardys, but with heavy doses of hectic comedy. The message was very much subdued by the pacing and noise but it was obvious that like the more prestigious Hardys, the Higgins' brought comfort to its audience.

On the other hand, the Weavers were somewhat different in their appeal. They were definitely "down home" rural folk with deliberate musical interludes. As such, their attraction was closer to the Judy Canova series but contained its own form of uniqueness. In fact, their major attraction was that they were a proven hillbilly commodity. Republic knew what it wanted with the group and just how to package the series. The group made one earlier film for Warner Bros. with Humphrey Bogart entitled *Swing Your Lady* (1938), which moved Bosley Crowther to state that he was sorry to see the "richly idiomatic folk humors" of the Weaver Brothers and Elviry reputed to be the funniest team in vaudeville "subordinated to anybody."[5] However, the team was really at home with Republic and their films were right for the Republic rural audiences. They could have made films more frequently but were well off from radio and vaudeville and chose not to do so.[6] Nevertheless, the eleven films in their Republic series ran from 1938 to 1943 and were filled with bucolic humor which, while sometimes less acceptable to urban audiences, subtly brought home the message that simple rural folk by handling life decently and straightforwardly could overcome and even derive benefits from the sophisticated machinations of any greedy dehumanizing system. In all probability, urban viewers also appreciated the Weavers or Republic humor, but Republic aimed the product at the rural and small town markets.

The team began in medicine shows, progressed to vaudeville, and reached national stardom on the radio as "The Arkansas Travelers."[7] The formula used by Republic had Leon "Abner" Weaver as a small town philosopher supported by his brother Frank "Cicero" as a mute pantomimist, and June "Elviry" as a musically talented country girl. Later they were joined by Loretta, the daughter of Leon and June who usually portrayed a wide-eyed innocent. They were all musically inclined so each film contained interludes of hillbilly music including at least one number on the "musical" saw. Actually, the Weaver success served as a prelude to the national interest in country music in the mid-1940s which continued to be revived periodically into the 1970s. Roy Rogers even played support in two of their films as a young male lead early in his own career.[8]

The first in the Republic series was *Down in "Arkansaw"* (1938) with orchestra leader and songwriter Pinky Tomlin and Ralph Byrd. It was an interesting mixture of musical comedy and drama which carried a bit of obvious propaganda. In the Arkansas backwoods, a government representative succeeded in making the hillbilly people understand the benefits they would derive from a dam which would provide them with modern facilities. This basic plot, mixed with romance, music, and comedy, was essentially a variation on the theme used in the Mesquiteers action/adventure film, *New Frontier*.[9] At the same time, while the rural elements benefited at the film's conclusion for the audience's satisfaction, the picture argued more persuasively than the Mesquiteers film in favor of the government's conservation and rehabilitation projects. Defending their homesteads against redevelopment, the Weavers were won over by the clean-cut government agent's honesty and love for their daughter. By virtue of compromise and communication, just as in the Mesquiteers, the backwoods people were vindicated and both sides in the conflict were satisfied.

In Old Missouri (1940) also brought out the value of cooperation and the sagacity of rural wisdom. The Weavers were impoverished sharecroppers but when they went to the city, they found the landowner in equally bad straits. They changed places and Pa Weaver was able to expose the landowner's crooked partners and make his family behave more sensibly. The conditions of both the landowner and the sharecroppers were improved by the Weavers' handling of the situation.

In *Arkansas Judge* (1941) the dishonesty of a spoiled rich girl caused an innocent charwoman problems and led to a family feud before Judge Weaver could set things right and help justice triumph over the selfishness and thoughtlessness of the rich girl.[10] *The Old Homestead* (1940) had small town mayor Elviry handling big town gangsters as well as local criminals. In the end, the Weavers ended crime in "Farmington" as well as straightened out a romance. The circumstances changed from film to film but the music, the formula, the attraction, and the message remained constant. *Mountain Rhythm* (1943) added a liberal dose of World War II patriotism. The studio synopsis gives the plot, the atmosphere, and the message of this film:

> The Weaver family chooses farming as their way of helping the national war effort. Their purchase of a West Coast acreage formerly owned by a Jap family brings them into conflict with the snobbish students of a nearby boys' school. The Weavers win the long-drawn-out tussel [sic] which ensues, the boys are converted to manual war-work, and the scoundrelly headmaster is exposed as a troublemaker and an enemy agent and arrested.[11]

Thus, the appeal of the Weaver series was that of an honest and dedicated rural family overcoming the artificial and dishonest sophisticates with an end result of vindication for themselves and betterment for all except the forces of evil. Served up with music and comedy, and in this case timely and welcome patriotism, the Weavers' series hit an appropriate chord in its designated audiences.

Judy Canova was unique in that her two series at Republic, while not really of A quality, were given better budgets by the studio than most of their B efforts. Canova had early proved her talents and her films had special attraction. She herself has said that she came to Republic as "a proven commodity."[12] While mainly rural and small town in their appeal, her musicals did play larger theatres much as the "Special" Westerns of Autry and Rogers.[13] As such, Canova's films also received more notice upon occasion. Besides the obvious theme of a rural innocent having basic decency and folk wisdom to see her through her tribulations and conflicts with less honest and more pretentious adversaries, the Canova series also relied heavily on a direct variant of an archetypal folk story. In many of her pictures she started out crude, clumsy, and seemingly unattractive. From the bottom she rose to the top to become the well attired and successful heroine in the finale. In other words, she portrayed again and again the Cinderella story.[14] The classic story had the lowly heroine abused by her pretentious step-relatives. Through outside help, supernatural in the folktale, she became the center of attention but was forced to flee. The hero then searched her out and she was elevated to a position of honor. The Canova variants frequently hit most of these motifs with the supernatural aid being replaced by self-initiative or sympathetic friends. This parallel was not a conscious effort for "significance" and can probably be attributed to the universality of the tale. Its popularity was simply adapted to the Canova formula.

Canova herself recognized this and attributed her movie success partially to this image. She also admitted that there was a conscious effort to have her progress from loser to winner in most of her films, another theme with even more claim to universality. Canova was quite aware of her appeal to her audience and knew her films might have had a positive effect. She candidly commented, "Sure, they [her pictures] were fairy tales that had a little upbeat lesson. I started out as a plain Jane, an ugly duckling, and ended up as a beautiful girl decked out in fancy dresses. I was the heroine, the country bumpkin, honest and straightforward who won out in the end. Republic had the best background crews and production values for their kind of product . . . but I was a top money maker for Yates and I fought him on contracts. . . . My shows were popular."[15]

Contrary to popular belief, Judy Canova was not simply a rural comedian portraying herself. Like Autry and Rogers at the same studio, she picked and then molded her image although in her case it was more of her own choosing having been developed long before she received the attention of the studio. Republic simply capitalized on the perfect combination of the star's appeal and the tastes of the audience to which Republic directed its films. Canova was a trained singer and could handle opera, but by her own admission early determined that her road to success lay in hillbilly comedy. A born performer, she said that while the chances of being successfully noticed as a straight or operatic singer were not high, she early decided that she could garner attention with the comedy-musical approach and so she deliberately worked to become a success in that field. As she put it, "I wanted to be unique and set out to be the best in the hillbilly field."[16]

Born in Florida, Canova attained her original success along with her sister and two brothers in a family act in a New York City Greenwich Village night spot in 1932. Then, they were signed first by Rudy Vallee and later by Paul Whiteman for their radio shows. The Canovas went on to some vaudeville and a Broadway appearance in *Calling All Stars* (1934). The *New York Times* said in part "The sketch launched a quaint and enormously self-possessed girl named Judy Canova apparently a Hill Billie herself . . . She has a talent."[17] While not a success, the show led to a Warner Bros. contract where she played supporting roles most notably in the film *In Caliente* (1935), doing a hillbilly take-off on and immediately following a straight rendition of "The Lady in Red" musical number. After additional solo stage appearances, she returned with her family to Hollywood, this time at Paramount in 1937 where she had fair supporting roles in two films. After additional vaudeville and radio stints, the family appeared on NBC-TV on May 3, 1939, in an experimental broadcast which gave them the honor of being the first televised hillbilly act.[18] Canova then had a starring role in the Broadway hit, *Yokel Boy*, which led to her signing with Republic.

Canova maintained that she preferred the lead in low-budget productions than to be a supporting player at a major studio.[19] And this was her destiny at Republic. All told she made thirteen films there in two series with a brief sojourn at Columbia in between. Of varying merit, they all were popular in the Republic strongholds because they cannily read their audience and delivered both the message and the required type of entertainment desired by their public.

Canova's first film in the Republic series was *Scatterbrain* (1940) and it included most of the elements which identified her successful movie formula. It was directed by Gus Meins, the same comedy trained veteran who helmed the Higgins Family series. *Scatterbrain* had a rather complex plot. A press agent planted a producer-director's girlfriend with an Ozark family in order to have her discovered as a natural talent, play a hillbilly heroine in the producer's film, and become a star. The actress was planted with Judy Canova and her "pappy," only it was Judy who was signed by error. The press agent and producer plan to marry her off and thus get rid of the competition but finally her screen test proved her true talent and they made her a real star.[20]

Canova started out loud, boisterous, and crude, wearing calicos and pigtails. Although friendly and funny, she was definitely at a disadvantage as the Hollywood schemers tried various tricks to undo and discourage her. But she and her cantankerous father were vindicated when she became a sensation and everyone, including her previous adversaries, recognized her worth. Elements of both the rural/city conflict and the Cinderella fantasy are obvious. The advertising campaign incorporated both with the copy, "Here's Judy Canova, the hayseed glamour girl . . . she's the mountain sugar who raises cain," and "So, yer agoin' to that city of glamour—Hollywood? I figure it this way—what have those stars got that I ain't got?"[21] A contemporary review pinpointed the audience attraction of the picture, "Judy Canova displays sufficient personality and ability in her backwoods character to indicate sticking around for several pictures and possible box office rating for the rural and family houses as time goes on."[22] On the basis of this film's success, Yates signed Canova to a five-year contract and she was considered a major property.

For her second film with the studio, Republic utilized as a springboard an old Broadway play, *Sis Hopkins*. Released in 1941, the film proved to be an outstanding success and is the classic example of the Canova film formula. Canova, through naivete, assumed an uncle was penniless and invited him to her farm. In reality he was wealthy and retired. When she was burned out he reciprocated much to the disdain of his socially conscious wife and selfish daughter.[23] Canova eventually proved her worth and was literally the center of attention at the film's conclusion.

It was the perfect Cinderella theme complete with degradation amongst plenty, evil pseudo-stepmother and daughter, fairy goduncle, flight from grace following her supposed disgrace, and ultimate happy ending. The second theme was also clearly present—the refreshingly honest underdog country bumpkin against the artificial city dwellers and collegiates with the former proving her worth and receiving recognition. Canova even sang a song entitled: "That Ain't Hay (It's the U.S.A.)," a direct glorification of the rural American in deflating the pretentious college boys.

The film was handsomely mounted for a B and included in its cast: Charles Butterworth, a well-known comedy character actor; Susan Hayward, soon to achieve star status; Bob Crosby, musical band leader turned actor; and Jerry Colonna, the famous comedian, in its cast. It was reviewed extensively for a Republic production and even the careful *New York Times* found it acceptable although the reviewer commented that the vehicle was quite old and ordinary.[24] In addition to the comedy and pathos, the film included hillbilly, swing, and popular music and even one operatic selection for Canova. *Sis Hopkins* was extremely successful having been reissued four times. Its influence was felt throughout the entire series. It also led to Canova demanding and receiving script, cast, and director approval and co-ownership in her pictures—a development quite unusual at Republic and shared only by John Wayne at a later date according to Canova.[25]

Canova's third release for Republic, *Puddin' Head*, came only three months after *Sis Hopkins* and bore a resemblance to *Scatterbrain*. The story line involved the attempt of a New York radio station to get Canova's farm through a phony romance, a fake "haunting," and finally a specious radio contract. Of course Canova proved worthy of a proper contract and achieved success complete with glamorous apparel in the closing numbers.[26] She even proved to be a better person than her tormentors by giving the conniving radio people the necessary land gratis. This film also had most of the necessary elements to the Canova formula and the mold was set. The Canova entries moved steadily if unsurprisingly along the same proven track. Along with Wayne, Rogers, and Autry, Canova was by this time part of Republic's established top lineup.

One other entry from Canova's first Republic series should be mentioned in that it reflected that other major theme so near and dear to Republic, Herbert Yates, and their audience. *Joan of Ozark* (1942) co-starred another wide and loudmouth comedy star, Joe E. Brown, and centered around Canova accidentally shooting a pigeon carrying a Nazi spy message, thereby becoming a national hero.[27] The Nazis set out to kill her as an object lesson. She was lured to a night club which was a Nazi front on the pretense of assisting G-men where she was to be killed. After the obligatory comedy mix-ups she turned the tables, uncovered the spy ring, and even ended up destroying a Japanese submarine. While played for laughs, the patriotic message was there. One of Canova's songs was even entitled "The Lady at Lockheed" and the Republic synopsis of the film succinctly stressed this emphasis. "The 'Ozark Thrush' became a national heroine by exposing the operations of a Nazi spy ring, her antics proving a real nemesis to the Axis."[28] It is safe to say that very few, if any, of the Republic series missed having at least one patriotic entry in their course.

In 1942 and 1943, Canova turned out four films for Republic and one on loan out to Paramount. Then for financial and personal reasons she signed with Columbia where in 1946 she did three pictures. However, at Columbia her budgets and production values were even less than at Republic where the budgets for and support of her series had varied because of personal conflicts within the studio.[29] As a result, Canova was off the screen until 1951 when Republic rehired her for six additional pictures through 1955. During the intervening period she kept busy with personal appearances, troop entertainment, and her radio show which, if anything, surpassed the success of her movies. It ran from 1943 through 1953 first on CBS and then NBC and she was voted "Queen of the Air" in 1949.[30]

Canova's second series at Republic was essentially similar to her early pictures and is considered a second series only because of her intervening work at Columbia. She was co-owner and, while the opening entries were in color, black and white soon returned as budgets again were cut this time in line with the prevalent policy at Republic in the 1950s. *Variety* commented that *Honeychile* (1951), the first entry, "figures as okay top-of-the-bill material for the smaller runs, particularly rural or small-town trade."[31] Apparently, Republic still knew the market as far as audience estimation was concerned. Basically, however, the later Canova vehicles were seen as second billing pictures in most areas.

The Canova formula and Republic's pacing held true to the very end of her series. The final entry, *Lay That Rifle Down* (1955), had Canova as the hillbilly drudge at her greedy aunt's hotel. She took a charm course, invented an imaginary prince charming, and took up with a confidence man. He and his confederates attempted to take over a farm upon which Canova had been supporting orphans. But Canova converted him, captured his accomplices, and discovered that there was oil on the property. The film blended both of Canova's attractions. It opened with the obvious Cinderella motif and shifted into the honest and charitable country girl outwitting the slick city crooks for a happy ending. Always aware of the value of public exposure throughout her career, Canova went on the road whenever possible to retain her rapport with her audience. The *New York Times*, in discussing how Republic retained a hold on its audience in competition with larger studios, noted, "Republic has a[n] . . . effective formula for making itself and its stars known to audiences—the personal appearance tour—Judy Canova, a headliner in variety houses for years, makes personal appearances between her chores at the studio. . . . To encourage its stars to keep up the good work Republic does not share in the proceeds from their outside engagements."[32] Her appearances were so popular that they sometimes made the papers when she was only passing through.[33] However, Canova was not only interested in the profits; she also understood the value of the publicity her shenanigans elicited. In 1941, she and Gene Autry appeared at the White House and Judy accepted a cigar after the luncheon, President Roosevelt even supposedly asking her if she wanted a light.[34] Apocryphal or not, the story fit Canova's image of the refreshingly direct hillbilly and solidified her appeal while bringing forth the desired publicity.

Canova controlled her image from the beginning and understood the attraction of her movies. A national magazine article at the height of Canova's popularity made much of the fact that she was the top hillbilly star and in demand in the Midwest and Southern markets.[35] Albert S. Rogell, who directed two of the Canova films, one at Republic and one at Columbia, was of the opinion that both aimed at the same audience but that Republic did a better job on this kind of film. He also states that while these films were simplistic they also contained "the teaching of the Church reduced to individual actions but the preachment was minimum and the pictures moved."[36] Barry Shipman, who wrote the last three of the second Canova series at Republic was a bit more pragmatic: "I even did a few of the Canova country-hick things. They weren't anything great. They were fairly set but they were a lot of fun."[37] However, Shipman also feels that much of this routine writing for the Westerns and other Bs did have more effect than he or others realized at the time. He stoutly maintains, moreover, that any such audience effect was positive.

Following her successful career at Republic, Canova continued her personal and television appearances, did one other movie (*Adventures of Huckleberry Finn*, Metro Goldwyn Mayer, 1960), and spent a great deal of time in charitable activities, particularly the March of Dimes. She had been quite aware of the public acceptance of her screen personality from the very beginning and actively communicated with her audience during the height of her career.[38]

The B comedy series usually with musical interludes at Republic therefore did play not only a role in the studio's production schedules but also in the studio's image and the way in which it affected its audience. Whether it was a reinforcement of family unity, a glorification of rural values, or a paean to the efficacy of the Cinderella myth, the messages were all related to the effectiveness of American tradition. For example, the continuing equation, especially at Republic, between conservative, rural common sense philosophy and flag waving patriotism versus the liberal urban atmosphere of hollow cynicism and decadence often related to subversion or at least irreverence toward country was quite clear not only in the Canova and Weaver family vehicles but also in most of the Western series as discussed in the previous chapter. The general beliefs of the middle American strata as interpreted by the studio were reflected in all B series at Republic because this type of entertainment was what their audience patronized. In the final analysis the B musical and comedy series were in much the same mold as the B Western series. The emphasis and the approach varied to fit the type of film but the overall aura was a restatement and a reinforcement of American values.

As demonstrated, the Republic studio excelled in the areas of serials, series Westerns, and rural comedy musical series. These are the products which are so well remembered by the fans and it is here that the impact which Republic had will be found. However, while these are the important group films, Republic also produced hundreds of individual B films, some of which were good, a few of which may have been excellent, and many of which were frankly routine. Although these films, along with the occasional A venture, were in most instances not as much a part of the image of Republic as the series, they still made up a significant part of the studio's output.

The Republic ventures into A production were summarized in Chapter 1. The studio's main emphasis on non-series Bs fell into three general areas. First, there were many individual comedies. Secondly, the studio released several satisfactory non-series program musicals. Finally, and most important, Republic relied heavily on action, mystery, and melodrama in non-series productions. As one authority put it, "Action films were made at Republic, but not exclusively—they were trying anything, and everything, to grab the mass audience."[39] And some of these individual efforts proved quite effective.

In the areas of comedy and musical productions, Republic tried for solid family entertainment from the very beginning. In 1936 they released *Follow Your Heart* with opera star Marion Talley. It was light on comedy and heavy on music. In contrast, that same year they put out *Sitting on the Moon* starring Roger Pryor, minor leading man of the 1930s, and Grace Bradley, a B leading lady, which was aimed at the popular music audience and concerned young lovers threatened by a blackmailing hussy. And in 1937 there was *The Hit Parade* with singer Frances Langford and big band names based on the famous weekly radio series. While basically a high budgeted B, this film was successful enough to merit follow-ups such as *Hit Parade of 1941, 1943, 1947,* and *1951.* All received fair to good although not sensational reviews in the *New York Times* save the last which was ignored.[40] This long string of productions might have qualified the "Hit Parade" as a series, but so much time elapsed between each and the plots and characters were for the most part unrelated. In addition, each production was later released under separate and unrelated titles for legal reasons thus destroying any series illusion.

Republic often utilized the services of actors and actresses on the decline in many of their Bs. Jane Frazee, who ended up in Roy Rogers pictures, did occasional non-Western musicals for the studio such as *Melody and Moonlight* (1940), *Moonlight Masquerade* (1942), and *Rosie the Riveter* (1944).[41] Ruth Terry, B actress and character performer, also did musicals at the studio in addition to straight acting and starred in such routine musical vehicles as *Sing, Dance, Plenty Hot* (1940), *Rookies on Parade* (1941) with bandleader Bob Crosby, *Youth on Parade* (1942), and *Pistol Packin' Mamma* (1944). There were two Earl Carroll review musicals (1945 and 1946) and several Ice Capade entries starring the ice skating champion, Vera Hruba Ralston.[42]

Republic also put specialty acts from radio, fairs, and other local entertainment sources into their B musicals to boost box office returns and publicity in their areas of popularity. For example, *Hoosier Holiday* (1944) starred Dale Evans but included the musical group the Hoosier Hot Shots. The group was prominently emphasized, the advertisements were larger than normal, and the play dates were quite successful when the film was shown in such middle American locales as Indiana.[43] None of these B musicals were epochal productions and few were more than light entertainment although many had heavy patriotic themes and sequences in keeping with the Yates dictum. Still they were workmanlike productions and represented a minor emphasis in the overall Republic schedule. Few of them contained elements of true "Stürm und Drang" and all carried the theme that decent people doing right will end up happy.

Even more effective among Republic's non-series film programs were the various mystery melodramas produced by the studio to fill its yearly schedules. Because these films leaned heavily on action and pacing by their very nature, Republic seemed quite at ease in turning them out. They not only predominated in the non-series area, but they were usually more successful. For example, *The President's Mystery* (1936) was written by the famous Nathanael West and Lester Cole and based upon a suggestion by Franklin D. Roosevelt for a series of stories in *Liberty* magazine. It involved a man starting a new life but having to face up to the old when his ex-wife was murdered. He did the right thing and ended up happily with a new wife and a new life. In the process of creating his new life, he became involved with a strike-bound factory in New England and the subject of strikes was of course sensational given the state of the economy and the union movements in the 1930s. Nonetheless, the picture was not really outstanding, rather self-conscious, and the *New York Times* called it only "interesting."[44] In his two years at Republic, West contributed to at least a dozen films of which nine have been identified. While he was never really committed to his writings there, he did absorb much of the background experiences which went into his well-known pessimistic novel on Hollywood, *The Day of the Locust*.[45]

Hearts in Bondage, a Civil War tale from 1936, was the only directorial effort of actor Lew Ayres. It was not remarkable but had fine special effects. Famed director James Cruze, who handled such famous films as *The Covered Wagon* (1923) and *I Cover the Waterfront* (1933), ended his career at Republic with such journeymen but acceptable B productions as *The Wrong Road* (1937), *Prison Nurse, Gangs of New York*, and *Come On Leathernecks* (1938)—three crime films and a military action piece. Cruze was an example that the studio frequently used talented and well-known actors or behind the scenes artists either on the way up or on the way down the popularity scale.

As was true of all other Republic efforts these melodramas also made heavy use of the patriotic themes as wartime approached. *Women in War* (1940), starring the well-known British actress, Wendy Barrie, concerned a woman who killed an officer to defend her honor and then vindicated herself in nursing service. It was one of the early films showing the London blackout under Nazi attack and contained considerable pro-British feeling. Both *Photoplay* and *Time* reacted favorably to its patriotism.[46] *Pride of the Navy* (1939) with James Dunn utilized torpedo boats as a backdrop for standard dramatics with a romantic triangle and was complete fiction but foreshadowed in emphasis John Ford's *They Were Expendable* at MGM six years later. *Pride's* patriotism was rampant and resembled a paid advertisement for the Navy.

In the area of pure mysteries, Republic also had a commendable record. *The Leavenworth Case* (1936) was based on a detective story by famed mystery writer Anna Katherine Green. *Who Killed Aunt Maggie?* in 1940 blended both comedy and mystery and was quite well received in the Republic strongholds according to famed character actor Walter Abel.[47] Republic also produced two Ellery Queen mysteries—one, *The Spanish Cape Mystery* (1935) with Donald Cook, was acceptable and the second, *The Mandarin Mystery* (working title, *The Chinese Orange Mystery*) (1936) with comic Eddie Quillan, was not, basically because Quillan was a bug-eyed comedian type.[48] The studio also did three rather mediocre "Mr. District Attorney" films based on the popular radio series—*Mr. District Attorney* (1941), *Mr. District Attorney in the Carter Case* (1941), and *Secrets of the Underground* (1942).[49] The last District Attorney entry was a murder mystery but involved home front defense, counterfeit war stamps, and the defeat of a major sabotage ring. These "mini-series" were interesting experiments but Republic's mystery-melodrama strength really remained in its frequent individual releases.

In the period from late 1940 to early 1942, Republic hit its stride and produced solid craftsmanlike Bs for a decade. The studio's professionalism showed in its individual products of the period as well as in its series. Most of the entries were between fifty and sixty minutes in length and were tailor-made for the lower half of the double bill although an occasional film became a hit with the critics or the public. The themes were, as usual, murder mysteries or war oriented military melodramas. A typical example, *London Blackout Murders* (1942), directed by George Sherman and written by Curt Siodmak involved the systematic murders of members of a Nazi spy organization.[50]

With war, Republic's hundred percentism accelerated as a major motif in single entry films. The plot to *Remember Pearl Harbor* was really nothing unusual and was used on four other occasions at Republic. In many respects the story line was secondary in that the film was rushed into release in May, 1942, for its exploitation value—a fact recognized and criticized by the *New York Times*.[51] But the blatancy of its message is obvious in its summary from the studio's files: "The heroic sacrifice of a young American soldier at the Philippine Army Post and his brilliant strategy prevent the Japanese from landing reinforcements during those fatal, first hours of the Pearl Harbor disaster."[52] As would be expected, it played well in the traditional Republic strongholds.[53] *My Buddy* (1944), another rather unusual example of Republic's use of patriotism, portrayed a World War I veteran portrayed by Don "Red" Barry forced to turn to crime and eventually killed. The plight of returning veterans was the major theme and the prologue tied the tale in neatly with the parallel situation facing the country in 1944.

Patriotism as related to the value of the American way of life continued to be a major emphasis at Republic even after World War II. *The Red Menace* (1949) was basically an exploitation film in which Yates took a special interest.[54] While a propaganda film aimed at a specific problem, the picture had further importance. The summary from Republic's files illustrated how this film included all the values that the studio emphasized through the years: "A young war vet, resentful of the crooked deals he has had from housing project crook promoters, joins the Communist movement in the misguided belief that it will bring him redress for his grievances. He soon discovers his mistake, and, with the girl he loves, finds freedom and human tolerance in an American country town."[55] Rugged individualism, sacrifice, the saving grace of honesty, evil city influence, freedom in a rural environment, justice, law and order, and patriotism were all apparent in an obvious but effective little romantic melodrama.

Message films are based on topical social issues and hence are important gauges of popular social thought.[56] Thus, *The Red Menace* was not only a good summary of Republic's interpretation of middle American values in general, but was also a barometer of concerns of the United States during the Cold War period of the late 1940s and early 1950s. But, simply because the film tied in with the mentality of the mass audience of the era did not necessarily mean that it was an effective film and some found its blatancy offensive. Bosley Crowther said in part:

> [I]t looks as though that studio, on the word of its president, Herbert Yates, meant it to be a solemn warning against 'insidious forces' that imperil our country from within. But the ineptitude of the plotting and the luridness with which it is played render the "menace" unimpressive and the perpetrators oddly absurd. . . .
>
> The most effective demonstration of charges against the Communists that the film provides is the disclosure of how the party allegedly abuses and intimidates those members who endeavor to break away. And for this, at least, the picture has a certain validity.[57]

Despite these reservations, *The Red Menace* had good play-dates in the Midwest and South and adequately mirrored and contributed to the McCarthy paranoia of the era. It mirrored the McCarthy mentality by the mere fact of being topical. It contributed by emphasizing the "menace" and reinforcing the message for those who were willing to accept it.

These and many other similar entries from Republic in the musical, mystery, melodrama, or military vein were frequently ordinary and quickly forgotten but they were also adequate and some were surprisingly good. They usually had the same messages and the same audience appeal of the Republic series but they lacked long term impact. The series and serials usually made more of an impression over the long run because they were more identifiable and thus more memorable. But, just as the series and serials declined in quality especially in the early 1950s, so too did the individual entries. While the subject matter remained the same, production was rushed, short-cut techniques were used, stock film was relied upon, and quality plots were less noticeable. The actors were also an indication of the change. In the heyday of the B films such well-known actors and actresses as Ramon Novarro, Francis Lederer, Ethel Barrymore, Edward Everett Horton, Richard Arlen, and Eric von Stroheim made occasional singles for Republic while in the declining days the stars were Rod Cameron, Robert Rockwell, Scott Brady, Don Megowan and similar performers who rarely even got a chance at the majors.[58]

There were of course some good Bs in the last years such as *Fair Wind to Java* (1953) with Fred MacMurray, Vera Ralston, and a good supporting cast. A seafaring yarn in color and with good special effects, Republic would have liked it to be an A but the principals were miscast and it became an acceptable B which was not a critical success.[59] *Stranger at My Door* (1956) was an unusual little minister versus outlaw morality play starring a B lead and A support actor MacDonald Carey and Skip Homier, a child actor turned character actor. Directed by William Witney and written by Barry Shipman, the story had an outlaw (originally meant to be Jesse James but changed due to legal complications) fall in love with a preacher's young wife and help the family while the preacher tried to convert the outlaw to the path of God. While there were some fine action sequences, the stress was on human emotions and conflicts. The spiritual mood prevailed. The film brought forth good reviews in *Variety*[60] and *The Hollywood Reporter*[61] and even unsolicited letters of praise. One said in part, "This picture must appeal to people of all age groups and all religions. Without a doubt this picture is worthy of more publicity and mention [than] it has received so far. . . . Why is it that millions can be spent for overated [sic] pictures, when here in our own back yard [the letter came from Glendale, California] someone can make a picture for 'Peanuts,' so to speak and have the so-called spectaculars beat a thousand ways."[62] This film was representative of what is meant by a B "sleeper," a routine offering that became more popular than was predicted.

But such "sleepers" as well as even nominally good B movies became less and less frequent as the production schedule at Republic decreased. Good, bad, or indifferent, the individual B pictures at Republic went the way of the B series, but they were all a part of the Republic schedule and continually presented positive interpretations on life in a variety of formats.

Notes

1. L111 (May, 1939), p. 63.
2. "Republic Productions, Inc. Produced Properties," p. 30.
3. Other examples include *The Covered Trailer* (1939) emphasizing family cooperation and loyalty, *Grandpa Goes to Town* (1940) concerning the family's good reputation, and *Meet the Missus* (1940) with Grandpa even considering a loveless marriage to save his son from disgrace. "Republic Productions, Inc. Produced Properties," pp. 32, 62, 102.
4. Miller, *B Movies*, p. 108.
5. *New York Times*, January 27, 1938.

6. *New York Times*, February 2, 1941.

7. Charles K. Stumpf, "The Weaver Brothers and Elviry," *Film Collector's Registry*, V (May, 1973), p. 10.

8. *Jeepers Creepers* (1939) and *Arkansas Judge* (1940).

9. See p. 163. This was an obvious theme of Autry's *Rovin' Tumbleweed* (1930), p. 143 and Rogers' *Under Western Stars* (1938), p. 150.

10. *Atlanta Constitution*, February 20, 1942.

11. "Republic Productions, Inc. Produced Properties," p. 107.

12. Interview by Professor Milton Plesur, State University of New York at Buffalo, and author with Judy Canova, Los Angeles, California, May 15, 1976.

13. For example in Kokomo, Indiana, Canova's pictures played one of the two larger theaters out of six available on their initial run normally. See *Kokomo Tribune*, March 30, 1944.

14. Stith Thompson, *The Folktale* (New York: Dryden Press, 1951), pp. 126–128. Cinderella (Type 510A) is probably the best known of all folktales and more than five hundred versions have been collected in Europe alone.

15. Interview with Judy Canova, Los Angeles, California, May 15, 1976.

16. Interview with Judy Canova, Los Angeles, California, May 15, 1976.

17. December 14, 1934.

18. *Variety*, May 4, 1939. The Canovas were not singled out as a special group however. The network was simply using whatever acts were available in those early broadcasts, and the family happened to be in New York City thus becoming the first television hillbillys by accident.

19. Interview with Judy Canova, Los Angeles, California, May 15, 1976.

20. "Republic Productions, Inc. Produced Properties," p. 147.

21. *Elwood* [Indiana] *Call-Leader*, October 1, 1946 and October 3, 1946. Reissue booking.

22. *Variety*, August 4, 1940.

23. Although she was ridiculed by the family and unhappy in her surroundings, he stood by her and enrolled her in his snobbish daughter's college. Because of her talent, Canova was given a major role in the college musical and the daughter's role was cut proportionately. The daughter, in an attempt at sabotage, involved the innocent hillbilly in a burlesque show but her expulsion from college was cancelled when the uncle came to her aid. Canova was the hit of the college show and even wore fancy clothing in the finale.

24. May 1, 1941.

25. Interview with Judy Canova, Los Angeles, California, May 15, 1976.

26. *Elwood* [Indiana] *Call-Leader*, January 20, 1949. Reissue booking.

27. *Elwood* [Indiana] *Call-Leader*, October 20, 1942.

28. "Republic Productions, Inc. Produced Properties," p. 83.

29. Interview with Judy Canova, Los Angeles, California, May 15, 1976. Yates took a personal interest in Canova and when she did not reciprocate, she indicated that he had her budgets cut. Actually, the budgets on five of her first seven pictures

increased slightly but the personal conflicts were apparently real. Had she not been so popular, he would have taken other steps she felt.

30. Richard Gertner, ed., *International Television Almanac* (New York: Quigley Publishing, 1976), p. 37.

31. Undated clipping in the Judy Canova clipping file of the Margaret Herrick Library at the Academy of Motion Pictures Arts and Sciences, Los Angeles, California.

32. February 2, 1941.

33. *Atlanta Constitution*, January 19, 1942, noted "Atlanta Gets Brief Look at J. Canova" when she made a half hour stopover there. Atlanta, though a large city, reflected Southern interest and gave Republic stars good coverage.

34. James Robert Parish, *The Slapstick Queens* (New York: Castle Books, 1973), p. 214.

35. Kyle Crichton, "Hillbilly Judy," *Colliers*, CIX (May 16, 1942), p. 17.

36. Interview with Albert S. Rogell, Republic director, Los Angeles, California, May 5, 1976.

37. Interview with Barry Shipman, Republic writer, San Bernardino, California, May 11, 1976.

38. Interview with Judy Canova, Los Angeles, California, May 15, 1976.

39. Miller, *B Movies*, p. 106.

40. May 31, 1937; August 18, 1940; April 16, 1943; May 5, 1947. The ads from the 1943 entry with John Carroll and Susan Hayward offered, "Gay Tunes! Sparkling Comedy! Blended into the season's brightest hit!," *Kokomo* [Indiana] *Tribune*, June 11, 1943.

41. The last named film was a lighthearted but patriotic musical based on a real event of the war. The plot had to do with housing shortages, war production, and romantic entanglements. Rosina B. (Bonavita) Hickey, the real Rosie the Riveter, has commented, "It was such a different world then. Jennie [her partner] and I were the same as all the people we knew. We worked hard because that's how we were brought up and because we believed in what our country was fighting for. We were very patriotic. Everyone was." [Richard Lamparski, *Lamparski's Whatever Became of . . . ?* (New York: Bantam, 1976), p. 271.] The *Elwood* [Indiana] *Call-Leader* gave the patriotic theme a big emphasis, August 22, 1944.

42. The first entry, *Ice Capades*, listed her as Vera Hruba, her Czech name, in a supporting role. *Atlanta Constitution*, Thursday, January 1, 1942. However, she soon attained star status both in ice skating movies and other vehicles at Republic. See Chapter 1, pp. 17–19.

43. *Elwood* [Indiana] *Call-Leader*, Tuesday, May 9, 1944; Wednesday, May 10, 1944; and Thursday, May 11, 1944.

44. October 4, 1936.

45. Tom Dardis, *Some Time in the Sun* (New York: Charles Scribner's Sons, 1976), p. 154.

46. *Photoplay*, LIV (July, 1940), p. 61, and *Time* XXXV (June 17, 1940), p. 86.

47. Interview with Walter Abel, by Professor Milton Plesur, New York City, March 1, 1976.

48. Miller, *B Movies*, p. 113.

49. "Republic Productions, Inc. Produced Properties," pp. 105, 149.

50. *Commonweal*, XXXVII (January 22, 1943), p. 351.

51. June 4, 1942.

52. "Republic Productions, Inc. Produced Properties," p. 132.

53. *Elwood* [Indiana] *Call-Leader*, November 20, 1942.

54. A publicity brochure was released with this B picture which shows Republic's and Yates' patriotic motivation. Although lacking subtlety, Yates' statement shows much about the man, his studio, and the times.

> The picture, "The Red Menace," was produced by Republic Productions, Inc., as our effort to assist in the fight against Communism and any other "Ism," whose purpose is to destroy our form of government by force and violence, bloodshed and terror.
>
> It must be evident to every sincere American citizen that our country and our American way of life are being imperiled by insidious forces from within and from without. Not long ago, one great American stated: "The Communists Have Been, Still Are and Always Will Be a Menace to Freedom, to Democratic Ideals, to the Worship of God, and to America's Way of Life."
>
> Within the past two weeks, another great American has declared: "The Communist Party and the Communist World Movement Have a Fixed Objective. That Objective Is World Domination Through Revolution. It Is a Long Range Objective, That Objective Will Never Change, Because If It Did, Communism Would Die."
>
> It is to combat this evil that was produced. Even though the picture was made behind closed doors, and there has been no public showing to date, Republic Studios and the Writer Have Already Been Attacked by the Daily People's World, a Communist Paper Published in San Francisco, and the Daily Worker, A Communist Paper Published in New York.
>
> The attack is more than on open threat. It is an effort to intimidate Republic Pictures and to stifle its right of freedom of speech. We accept the challenge of The Communist Party and its Fellow Travelers, and we declare that the Republic organization will do everything in its power, regardless of expense or tribulations, to make certain that "The Red Menace" Is Shown in Every City, Town and Village in The United States of America and Other Countries Not Under Communist Control.
>
> > Herbert J. Yates
> > President
> > Republic Productions, Inc.

55. "Republic Productions, Inc. Produced Properties," p. 133.

56. White and Averson, *The Celluloid Weapon*, book jacket rephrased, p. 260. *The Red Menace* is given as an example of the anticommunist film of the period on pp. 123–124.

57. *New York Times*, June 27, 1949.

58. These are good actors but lacked the popularity or versatility of earlier Republic stars. For example, Rod Cameron remained a B Western lead and television star (*State Trooper*) for most of his career; Robert Rockwell is best remembered as a

supporting actor in *Our Miss Brooks* on television. Brady fared better but was reduced to playing character supporting roles on *Police Story* and in television movies in the 1960s and 1970s. Don Megowan was a stuntman who played in inexpensive science fiction films such as *The Werewolf* (1956) and occasional guest roles on *The Lucy Show* on television.

59. *New York Times*, August 28, 1953.

60. *Variety*, April 14, 1956, "Republic has an exceptionally well-done family trade offering . . . strong inspirational values . . . raise it considerably above . . . the average program entry."

61. *The Hollywood Reporter*, April 14, 1956, "a theme that lifts it well out of the ordinary class and into a niche where it deserves to be considered with very special interest."

62. Letter to the author from Barry Shipman, February 1, 1976. Shipman sent the original studio-issued circular on this film. The trade reviews, testimonials, and fan letter were included. Witney also recalls this film as his favorite because it dealt with "relationships." Francis M. Nevins, Jr., "William Witney," *Films in Review*, p. 538.

CHAPTER NINE

~

The Republic Legacy:
Summary and Conclusion

In the present study the importance of the B film and the philosophy of Republic Pictures as demonstrated in the output of such movies have been examined. As the largest and most efficient of the independent studios Republic probably had a major influence on a segment of the great American audience and while it did not contribute dramatically to the film industry in a major way, the studio did at the same time make a subtle but significant contribution through the years.

Leo Rosten, perceptive observer of the Hollywood scene, recognized the basic contribution of the movie colony in its heyday. "Our values are extended to the strident and the unmistakable in Hollywood's way of life. It is for this reason that a study of Hollywood can cast the profile of American society into sharper relief."[1] Thus, in other words, its values reflect those of the wider culture. But in addition to reflection, the movies also serve as a reinforcement factor. Rosten pointed out that the very success of Hollywood lies both in the skill with which it reflects the assumptions, the fallacies, and the aspirations of an entire culture and also that through movies, it *reinforces* "our typologies . . . with overpowering repetitiveness."[2]

Herein lays the importance and significance of Republic and its product. It mirrored and, in doing so, reinforced the values of a large segment of the American people in terms and stories which they could understand, appreciate, and enjoy for entertainment's sake. Thus it can be said that while Republic perhaps did not have a major role in reflecting or influencing American culture as a whole, it did reinforce certain values for a particular audience and was particularly well received in the "Bible Belt." The Republic product at its best served as a cultural document—certainly not in terms of reflecting the West, the War, the police work, or rural life as it was—but rather in mirroring the artificial excitement, the slick action, and the escapist fantasies that its audience, especially the young and unsophisticated, wanted from their entertainment in the 1930 and 1940s. Simultaneously and because of their success with this type of product, Republic reinforced the ethical and moral standards of the times and reinforced the value system which the audience needed and which supported them during those two decades of instability.

Undoubtedly, Republic's understanding of the power of the B film was most evident in its excellent serials and the genre leading Autry, Rogers, and Canova movies. After 1939, John Wayne provided some strength for the studio's ventures into As but not with the consistency of their thrust into the B area since Wayne, while under exclusive contract, was loaned out regularly at very profitable rates.

Photoplay, which in the 1930s and 1940s was the most astute fan magazine, recognized the Republic contribution when it discussed the potency of Gene Autry in 1938 as the studio was solidifying its program:

> Gene and his quiet staggering success is both a lesson and a promise. The lesson is never again to forget the down-to-earth people upon whom the movies have always depended. The promise is the unlimited rewards to come from pictures prepared to please them. . . . A Gene Autry can sell many stars far more famous than himself in more territories than you ever imagined. He can swell the returns from their pictures and build their names, too, in that now very respectable orphans' home of the movies—the once lowly sticks.[3]

Given this Republic impact upon the B audience, what were the specific values that the studio's films so successfully promulgated? Obviously, Republic religiously followed the dictates of the Motion Picture Production Code.[4] Good always won out and there was no confusing good and evil in a Republic production. The studio couched it in action and comedy but the message was always prominent. But, as has been consistently shown, Republic went well beyond the simple guidelines of good over evil. A combination of President Yates' convictions, the desires and needs of the audience, and the accepted beliefs of the era all meshed to provide other messages, usually outright but sometimes slightly less immediately obvious.

These messages permeated the entire spectrum of Republic productions from serials to A films. A final comparative example will illustrate that the message was observable throughout the firm's entire output although perhaps more obvious in the B segment. Whatever message any film had was most concentrated in the thirty-second to two-minute trailer created to attract the audience and to give that audience a massive dose of whatever the film had to offer in a short period. With this factor in mind, compare select passages from the "coming attractions" of two representative Republic films of the same year. One is an example of Republic's specialty; the other is from a Republic prestige production. The first is from the last meritorious serial in terms of new ideas and production values released in 1949 before the final decline of that genre—*King of the Rocket Men*. That same year the studio also released one of its more successful and well-known A productions, a John Wayne vehicle entitled *Sands of Iwo Jima*.

The trailer for *King of the Rocket Men* was very loud, very brassy, and designed to take away the breath of the audience. It opened with four different shots of the film's best special effects showing the hero flying through the air while the titles emblazoned across the screen: "He's Coming Your Way . . . The Jet-Propelled Phantom of the Sky! Fearless Enemy of Spies and Saboteurs! King of the Rocket Men." The scene changed to a fight sequence between three heavies, two heroes, and the heroine while a deep-voiced narrator intoned, "When a gang of foreign agents plot to kill the leading scientists of the world . . . Jeff King, thunderbolt of the air . . . wrecks their plans by his heroic action. . . ." during which the visual returned to the flying hero in exciting shots of him flying close to the ground.[5] And this was merely the first seven shots of the short trailer. The emphasis was blasted out with an unsubtle blatancy which was nonetheless effective in reaching its audience. The action continued on for a total of twenty-three separate shots but the opening seven with accompanying titles and narration give the serial's drift sufficiently—an action-packed paeon to self-reliance, rugged individualism, patriotism, and the fight for law and order.

In comparison, the *Sands of Iwo Jima* trailer, while naturally striving to hold the attention, was much more subdued and aimed at adult viewers but the themes were surprisingly similar. It opened with a shot of a marine camp and the hero and his squad marching out to an off-screen chorus singing the Marine Hymn while the titles rolled up the screen proclaiming: "Republic Studios Proudly Dedicates One of the Truly Great Motion Pictures Ever to Reach the Screen. . . . To the Fighting'est Most lovable Bunch of Guys in the World. . . ." A few scenes later, John Wayne as Stryker was seen standing in the center of his squad saying, "I'm gonna ride ya tell ya can't stand up, but when ya do stand up, you're gonna be Marines!" Over scenes of Marine training, the narrator came in, "These are your boys . . . whom John Wayne, as Sergeant Stryker, forged into fighting men. . . ." The trailer concluded with scenes of Marine combat, interspersed with Wayne in an action shot, the sound of punctuated gunfire, and the titles stating: "An Inspiring Human Story Makes the Mightiest of Motion Pictures! . . . Starring John Wayne . . . His Greatest Performance! . . . His Biggest Picture! . . . 'Sands of Iwo Jima' . . . A Republic Production." The final visual showed Marines and tanks at the foot of Suribachi with the Marine flag superimposed over the whole scene.[6]

This trailer was a bit less brassy and fast paced and, in keeping with its "class," was more complex. But the similarity in values is evident. Even with the example recounting only about half the content, this excerpt showed that the Republic As included the same ideals—patriotism, self-reliance, rugged individualism, defense of the American way of life. Of course, as would be expected, in the A productions there were also other values in addition to the basics and all were presented with more maturity and therefore perhaps more subtlety than in a B. For example, in *Sands*, war is presented not only for patriotic effects and action sequences but also with much more realism and with more consideration of its effects on human emotions than would be usual in a formula B. And the hero was a flawed man with personal problems.[7]

Sophistication, maturity, and expense aside, the Republic As were not that different from Republic Bs in terms of basic message. Indicatively, the audience for the Republic Bs could usually appreciate the Republic A. While the basic themes remained the same, each B genre developed different approaches and emphases.

The serials first and foremost brought out the virtues of self-reliance and rugged individualism as the hero/heroine battled against overwhelming odds to overcome the usually much more imaginative and always more aggressive forces of evil. The tribulations also frequently underwrote the value of leadership and initiative. The whole point could be summarized as integrity. Secondly, the serials drew deeply upon the virtue of patriotism and self-sacrifice for one's companions and country. Finally, the chapterplays relied upon the themes of justice and law and order.

The Western series emphasized much the same messages as the serials but in a different priority and with a few additions. The main theme in Republic Westerns seemed to be justice and law and order coupled with rugged individualism—but individualism tempered with cooperation when appropriate. There was also a strong undercurrent of the importance of defending the underdog—rarely emphasized in the serials. Of course, the Westerns also utilized patriotic materials whenever possible, perhaps not as much as serials but worthy of comment nonetheless. Lastly, the glorification of rural values was clear in the studio's Western output.

The series comedies shared some of the preceding themes, but given the different mood, the approach was usually altered. The comedies tended to stress domestic and social values rather than the aggressive life and death struggles prevalent in the other two genres. The primary message of the comedy tended to be integrity but integrity through family unity. Rural values were a strong second priority. Also, honesty seemed to be singled out more than in Westerns and serials. Much has been made of the Cinderella theme and, in some respects this is another description for the defense of the underdog and the belief in the strength of the common man. Finally, the comedies did not escape the inclusion of patriotic plots and themes although they were presented in a lesser degree than in serials and Westerns.

There were of course other messages in the Republic product and even occasional lapses and contradictions in those listed above, but these were the primary themes. These values, packaged to reach the Republic audience, also fit the needs of the times—the insecurity and dehumanization of the Great Depression, the normal and even commendable chauvinism of the Second World War, and the paranoia of the McCarthy era—altered slightly to fit each period. It was good versus evil with a heavy dose of patriotism and, when all of the themes and examples are summarized, it came down to the fact that the message of Republic, and Hollywood, was a politicized version of the Protestant Ethic, a major force in American history.

Secondarily, the studio offered a contribution to the industry as a training ground for professionals which functioned as a "baptism of fire." Republic may not have been a power within the Hollywood hierarchy, but it did provide certain significant services to the other studios under the contributions of journeymanship, craftsmanship, and technical excellence. It was indirect, unplanned, and perhaps even unsuspected at the time but was quite identifiable in retrospect. This fact has been acknowledged by many movie people on both sides of the camera.

Character actor I. Stanford Jolley, who appeared in over five hundred films, many of which were for Republic, summed up the value of Republic in teaching efficiency within the industry:

> Serials and the budget westerns were such wonderful training grounds for actors and directors alike. You had to learn fast to stay in the business; you had to learn well. To help you better understand what I am saying, allow me to illustrate. The high professionalism and teamwork at a small studio like Republic, with limited finances, could result in up to 100 scenes a day. While over at, say, MGM if they got 10 scenes a day it was a small miracle![8]

In other words, Republic's schedule resulted in professional productions and technical excellence under pressure. But the studio taught more than just speed. Republic's rapid schedule, low budgets, and areas of specialization taught its actors and technical crews basic fundamentals valuable throughout the industry. John Wayne, whose recognition of Republic's value to his career has been cited previously, also admitted the value of the Bs as a training ground. He felt that the essential ability to handle dialogue was the most valuable lesson he received from his B career. "The quickie westerns taught me how to speak lines . . . straight lines. . . . The biggest difference between a B western and an A western is in how they tell the story. The B picture has to do it with stretches of talk, straight exposition. Every once in a while they stop the action and the hero or somebody explains the background or why somebody came to town."[9]

On the other side of the camera, director Joseph Kane, who received his start at Republic and became the "house director," observed that he and others learned the value of the ability to make decisions at Republic. "Action takes quite a lot of time. . . . You have to know exactly what you're going to do. . . . So you don't waste any time. As soon as you say, 'Cut! Print!' you move to the next setup right away. You don't hesitate. And you don't change your mind. As soon as you set something up, the whole damn crew leaps at it and starts getting it ready. . . . They're working hard and you don't want to fool around. . . . And keep going, keep moving."[10] Kane credited his action-oriented years at Republic with making possible his later transition to television, which also thrives on pressure and speed.

Another B director who frequently worked at Republic stressed that the studio taught teamwork. After recounting how he worked with the actors and technicians to make an action sequence in a Red Ryder vehicle (*Sheriff of Las Vegas*, Republic, 1944) more interesting and out of the ordinary, Lesley Selander pointed out, "Now this might not seem like anything on a little Western. But it showed the care, interest, and, family-like attitude we all had then. We were a team, even on a budget Western it made no difference."[11]

In the area of writing, Barry Shipman, who wrote Westerns and other Bs at Republic, saw the Western format as a creative form of writing and valuable to his career. "The Western writer, that is, one who makes a career of writing outdoor action films, is a breed all his own. . . . To me it offers the challenge that faces any writer of fiction and actually has more fulfillment for my creative instinct than any other form of film. Besides, it allows me more freedom."[12] Shipman still feels that his years with Republic where he started writing serials and progressed through all B genres, were valuable professionally.[13] Although it seems a contradiction, the formula writing on B pictures did provide creative freedom within the format and it taught discipline.

In a realm of movie technology—that of special effects—the Lydecker brothers at Republic were considered to be the best. Ted Lydecker was very enthusiastic about his Republic career:

> My business was the most fantastic there was. Everything was new everyday. You were your own little world of explosions and miniature cars and planes. People don't understand or realize what we did, Howard and I. It was kind of like Walt Disney when he first started. Everything he did was your own way. I wish we could do that kind of stuff today. It was wonderful and nerve-wracking! We worked on a weekly schedule for the serials. The miniatures and climaxes were all done at the last minute. We never got a complete script in advance. We would make up a budget but there were always changes. On features, the effects were always done after the picture was completed.[14]

In certain respects, the special effects people controlled the end product and the scheduling. Ted Lydecker elaborated on another occasion that although they worked well with the other Republic personnel, the brothers and their assistants knew that acceptable special effects took time especially when the budget was limited. Therefore, since the effects were done last, the special effects people exerted a great deal of influence on the final product.[15] Regardless of their status, the effects of Republic were highly rated and the Lydeckers delivered on time when it was a crucial factor.

Even in the field of music, Republic made a contribution by training young musicians. Music was important at Republic and added a gloss and excitement lacking in other inexpensive productions. The studio made it a practice to score serials, Westerns, and other B films heavily. This meant that the music was frequently mass produced or drawn from stock. Stanley Wilson, who became Executive Musical Director at Universal and who was a well-known cinema composer, said of his Republic period, "We were a very good highly overworked underpaid group of dedicated people. . . . It was the best training anyone ever had."[16]

Finally, in the field of stuntwork Republic utilized the best craftsmen and afforded them the opportunity to develop techniques. Not only did these men gain experience at Republic and train others in their field, but the major studios benefited also from their expertise. David Sharpe, one of the best who worked on innumerable Republic pictures, pointed out that his crew of stuntmen and second unit directors moved freely between the independents and the majors since Warners, MGM, Twentieth, etc. could not afford to keep action units on the payroll constantly. This meant the action sequences in most of the major studio productions were clear and obvious reflections of the state of the art in B films, the primary environment for action sequences.[17] The film credits of many quality movies from the most prestigious studios reflects the inter-relationship between major and minor studios through the good offices of the action units.[18]

In the year 1943, Republic produced fifty-five films compared with MGM's twenty-seven and Warner Bros.' nineteen. With such a production schedule and its demonstrated technical excellence, it is no surprise that Republic offered its personnel a complete course in pragmatic filmmaking. As further proof, it can be pointed out that when the market for the B film declined in the early 1950s, many of the Republic personnel moved directly over to the fast paced, rapid delivery field of weekly television series.[19] Republic trained people remained in demand. In fact, Don Barry called Republic "a university for television production."[20]

Finally, Republic personnel not only had staying power, but many became leaders in their field of specialization. In addition to the actors who have been mentioned frequently in earlier chapters, representative Republic workers who received recognition for their contributions included executive Michael Frankovich, who became a well-known production company head, and Robert Beche, who went on to the popular and long-lasting television series, *Gunsmoke*. Director William Witney, the famous serial director, made action films for both theaters and television until his death. Republic stalwart Allan Dwan was highly acclaimed by contemporary Peter Bogdanovich, and Edward Ludwig was yet another rediscovered director, having been discussed in *Take One*[21] and other scholarly film magazines. Academy Award winning stunt coordinator Yakima Canutt was still active until the early 1970s and another excellent stuntman, David Sharpe, was very active in television until his death. Cameramen Bud Thackery and Jack Marta did superior camerawork in television and were recognizable by their distinctive styles. Broadway musical composer Cy Feuer and multi-talented musician Victor Young both were Republic alumni as was television composer Stanley Wilson.

Thus, many Republic personnel remained active until death or retirement at the few studios which maintained a full schedule. Universal and Buena Vista for example utilized Republic trained people. As Ted Lydecker said, "My brother and I trained most of the special effects people who are now over at Universal."[22] These sentiments are echoed by a number of ex-Republic staff.

Republic and its product have undergone a rediscovery and appreciation over the last decade and there appears to be a continuing interest in its B output. Much of it is admittedly nostalgic but this does not remove the phenomenon from serious consideration. In a 1976 survey of serial favorites, thirty to forty years after they were released, eight out of the top ten and seventeen out of the top twenty were released by Republic.[23] Periodicals such as *Film Collector's Registry*, *Serial World*, *Yesterday's Saturdays*, and *Serial Report* were devoted to Westerns and serials and invariably rank Republic highly. Serious publications such as *Films in Review* and *Take One* have devoted space to the B revival. The Republic products are favorites at film conventions and are in continual television release, either in their original formats or in re-edited versions such as *Roy Rogers Presents the Great Movie Cowboys*. Republic stars, supporting players, and even behind-the-scenes personnel were also in demand at film conventions until their age caused many of them to cease traveling. A few are still making occasional appearances. Adrian Booth was guest of honor at Serialfest 2006 in Newtown, Pennsylvania, and was both a hit and most informative.

Peggy Stewart, Republic serial and B Western heroine, summed up the various reasons for Republic's appeal:

> It's kind of hard to say, the majority of people at the conventions that I've talked to, they love the memory. It's memorable, happy memories, good memories even if you didn't have a childhood that you particularly liked. You find people saying how they enjoyed that portion of their childhood.
>
> A lot of folks too have talked about the fact that there are no places to send their kids on Saturdays, no matinees so they have shown their Westerns to satisfy their kids. To give them shows, good shows, the Westerns and serials, show them right from wrong, the goodies and the baddies, the white hats and the black hats on Saturdays and it entertains them for a week.
>
> I also think the interest is because of morality. The Westerns and serials, particularly the Westerns had morality in them. People like this and they liked to be left on an affirmative note, not a negative note.[24]

Stewart covered the ground well—memories, straightforward entertainment, morality, affirmation. Republic filled a need and filled it well. It is true that other producers of B films also contributed both to the audience and to the industry to some degree. But Republic by all criteria made the most of the B niche. Would American society have been different without it? Perhaps not, but it might have been poorer. The existence of Republic and its role in the lives of at least two generations of moviegoers cannot be ignored.

Notes

1. *Hollywood: The Movie Colony, The Movie Makers* (New York: Harcourt Brace and Company, 1941), p. 5.

2. Rosten, p. 360.

3. Kirkley Baskette, "Pay Boy of the Western World," *Photoplay*, LII (January, 1938), p. 327.

4. Olga J. Martin, *Hollywood's Movie Commandments: A Handbook for Motion Picture Writers and Reviewers* (New York: H. W. Wilson Company, 1937; reprinted, Arno Press, 1977), p. 99.

5. *"King of the Rocket Men": Trailer Cutting Continuity* in Republic Studio Shooting and Continuity Scripts, Collection #979 in the Special Collections Library, University of California at Los Angeles.

6. *"Sands of Iwo Jima" Cross Plug Trailer Cutting Continuity* in Republic Studio Shooting and Continuity Scripts, Collection #979 in the Special Collections Library, University of California at Los Angeles.

7. For elaboration on the cinematic value of *Sands*, see Eyles, *John Wayne and the Movies*, pp. 119–120.

8. Jim Schoenberger, "An Interview with I. Stanford Jolley," *Film Collector's Registry*, VI (March, 1974), p. 4.

9. Zolotow, *Shooting Star: A Biography of John Wayne*, p. 113.

10. Quoted in McCarthy and Flynn, *Kings of the Bs*, p. 322.

11. Jon Tuska, ed. *Close Up: The Contract Director* (Metuchen, New Jersey: Scarecrow Press, 1967), p. 247.

12. *Hollywood Citizen-News*, July 21, 1952.

13. Interview with Barry Shipman, San Bernardino, California, May 11, 1976.

14. Dan Daynard, "The Lydeckers, Masters of Miniature Mayhem," *The New Captain George's Whizzbang*, III (n.d.), p. 7.

15. Interview with Theodore Lydecker, Los Angeles, California, May 17, 1976.

16. Dan Daynard, "The Film Music of Stanley Wilson," *The New Captain George's Whizzbang*, IV (n.d.), p. 15.

17. Interview by Mark Hall, California State University at Chico, with David Sharpe, August, 1976, sponsored by the American Film Institute.

18. Undated letter from Mark Hall, August, 1976.

19. Robert Sklar, *Movie Made America*, p. 282.

20. Interview with Donald Barry, Los Angeles, California, May 6, 1976.

21. Alan Collins, "Edward Ludwig: The Quiet Revolutionary," *Take One*, IV (May–June, 1972), pp. 27–28; John H. Dorr, "Allan Dwan," *Take One*, IV (May–June, 1972), pp. 8–9; and Peter Bogdanovich, *Allan Dwan: The Last Pioneer* (New York: Praeger, 1971).

22. Interview with Theodore Lydecker, Los Angeles, California, May 17, 1976.

23. "Spy Smasher Tops Serial Poll," *Film Collector's Registry*, No. 61 (February, 1976), p. 4.

24. "An interview with Peggy Stewart," *Western Corral*, No. 1, p. 18.

EPILOGUE

~

The Later Years

Although for all practical purposes, Republic was out of the theatrical film production by the late 1950s, the company did create Hollywood Television Service (HTS) in 1950 for purposes of making Republic productions available to the growing television market. Of course, the Republic backlog of over 380 Westerns and 66 serials formed the backbone of this service (when said films were contractually still available for distribution[1]). However, HTS also made new products available to the expanding television market.

The first was a science fiction series (theatrically released as featurettes in 1953, television release 1955) entitled *Commando Cody—Sky Marshall of the Universe*. Not only was the title character lifted out of the Republic serial universe, each episode played like a serial chapter except that the cliffhanger came at midpoint and was resolved after the commercial break. Each episode then became a stand alone adventure.

Other Hollywood Television Service series include *Stories of the Century* (starring a pre-*Dallas* Jim Davis), *The Adventures of Fu Manchu*, *Frontier Doctor* (starring Rex Allen, one of Republic's last B cowboy heroes), and *Stryker of Scotland Yard*. While Republic's last theatrical feature, *Spoilers of the Forest*, was released in 1956, these television series continued to circulate for several years. A few other feature films were produced on the lot using Republic personnel but were not technically Republic productions.[2]

In 1959, Herbert Yates sold off the Republic Studios but that was not the end of the Republic name. Distribution rights remained and a somewhat confusing trail of organizational changes followed over the years.

In 1960, film or lot rentals accounted for approximately 20% of the income of Republic Pictures Corporation, while the rest came from film processing (Consolidated Film Industries, dates from the early days of Republic, see Chapter 1) and plastics (Consolidated Molded Products Company).[3] In 1967 National Telefilm Associates (NTA) purchased the entire Republic backlog for distribution and technically Hollywood Television Services ceased to exist. In 1963, CBS Television leased the Republic lot and took over many remaining personnel. In 1967, they completed the purchase.

But the Republic image of old had one last gasp. Based on the *Batman* television success in the 1960s, Republic's serials were re-edited and released to television in 100-minute feature-length presentations. The *Raiders of the Lost Ark* (1981) craze and its sequels and rip offs added to the interest in Republic stock in trade. In 1985 NTA revived the old Republic name and logo and Republic Pictures Corporation once again came into existence. They even went back into production, handling the well received *Beauty and the Beast* television series and other releases. Blockbuster/(Spelling Entertainment Group) Aaron Spelling Productions purchased the Republic output. They were sold to Paramount Pictures (Viacom) which currently handles Republic distribution under the title of Worldvision.[4] Both the Republic Archives and the Jack Mathis papers are housed at Brigham Young University under the curatorship of James D'Arc.

This brings us up to date on Republic's fate. However, the later corporate changes and even the later productions influenced by the renewed interests in serials are a far cry from the solid cultural influences of the early Republic product. The point is that the 1930s and 1940s serials, B westerns, and other action oriented features were created by a small studio staffed by hardworking and able craftsmen interested only in turning out a quality and saleable product for the vast filmgoing community in order to pay their bills. These films had the underlying messages that honor, loyalty, freedom, and family were important to the American community—perhaps because the films' creators had the same value system. The messages were frequently unconscious and rarely pounded home.

But to the theatergoing public of the late Depression, World War II, and the Cold War era of the late 1940s and early 1950s, the messages struck home. They were the same messages taught in the homes, the schools, and the religious community. However, perhaps because they were presented in heroic, action-packed packages with excellent stuntwork and editing and backed by exciting musical scores, these positive messages were absorbed by the children, the working class, and general moviegoers in a painless and subtle way that the viewer never registered. But they did influence three generations of moviegoers and helped support the American ideals—more identifiable at that time than in today's era. As such, maybe Republic never intended to be an influence on its audience, but it was a positive reinforcement of what our country represents nonetheless.

Notes

1. Gene Autry, Roy Rogers, and Bill Elliott fought the release of their films to television but these claims were eventually settled in court.

2. Mathis, Jack. *Republic Confidential, Volume I, the Studio* (Barrington, Illinois: 1989), p. 439.

3. Ibid, p. 512.

4. Interview with Barry Allen, in charge of the Republic project, at Paramount, August 6, 2004.

APPENDIX A

~

Republic Serials

Darkest Africa (1936)
Undersea Kingdom (1936)
The Vigilantes Are Coming (1936)
Robinson Crusoe of Clipper Island
  (1936)
Dick Tracy (1937)
The Painted Stallion (1937)
SOS Coast Guard (1937)
Zorro Rides Again (1937)
The Lone Ranger (1938)
Fighting Devil Dogs (1938)
Dick Tracy Returns (1938)
Hawk of the Wilderness (1938)
Lone Ranger Rides Again (1939)
Daredevils of the Red Circle (1939)
Dick Tracy's G-Men (1939)
Zorro's Fighting Legion (1939)
Drums of Fu Manchu (1940)
Adventures of Red Ryder (1940)
King of the Royal Mounted (1940)
Mysterious Doctor Satan (1940)
Adventures of Captain Marvel
  (1941)

Jungle Girl (1941)
King of the Texas Rangers (1941)
Dick Tracy vs. Crime Inc. (1941)
Spy Smasher (1942)
Perils of Nyoka (1942)
King of the Mounties (1942)
G-Men vs. the Black Dragon
  (1943)
Daredevils of the West (1943)
Secret Service in Darkest Africa
  (1943)
The Masked Marvel (1943)
Captain America (1944)
The Tiger Woman (1944)
Haunted Harbor (1944)
Zorro's Black Whip (1944)
Manhunt of Mystery Island (1945)
Federal Operator 99 (1945)
The Purple Monster Strikes (1945)
The Phantom Rider (1946)
King of the Forest Rangers (1946)
Daughter of Don Q (1946)
The Crimson Ghost (1946)

Son of Zorro (1947)
Jesse James Rides Again (1947)
The Black Widow (1947)
G-Men Never Forget (1948)
Dangers of the Canadian Mounted (1948)
Adventures of Frank and Jesse James (1948)
Federal Agents vs. Underworld, Inc. (1949)
Ghost of Zorro (1949)
King of the Rocket Men (1949)
The James Brothers of Missouri (1950)
Radar Patrol vs. Spy King (1950)

The Invisible Monster (1950)
Desperadoes of the West (1950)
Flying Discman from Mars (1951)
Don Daredevil Rides Again (1951)
Government Agents vs. Phantom Legion (1951)
Radar Men from the Moon (1952)
Zombies of the Stratosphere (1952)
Canadian Mounties vs. Atomic Invaders (1953)
Trader Tom of the China Seas (1954)
Man with the Steel Whip (1954)
Panther Girl of the Kongo (1955)
King of the Carnival (1955)

~

Republic's Three Mesquiteer Series

The Three Mesquiteers (1936)
Ghost Town Gold (1936)
Roarin' Lead (1936)
Riders of the Whistling Skull
  (1937)
Hit the Saddle (1937)
Gunsmoke Ranch (1937)
Come On Cowboys (1937)
Range Defenders (1937)
Heart of the Rockies (1937)
Trigger Trio (1937)
Wild Horse Rodeo (1937)
Purple Vigilantes (1938)
Call the Mesquiteers (1938)
Outlaws of Sonora (1938)
Riders of the Black Hills (1938)
Heroes of the Hills (1938)
Pals of the Saddle (1938)
Overland Stage Raiders (1938)
Santa Fe Stampede (1938)
Red River Range (1938)
Night Riders (1939)

Three Texas Steers (1939)
Wyoming Outlaw (1939)
New Frontier (1939)
Kansas Terrors (1939)
Cowboys from Texas (1939)
Heroes of the Saddle (1940)
Pioneers of the West (1940)
Covered Wagon Days (1940)
Rocky Mountain Rangers (1940)
Oklahoma Renegades (1940)
Under Texas Skies (1940)
Trail Blazers (1940)
Lone Star Raiders (1940)
Prairie Pioneers (1941)
Pals of the Pecos (1941)
Saddlemates (1941)
Gangs of Senora (1941)
Outlaws of the Cherokee Trail
  (1941)
Gauchos of El Dorado (1941)
West of Cimarron (1941)
Code of the Outlaw (1942)

Raiders of the Range (1942)
Westward Ho! (1942)
Phantom Plainsmen (1942)
Shadows on the Sage (1942)
Valley of Hunted Men (1942)

Thundering Trails (1943)
Blocked Trail (1943)
Santa Fe Scouts (1943)
Riders of the Rio Grande (1943)

APPENDIX C

~

Gene Autry's Republic Appearances

Tumbling Tumbleweeds (1935)
Melody Trail (1935)
The Sagebrush Troubadour (1935)
The Singing Vagabond (1935)
Red River Valley (1936)
Comin' Round the Mountain
  (1936)
The Singing Cowboy (1936)
Guns and Guitars (1936)
Oh Susannah! (1936)
Ride, Ranger, Ride (1936)
The Big Show (1936)
The Old Corral (1936)
Round-Up Time in Texas (1937)
Git Along Little Doggies (1937)
Rootin' Tootin' Rhythm (1937)
Yodelin' Kid from Pine Ridge (1937)
Public Cowboy No. 1 (1937)
Boots and Saddles (1937)
Manhattan Merry-Go-Round
  (1937) [guest appearance]
Springtime in the Rockies (1937)
The Old Barn Dance (1938)

Gold Mine in the Sky (1938)
Man from Music Mountain (1938)
Prairie Moon (1938)
Rhythm of the Saddle (1938)
Western Jamboree (1938)
Home on the Prairie [Ridin' the
  Range] (1939)
Mexicali Rose (1939)
Blue Montana Skies (1939)
Mountain Rhythm (1939)
Colorado Sunset (1939)
In Old Monterey (1939)
Rovin' Tumbleweeds (1939)
South of the Border (1939)
Rancho Grande (1940)
Gaucho Serenade (1940)
Carolina Moon (1940)
Ride, Tenderfoot, Ride (1940)
Melody Ranch (1940)
Ridin' on a Rainbow (1941)
Back in the Saddle (1941)
The Singing Hills (1941)
Sunset in Wyoming (1941)

Under Fiesta Stars (1941)

Down Mexico Way (1941)

Sierra Sue (1941)

Cowboy Serenade (1942)

Heart of the Rio Grande (1942)

Home in Wyoming (1942)

Stardust on the Sage (1942)

Call of the Canyon (1942)

Bells of Capistrano (1942)

City Sue (1946)

Trail to San Antone (1947)

Saddle Pals (1947)

Twilight on the Rio Grande (1947)

Robin Hood of Texas (1947)

APPENDIX D

~

Roy Rogers' Republic Appearances

Tumbling Tumbleweeds (1935)—
  Autry
The Big Show (1936)—Autry
The Old Corral (1936)—Autry
Wild Horse Rodeo (1937)—Three
  Mesquiteers
The Old Barn Dance (1938)—
  Autry
Under Western Stars (Washington
  Cowboy) (1938) [first starring
  role]
Billy the Kid Returns (1938)
Come On, Rangers (1938)
Shine On, Harvest Moon (1938)
Rough Riders' Round-up (1939)
Frontier Pony Express (1939)
Southward Ho! (1939)
In Old Caliente (1939)
Wall Street Cowboy (1939)
The Arizona Kid (1939)
Jeepers Creepers (1939)—Weaver
  Brothers and Elviry
Saga of Death Valley (1939)

Days of Jesse James (1939)
Young Buffalo Bill (1940)
Dark Command (1940) [first A film
  appearance]
Carson City Kid (1940)
The Ranger and the Lady (1940)
Colorado (1940)
Young Bill Hickok (1940)
The Border Legion (1940)
Robin Hood of the Pecos (1941)
Arkansas Judge (1941)—Weaver
  Brothers and Elviry
In Old Cheyenne (1941)
Sheriff of Tombstone (1941)
Nevada City (1941)
Bad Men of Deadwood (1941)
Jesse James at Bay (1941)
Red River Valley (1941)
The Man from Cheyenne (1942)
South of Santa Fe (1942)
Sunset on the Desert (1942)
Romance on the Range (1942)
Sons of the Pioneers (1942)

Sunset Serenade (1942)
Heart of the Golden West (1942)
Ridin' Down the Canyon (1942)
Idaho (1943)
King of the Cowboys (1943)
Song of Texas (1943)
Silver Spurs (1943)
The Man from Music Mountain (1943)
Hands Across the Border (1944)
The Cowboy and the Senorita (1944)
Yellow Rose of Texas (1944)
Song of Nevada (1944)
San Fernando Valley (1944)
Lights of Old Santa Fe (1944)
Brazil (1944) [guest appearance]
Lake Placid Serenade (1944) [guest appearance]
Utah (1944)
Bells of Rosarita (1945)
The Man from Oklahoma (1945)
Sunset in El Dorado (1945)
Don't Fence Me In (1945)
Along the Navajo Trail (1945)
Song of Arizona (1946)
Rainbow Over Texas (1946)
My Pal Trigger (1946)
Under Nevada Skies (1946)
Roll On, Texas Moon (1946)

Home in Oklahoma (1946)
Out California Way (1946) [guest appearance]
Helldorado (1946)
Apache Rose (1947)
Hit Parade of 1947 (1947) [guest appearance]
Bells of San Angelo (1947)
Springtime in the Sierras (1947)
On the Old Spanish Trail (1947)
The Gay Ranchero (1948)
Under California Stars (1948)
Eyes of Texas (1948)
Night Time in Nevada (1948)
Grand Canyon Trail (1948)
Far Frontier (1948)
Susanna Pass (1949)
Down Dakota Way (1949)
The Golden Stallion (1949)
Bells of Coronado (1950)
Twilight in the Sierras (1950)
Trigger, Jr. (1950)
Sunset in the West (1950)
North of the Great Divide (1950)
Trail of Robin Hood (1950)
Spoilers of the Plains (1951)
Heart of the Rockies (1951)
In Old Amarillo (1951)
South of Caliente (1951)
Pals of the Golden West (1951)

APPENDIX E

~

Other Republic Series Discussed

The Higgins Family Series
   The Higgins Family (1938)
   My Wife's Relatives (1939)
   Should Husbands Work? (1939)
   The Covered Trailer (1939)
   Money to Burn (1939)
   Grandpa Goes to Town (1940)
   Earl of Puddlestone (1940)
   Meet the Missus (1940)
   Petticoat Politics (1941)

Weaver Brothers and Elviry Series
   Down in "Arkansaw" (1938)
   Jeepers Creepers (1939)
   In Old Missouri (1940)
   Grand Ole Opry (1940)
   Friendly Neighbors (1940)
   Arkansas Judge (1941)
   Mountain Moonlight (1941)

Tuxedo Junction (1941)
Shepherd of the Ozarks (1942)
The Old Homestead (1942)
Mountain Rhythm (1943)

Judy Canova Series
   Scatterbrain (1940)
   Sis Hopkins (1941)
   Puddin' Head (1941)
   Sleepytime Gal (1942)
   Joan of Ozark (1942)
   Chatterbox (1943)
   Sleepy Lagoon (1943)
   Honeychile (1951)
   Oklahoma Annie (1952)
   The Wac from Walla Walla (1952)
   Untamed Heiress (1954)
   Caroline Cannonball (1955)
   Lay That Rifle Down (1955)

~

Bibliography

Manuscripts and Original Republic Pictures, Inc. Material

Collections

Academy of Motion Picture Arts and Sciences. Los Angeles. Vertical File. Republic Studios and related headings.

"Republic Pictures Studio: The Fastest Growing Organization in Film Industry." *The Hollywood Reporter*, 1938.

American Film Institute. Los Angeles. Vertical File. Republic Studios and related headings.

National Telefilm Associates. Los Angeles, Republic collection.

"History of Republic Pictures." n.d. Manuscript. 4 pp. *Ten Years of Progress: Republic Pictures Corporation 10th Anniversary.* Los Angeles: Republic Pictures Corporation, [1945].

New York Public Library. Theatrical Section. Vertical File.

Republic 1935–36 Attractions Now Available! Los Angeles: Republic Pictures, 1935.

Republic Pictures Pressbook. 1935. (Microfilm reel ZAN-T8, reel 33).

University of California at Los Angeles Special Collections Library. Collection 979. Republic Continuity Scripts and Shooting Scripts.

Dick Tracy's G-Men. Continuity Script. No. 896. August, 1939.

The Fighting Devil Dogs. Continuity Script. No. 1740. April, 1938.

"King of the Rocket Men" Trailer Cutting Continuity.

"Sands of Iwo Jima" Cross Plug Trailer Cutting Continuity.

Stranger at My Door. Shooting Script.

University of California at Los Angeles Theater Arts Library.

"Producer-Interest Stories; SWG Credits; Story Purchases; Pictures Cleared." Hollywood: Republic Pictures Corporation, 1957 [?].

"Republic Productions, Inc. Produced Properties." Story Department. January 1, 1951.

"Summaries on: Unproduced Autrys, Produced Rogers [etc.]: Themes on: Unproduced Westerns; Produced Properties." Hollywood: Republic Pictures Corporation, 1953 [?].

University of Wyoming Library. Collection 5189. Duncan Renaldo Collection.

The Lone Ranger Rides Again. Shooting Script. No. 1009. January, 1939.

Secret Service in Darkest Africa. Shooting Script. No. 1295. June, 1943.

Other Republic Pictures, Inc. Material with Locations

Pressbooks. Published by studio for theater use.

Heart of the Golden West. Hollywood: Republic Pictures, 1942. Jack Mathis. Northbrook, Illinois.

Heroes of the Saddle. Hollywood: Republic Pictures, 1940. Jack Mathis. Northbrook, Illinois.

Spoilers of the Plains. Hollywood: Republic Pictures, 1951. Jack Mathis. Northbrook, Illinois.

Still Manuals. Published by studio for theater use.

Bells of Rosarita. Hollywood: Republic Pictures, 1945. Jack Mathis.

Canadian Mounties vs. Atomic Invaders. Hollywood: Republic Pictures, 1953. Jack Mathis.

Captain America. Hollywood: Republic Pictures, 1944. Jack Mathis.

The Crimson Ghost. Hollywood: Republic Pictures, 1946. Jack Mathis.

Dangers of the Canadian Mounted. Hollywood: Republic Pictures, 1948. Jack Mathis.

Drums of Fu Manchu. Hollywood: Republic Pictures, 1940. Jack Mathis.

G-Men Never Forget. Hollywood: Republic Pictures, 1948. Jack Mathis.

G-Men Vs. The Black Dragon. Hollywood: Republic Pictures, 1943. Jack Mathis.

Government Agents vs. Phantom Legion. Hollywood: Republic Pictures, 1951. Jack Mathis.

The James Brothers of Missouri. Hollywood: Republic Pictures, 1950. Jack Mathis.

Jesse James Rides Again. Hollywood: Republic Pictures, 1947. Jack Mathis.

In Old Monterey. Hollywood: Republic Pictures, 1939. Jack Mathis.

King of the Cowboys. Hollywood: Republic Pictures, 1943. Jack Mathis.

King of the Mounties. Hollywood: Republic Pictures, 1942. Jack Mathis.

King of the Rocket Men. Hollywood: Republic Pictures, 1949. Jack Mathis.

Manhunt of Mystery Island. Hollywood: Republic Pictures. 1945. Jack Mathis.

The Masked Marvel. Hollywood: Republic Pictures, 1943. Jack Mathis.

My Pal Trigger. Hollywood: Republic Pictures, 1946. Jack Mathis.

The Purple Monster Strikes. Hollywood: Republic Pictures, 1945. Jack Mathis.

Rovin' Tumbleweeds. Hollywood: Republic Pictures, 1939. Jack Mathis.

Secret Service in Darkest Africa. Hollywood: Republic Pictures, 1943. Jack Mathis.

South of the Border. Hollywood: Republic Pictures, 1939. Jack Mathis.

Springtime in the Sierras. Hollywood: Republic Pictures, 1947. Jack Mathis.
Spy Smasher. Hollywood: Republic Pictures, 1942. Jack Mathis.
Zombies of the Stratosphere. Hollywood: Republic Pictures, 1952. Jack Mathis.

Miscellaneous Republic Pictures, Inc. Material
Republic Pictures: 16 MM Program. Hollywood: Republic Pictures, [1950]. Author's collection.
Republic Reporter, The. Company journal. I (April 11, 1939): 11 to I (January 9, 1940): 37. Alan Barbour. Kew Gardens, New York.
Wood, Thomas. "Corn in the Can." Manuscript. 1941. In the Serials clipping file at the Margaret Herrick Library of the Academy of Motion Picture Arts and Sciences. Los Angeles.
Yates, Herbert J. *The Red Menace*. Promotional brochure. Hollywood: Republic Pictures, 1949. Author's collection.
Yates, Herbert J. *Republic Pictures Corporation Annual Report*. January 31, 1951. Hollywood: Republic Pictures, 1951. Author's collection.

Films Views
(Listed Chronologically within Subject)

Serials
Undersea Kingdom (1936).
SOS Coast Guard (1937).
Fighting Devil Dogs (1938).
Daredevils of the Red Circle (1939).
Dick Tracy's G-Men (1939).
Zorro's Fighting Legion (1939).
Mysterious Doctor Satan (1940).
Adventures of Captain Marvel (1941).
Spy Smasher (1942).
Perils of Nyoka (1942).
G-Men vs. the Black Dragon (1943).
The Masked Marvel (1943).
Captain America (1944).
The Tiger Woman (1944).
Manhunt of Mystery Island (1945).
The Purple Monster Strikes (1945).
Daughter of Don Q (1946).
The Black Widow (1947).
King of the Rocket Men (1949).
Flying Disc Man from Mars (1951).
Zombies of the Stratosphere (1952).

Canadian Mounties vs. Atomic Invaders (1953).
Panther Girl of the Kongo (1955).

B Series Films

Hit the Saddle—Three Mesquiteers (1937).
New Frontier—Three Mesquiteers (1939).
Tumbling Tumbleweeds—Gene Autry (1935).
The Big Show—Gene Autry (1936).
In Old Monterey—Gene Autry (1939).
Sioux City Sue—Gene Autry (1946).
Under Western Stars—Roy Rogers (1938)
Bells of Rosarita—Roy Rogers (1945).
Don't Fence Me In—Roy Rogers (1945).
My Pal Trigger—Roy Rogers (1946).
Home in Oklahoma—Roy Rogers (1946).
Scatterbrain—Judy Canova (1940).
Roy Rogers Presents the Great Movie Cowboys. Syndicated television series of B
    Western movies shown on WNED-TV. Buffalo, New York. Fall 1976–Spring
    1977. National Telefilm Associates.

A Films

Man of Conquest (1939).
Dark Command (1940).
Wake of the Red Witch (1948).
Macbeth (1948).
Sands of Iwo Jima (1949).
The Quiet Man (1952).
Johnny Guitar (1954).

Soundtrack Tapes
(Listed Chronologically)

Adventures of Captain Marvel. (1941). Tape of soundtrack in author's collection.
Spy Smasher. (1942). Tape of soundtrack in author's collection.
G-Men vs. the Black Dragon. (1943). Tape of soundtrack in author's collection.
D Day on Mars (feature version of *The Purple Monster Strikes*). (1945). Tape of sound-
    track in author's collection.
Lost Planet Airmen (feature version of *King of the Rocket Men*). (1949). Tape of sound-
    track in author's collection.
Missile Monsters (feature version of *Flying Disc Man from Mars*). (1951). Tape of
    soundtrack in author's collection.

Interviews

Abel, Walter. Actor. New York. Interview by Milton Plesur, Professor of History, State University of New York at Buffalo and author. March 1, 1976.

Abrams, Morris R. Republic script supervisor and assistant director. Los Angeles. May 17, 1976.

Alyn, Kirk. Republic actor. Los Angeles. May 11, 1976.

Barry, Donald "Red." Republic actor. Los Angeles. May 6, 1976.

Bennet, Spencer G. Republic director. Los Angeles. May 10, 1976.

Bennett, Bruce. Republic actor. Los Angeles. Telephone interview. May 7, 1976.

Bernds, Edward. Columbia director. Los Angeles. May 6, 1976.

Booth, Adrian. Republic actress. Newton, Pennsylvania. May 2006.

Canova, Judy. Republic actress. Los Angeles. Interview by Milton Plesur, Professor of History, State University of New York at Buffalo and author. May 15, 1976.

Chapman, Marguerite. Republic actress. Los Angeles. Interview by Milton Plesur, Professor of History, State University of New York at Buffalo and author. May 15, 1976.

Glut, Donald F. Movie historian and television writer. Los Angeles. May 10, 1976.

Hagner, John. Stuntman director of Stuntman's Hall of Fame. Los Angeles. Telephone interview. May 10, 1976.

Hall, Mark. Instructor, Chico State College. Los Angeles. May 15, 1976.

Harmon, Jim. Writer. Los Angeles. May 10, 1976.

Hills, Rowland "Dick." Republic business office manager. Los Angeles. May 13, 1976.

Kirkpatrick, Ernest. National Telefilm Associates, Technical Services and Republic's Hollywood Television Service Division. Los Angeles. May 12, 1976.

Lamparski, Richard. Writer. Los Angeles. Telephone interview. May 6, 1976.

Livingston, Robert. Republic actor. Los Angeles. Telephone interview. May 8, 1976.

Lydecker, Theodore. Republic special effects expert. Los Angeles. May 17, 1976.

Nibley, Sloan. Republic writer. Los Angeles. May 4, 1976.

Ralston, Vera Hruba (Mrs. Charles Alva). Republic actress. Santa Barbara, California. Telephone interview. May 10, 1976.

Rogell, Albert S. Republic director. Los Angeles. May 5, 1976.

Rush, Art. Roy Rogers' manager. Los Angeles. Telephone interview. May 6, 1976.

Sharpe, David. Republic stuntman. Los Angeles. Interview by Mark Hall for the American Film Institute. August, 1976.

Shipman, Barry. Republic writer. San Bernardino, California. May 11, 1976.

Siegel, Sol C. Republic producer. Los Angeles. Telephone interview. May 5, 1976.

Slide, Anthony. Film scholar. American Film Institute. Buffalo, New York. January 18, 1975.

Stewart, Peggy. Republic actress. Los Angeles. May 18, 1976.

Stirling, Linda. Republic actress. Los Angeles. May 13, 1976.

Waggoner, Rex. National Telefilm Associates, Publicity Director. Los Angeles. May 12, 1976.

White, William. Associate Professor, Chico State College. Chico, California May 15, 1976.

Newspaper Articles

"Allege 18 Vera Ralston Films Flopped: Movie Head Sued Over Actress-Wife," *New York Herald Tribune*, October 30, 1956.

"Asks Receiver for Republic Film Studio," *New York Post*, August 20, 1958.

"Atlanta Gets Brief Look at J. Canova," *Atlanta* (Georgia) *Constitution*, January 19, 1942.

Buckley, Tom, "'The Day of the locust': Hollywood, by West, by Hollywood," *New York Times Magazine*, June 2, 1974, pp. 10–13.

"C.B.S. Buys Studio," *New York Times*, February 24, 1967.

"C.B.S. Gets 10-Year Lease on Coast Republic Studio," *New York Times*, May 4, 1963.

"Carr, Johnston Leaving Outfit," *Variety*, December 18, 1936.

Darst, Stephen, "Old Film Serial Director Decries Sex and Violence in Movies of Today," *St. Louis Review*, n. d. [1975].

"Exhibs Seize on Serials to Woo Tots Away from Telesets," *Variety*, November 9, 1950.

"Exit (As Expected) of Republic from MPEA First in O'Seas Body's History," *Variety*, December 11, 1957.

"Fading, Fading—One-Man Rule; Yates' Republic Exit Latest Instance," *Variety*, July 8, 1959.

"Figure Skating Bug Hits Republic Head," *New York Morning Telegraph*, June 14, 1941.

"Film Group Changes Its Corporate Name," *New York Times*, April 13, 1935.

"Film Guilds Warn Republic Studios," *New York Times*, January 22, 1958.

"Film Partners in Quick Rise," *New York World-Telegraph*, April 27, 1935.

"Fred Brannon" (Obituary), *Variety*, April 15, 1953.

"Gene Autry of Westerns Goes Over Big with Fans," *New York World-Telegraph*, May 14, 1938.

"Gene Autry's Advice to Youth in Wartime." Unidentified Sunday supplement article, *circa* 1942. In the Theatrical Section of the New York Public Library.

Greenbaum, Lucy, "Sinatra in a Sombrero," *New York Times Magazine*, November 4, 1945, p. 42.

Haber, Joyce, "Roy's Not Ready to Ride into the Sunset," *Los Angeles Times*, Calendar, April 21, 1974.

Hanna, David, "The Little Acorn Has Grown," *New York Times*, February 2, 1941.

Haugland, Vern, "Don Barry Is Western Star No. 5 After Short, Swift Rise in Films." Unidentified newspaper, November 8, 1942. In the Donald Barry clipping file at the Theatrical Section of the New York Public Library.

"Hedda Hopper's Hollywood," *Los Angeles Times*, May 31, 1942.

"Herbert Yates" (Obituary), *Variety*, February 9, 1966.

"Herbert Yates, Founder of Republic Pictures" (Obituary), *New York Herald Tribune*, February 5, 1966.

"Herbert Yates of Republic Films, Developer of Cowboy Stars, Dies" (Obituary), *New York Times*, February 5, 1966.

Hirshey, Gerri, "Roy Rogers Rides Again," *The New York Sunday News*, Leisure, December 28, 1975.

"Home, Home on the Ranch," *Atlanta* (Georgia) *Constitution*, *This Week*, June 14, 1942, p. 14.

"Ideas: Spy Smasher Triumphs Again," *Edwardsville* (Illinois) *Intelligencer*, November 29, 1973.

"In the Big Time," *New York Times*, September 7, 1941.

"Investors Sue Yates," *New York Times*, October 30, 1956.

"'King of the Serials' to do 100th Film," *New York Herald Tribune*, October 31, 1952.

Levitas, Louise, "A Stranger in Pitchman's Gulch: Roy Rogers, the Cowboy Star, Gets Not a Tumble, Despite Full Regalia," *PM*, May 20, 1941.

"Little Dogies Git Along," *New York Times*, August 4, 1940.

Martinez, Al, "Roy Rogers and Gene Autry: Two Old-Time Cowboy Stars Reflect a Heroic Age," *Los Angeles Times*, February 27, 1977, see. CC, Part II, pp. 3, 5–6.

"Myers, Rembusch Blast Rep on Plan for Selling to TV," *Variety*, June 13, 1951.

"New Suit Seeks Liquidation of Republic Pic," *Variety*, August 27, 1958.

"New Supplier of 'Kid Matinee' Pies," *Variety*, July 12, 1974.

"News of the Screen," *New York Sun*, July 8, 1936.

Parsons, Louella O., "In Hollywood—Vera Ralston," *New York Journal American*, February 8, 1943.

Pelswick, Rose, "Republic Steps Up with Texas Epic," *New York Journal American*, April 23, 1939.

"Plastics the Charmer in Bettered Earnings Picture for Republic," *Variety*, October 12, 1960.

Redelings, Lowell E., "The Hollywood Scene: Men Behind the Scenes," *Hollywood Citizen-News*, July 21, 1952.

"Rep's Old Pix in 'New' Dress," *Variety*, February 10, 1954.

"Rep's Sale to TV Cues Interest in Wall Street," *Variety*, June 13, 1951.

"Republic Aims Its Films at Heart of America," *Variety*, Ninth Anniversary Edition, October 29, 1942.

"Republic Doubles Budget for '52–53," *New York Times*, July 23, 1952.

"Republic Enters Field of Feature Pictures," *New York World Telegraph*, July 13, 1938.

"Republic Film Plans," *New York Times*, October 3, 1953.

"Republic Is Adding Four Sound Stages," *New York Times*, June 16, 1953.

"Republic Okays Old Films for Tele; Editing, Rescoring to Fit TV Needs," *Variety*, June 13, 1951.

"Republic Pictures Plans 50 Features in Season," *New York Herald Tribune*, April 6, 1939.

"Republic Pictures to Spend $2,500,000," *New York Times*, February 18, 1942.

"Republic Pictures Upheld in Autry, Rogers Suits," *Wall Street Journal*, June 9, 1964.

"Republic Plans Major Scale Return to TV Productions; Seeks Key Men," *Variety*, August 9, 1959.

"Republic Raises Production List," *New York Times*, February 3, 1965.

"Republic Sets Biggest Slate," *New York Morning Telegraph*, March 4, 1941.

"Republic Sets Budget for Features, Westerns, Serials," *New York Sun*, February 28, 1941.

"Republic Starts Cutback in Staff," *New York Times*, May 23, 1956.

"Republic Stepping High," *Variety*, Tenth Anniversary Edition, October 29, 1943, p. 456.

"Republic Studio to Resume Work," *New York Times*, January 8, 1957.

"Republic Studios Continue to Grow," *New York Times*, August 17, 1954.

"Republic Studios Expanding Plant," *New York Times*, June 14, 1957.

"Republic to Make 22 'De Luxe' Films," *New York Times*, January 14, 1954.

"Republic to Offer Independents Aid," *New York Times*, September 11, 1953.

"Republic to Rent Top Films to TV," *New York Times*, January 13, 1956.

"Republic Will Turn Out Escape Films, Says Yates," *New York World-Telegraph*, September 9, 1939.

"Republic's Bright New Outlook; Carter Quips About Old Nepotism," *Variety*, November 30, 1960.

"Republic's Chief, H. J. Yates Discusses Independent Pix," *New York Post*, May 2, 1939.

Roberts, William, "Cliffhangers," *Los Angeles Times*, November 20, 1946.

"Serials: Continued This Week," *Los Angeles Times*, January 20, 1965.

Shlyen, Ben, "For Present and Future," *Box Office*, January 15, 1968.

"62 Feature Films Listed by Republic," *New York Times*, May 30, 1940.

"Stockholder Sues to Close Republic Films," *New York Daily News*, August 20, 1958.

"Strongly Reported, Flatly Denied: Richard Altschuler Denies Republic Closedown of Domestic Branches," *Variety*, February 12, 1958.

"Studio Enjoins Gene Autry: Says 'Horse Opera' Star Ran Away to Go on the Stage," *New York Herald Tribune*, February 4, 1938.

"Suit Calls Film Tycoon's Wife 9-1 Floperooll," *New York Daily News*, October 30, 1956.

"Theatrical Cliffhanger Serials of Yesteryear Still Sell 'Far Out,'" *Variety*, February 12, 1964.

Thirer, Irene, "It's Vera Ralston Now—Republic's Queen Takes 'Rib,'" *New York Post*, June 4, 1946.

"30 Writers Working at Repub, New High," *Variety*, August 16, 1939.

Thomas, Bob, "Roy Rogers Finds Happy Trails Far from the Movie Industry," *Los Angeles Times*, January 6, 1975.

"200G Rep Deal Releasing 104 Pix for TV Seen Breaking Log Jam," *Variety*, December 17, 1952.

"Two Old Cowboys Still Ride High," *Buffalo Courier-Express*, March 1, 1977.

"TV-Movie Tie-Ins Remain Confused," *New York Times*, May 15, 1952.

"Vera Ralston Finds Court's for Courting," *New York World Telegram and Sun*, June 15, 1962.

Whalen, David B., "Republic Pictures," *The Film Daily Cavalcade*, 1939, pp. 176–182. In the Republic Pictures clipping file at the Margaret Herrick Library of the Academy of Motion Picture Arts and Sciences. Los Angeles.

Wood, Thomas, "The Sad State of the Serial," *New York Times*, December 22, 1946.

"Writers Strike vs. Republic on TV Residuals," *Variety*, February 19, 1958.

Yates, Herbert J., "Top-Cost Pix Shed," *Variety*, January 7, 1953.

"Yates Wants Better B's from Republic," *Variety*, February 22, 1939.

Newspaper Use of Republic Advertisement for Special Films

Elwood (Indiana) *Call-Leader*, October 15, 1942; October 20, 1942; November 20, 1942; December 16, 1943; February 4, 1944; April 21, 1944; May 9, 10, 11, 1944; July 27, 1944; August 22, 1944; November 9, 1944; August 23, 1945; February 14, 1946; October 1, 1946; October 3, 1946; November 21, 1946; December 13, 1946; February 14, 1947; January 20, 1949.

Kokomo (Indiana) *Tribune*, June 10, 1943; June 11, 1943; December 16, 1943; March 30, 31, 1944; May 4, 1944; June 22, 23, 24, 1944; June 12, 1947; October 9, 1947; November 13, 1947; February 12, 1948; June 9, 1949; January 5, 1951; January 19, 1952.

Reviews of Movies

Apache Rose. *New York Times*, July 23, 1947.

Arkansas Judge. Atlanta (Georgia) *Constitution*, February 20, 1942.

Boots and Saddles. *New York Times*, November 8, 1937.

Call the Mesquiteers. *New York Times*, March 12, 1938.

Calling All Stars (Broadway theatrical play). *New York Times*, December 14, 1934.

Chatterbox. *New York Times*, July 2, 1943.

Crowther, Bosley. *My Pal Trigger*. *New York Times*, August 17, 1946.

Crowther, Bosley. *The Red Menace*. *New York Times*, June 27, 1949.

Crowther, Bosley. *Sis Hopkins*. *New York Times*, May 1, 1941.

Crowther, Bosley. *Swing Your Lady*. *New York Times*, January 27, 1938.

Fair Wind to Java. *New York Times*, August 28, 1953.

Hartung, Philip T. *London Blackout Murders*. *Commonweal*. XXXVIII (January 22, 1943): 351.

Heart of the Golden West. *Box Office*, November 16, 1942.

Heart of the Golden West. *Variety*, November 16, 1942.

Hi Ho Silver. *New York Post*, July 25, 1940.

Hit Parade. *New York Times*, May 31, 1937.

Hit Parade of 1941. *New York Times*, August 18, 1940.

Hit Parade of 1943. *New York Times*, April 16, 1943.

Hit Parade of 1947. *New York Times*, May 5, 1947.

Hit the Saddle. Variety, August 4, 1957.

Honeychile. Variety, 1951. Undated clipping in the Judy Canova clipping file at the Margaret Herrick Library of the Academy of Motion Picture Arts and Sciences. Los Angeles.

Ice Capades. Atlanta (Georgia) *Constitution*, January 1, 1942.

In Old Monterey. Variety, August 4, 1939.

King of the Cowboys. Box Office, April 5, 1943.

Manhattan Merry-Go-Round. New York Times, December 31, 1937.

Melody Ranch. New York Times, December 26, 1940.

Mishkin, Leo, *Rookies on Parade. New York Morning Telegraph*, May 22, 1941.

Mortimer, Lee, *Remember Pearl Harbor. New York Daily Mirror*, June 4, 1942.

My Wife's Relatives. Photoplay. LII (May, 1939): 63.

The President's Mystery. New York Times, October 4, 1936.

Rags to Riches. New York News, November 8, 1941.

Remember Pearl Harbor. New York Times, June 4, 1942.

Rovin' Tumbleweeds. Motion Picture Herald, November 25, 1939.

Santa Fe Stampede. New York Times, April 26, 1939.

Scatterbrain. Variety, August 4, 1940.

Sioux City Sue. New York Times, July 23, 1947.

South of the Border. Motion Picture Herald, December 16, 1939.

Stranger at My Door. Hollywood Reporter, April 14, 1956.

Stranger at My Door. Variety, April 14, 1956.

Three Texas Steers. Variety, July 2, 1939.

Under Western Stars. New York Times, June 25, 1938.

Utah. New York Times, March 12, 1945.

Winsten, Archer, *Rocky Mountain Rangers. New York Post*, June 27, 1940.

Winsten, Archer, *The Sombrero Kid. New York Post*, September 30, 1942.

Women in War. Photoplay, LIV (July, 1940): 61.

Women in War. Time, XXXV (June 17, 1940): 86.

Journal and Periodical Articles

Adams, Leo, ed. *Yesterday's Saturdays.* No. 1 (1972) to No. 6 (1975).

Barbour, Alan G., ed. *Screen Ads Monthly.* I (October, 1967): 1 to I (January, 1968): 4.

Barbour, Alan G. *Screen Nostalgia Illustrated.* No. I to No. 8 (1975).

Barbour, Alan G. *Serial Pictorial.* No. 1 to No. 8 (n. d.).

Barbour, Alan G., ed. *Serial Quarterly.* No. 1 (January–March, 1966) to No. 7 (July–September, 1967).

Baskette, Kirkley. "Pay Boy of the Western World." *Photoplay.* LII (January, 1938): 327–328.

Beaumont, Charles. "Don't Miss the Next Thrilling Chapter!" *Show Business Illustrated.* I (March, 1962): pp. 52–56, 78–80.

Black, Gregory and Koppes, Clayton R. "OWI Goes to the Movies: The Bureau of Intelligence's Criticism of Hollywood, 1942–43." *Prologue: The Journal of the National Archives*. VI (Spring, 1974): 44–59.

Blair, Earl W., Jr. "Meanwhile . . . at Republic." *Film Collector's Registry*. No. 70. (November, 1976): 12–13.

Blair, Earl W., Jr. "Reminiscing with Henry Brandon." *Those Enduring Matinee Idols*. II (December, 1972–January, 1973): 291–292.

Blair, Earl W., Jr. "Republic Today!" *Film Collector's Registry*. No. 68 (September, 1976): 11.

Blair, Earl W., Jr. "Rocketman Flies Again." *Film Collector's Registry*, No. 69 (October, 1976): 11–13.

"A Chill in Hollywood." *Newsweek*. XLVIII (November 12, 1956): 116.

Cocchi, John. "The Films of Allan Lane." *Screen Facts*. No. 19. IV (1968): 50–53.

Cocchi, John. "The Films of Roy Rogers and Gene Autry." *Screen Facts*. No. 5. I (1963): 47–61.

Cohen, Joan. "The Second Feature: The Rise and Fall of the B Movie." *Mankind*. V (June, 1976): 26–35.

Collins, Alan. "Edward Ludwig: The Quiet Revolutionary." *Take One*. IV (May–June, 1972): 27–28.

Connor, Edward. "The First Eight Serials of Republic." *Screen Facts*. No. 7. II (1964): 52–61.

Connor, Edward. "The Golden Age of Republic Serials." *Screen Facts*. No. 17. III (1968): 48–61.

Connor, Edward. "The Golden Age of Republic Serials (Part 2)." *Screen Facts*. No. 18. III (1968): 20–35.

Connor, Edward. "The Three Mesquiteers." *Screen Facts*. I (1964): 52–61.

"Continued Next Week." *Screen Thrills Illustrated*. I (June, 1962): 16–29.

Coons, Minard. "An Interview with Peggy Stewart." *Film Collector's Registry*. No. 57 (November, 1975): 5–9.

Coons, Minard, and Easterling, Allan. "The Jolley Villain: An Interview with I. Stanford Jolley." *Film Collector's Registry*. No. 67 (September, 1976): 3–6.

Crichton, Kyle. "Hillbilly Judy." *Colliers*. CIX (May 16, 1942): 17, 62–63.

Davy, Daryl. "Davy on 16 MM: William Elliott." *Film Fan Monthly*. No. 94 (April, 1969): 17.

Danard [sic], Donald. "Bennet's Serials." *Films in Review*. XIV (October, 1963). 8: 509.

Daynard, Don. "The Film Music of Stanley Wilson." *The New Captain George's Whizzbang*. No. 17 (n.d.): 15.

Daynard, Don. "The Lydeckers: Masters of Miniature Mayhem." *The New Captain George's Whizzbang*. No. 16 (n.d.): 2–8.

Daynard, Don. "Master of Miniature Mayhem: Chapter Two." *The New Captain George's Whizzbang*. No. 17 (n.d.): 28–29.

Daynard, Don. "The Perils of Linda." *The New Captain George's Whizzbang*. No. 18 (n.d.): 8–14.

Daynard, Don. "Roy Barcroft—Best of the Badmen." *The New Captain George's Whizzbang.* No. 7 (n.d.): 2–5.

Daynard, Don. "Shooting Down Some B-Western Myths." *The New Captain George's Whizzbang.* No. 18 (n.d.): 32.

Dorr, John H. "Allan Dwan." *Take One.* IV (May–June, 1972): 8–9.

"Double Mint Ranch." *Time Magazine.* XXXV (January 15, 1940): 47–48.

Dyer, Peter John. "Those First Rate Second Features." *Films and Filming.* II (September, 1956): 17–18.

Eisenberg, Michael T. "A Relationship of Constrained Anxiety: Historians and Film." *History Teacher.* VI (1973): 553–568.

Elkin, Frederick. "The Psychological Appeal of the Hollywood Western." *The Journal of Educational Sociology.* XXIV (October, 1950): 72–86.

Emery, F. E. "Psychological Effects of the Western Film: A Study in Television Viewing." *Human Relations.* XII (1959): 195–231.

Everson, William K. Review of B Movies by Don Miller. *Films in Review.* XXV (November, 1974): 564–565.

Everson, William K. "Serials with Sound." *Films in Review.* IV (June–July, 1953): 270–276.

Everson, William K. "Stunt Men." *Films in Review.* VI (October, 1955): 394–402.

"Fallen Republic." *Time Magazine.* LXXXIX (April 14, 1958): 59.

Farber, Manny. "Movie in Wartime." *New Republic.* CX (January 3, 1944): 18–20.

Fernett, Gene. "An Interview with Theodore Lydecker." *Film Collector's Registry.* V (November, 1973): 1, 6.

Fernett, Gene. "Jack English Looks Back." *Classic Film Collector.* No. 21 (Summer, 1968): 52, 55.

Fernett, Gene. "Nat Levine: The Serial King." *Views and Reviews.* I (Summer, 1969): 22–31.

Fernett, Gene. "Spencer Gordon Bennett [sic] Biography Off the Press." *Classic Film Collector.* No. 36 (Fall, 1972): 63.

Folsom, James K. "Western Themes and Western Films." *Western American Literature.* II (1967): 195–203.

Friedman, Norman L. "Studying Film Impact on American Conduct and Culture." *Journal of Popular Film.* III (Spring, 1974): 173–181.

Geltzer, George. "40 Years of Cliffhanging." *Films in Review.* VII (February, 1957): 60–68.

"Gene Autry's Cowboy Dictionary." *TV Guide.* I (October 2, 1953): 8–9.

Glut, Don. "Interview: Tom Steele." *The Tom Crier.* I (n.d.): 2.

Goodman, Mark. "The Singing Cowboy." *Esquire.* LXXIII. (December, 1975): 154–155, 240, 245–248.

Hagner, John G., ed. *Falling for Stars Newsletter.* I (January, 1965): I to IV (January, 1968): 1.

Hagner, John G., ed. *News and Views: The Hollywood Stuntmen's Hall of Fame.* I (June 10, 1976): 10 to I (Fall, 1976): 15.

Hagner, John G. "Yak: Super Stuntman." *Classic Film Collector*. No. 18 (Summer, 1967): 13.

Harper, Mr. "After Hours: Falling Idol." *Harpers*. CC (January, 1950): 99–101.

Hewetson, Alan. "Comics in Cinema." *Cinema*. V (1969): 2–7.

Hoffman, Eric. "Saturday Matinee Spy Hunters of World War Two." *Serial World*. No. 1 (1974): 8–9.

Hoffman, Eric. "The Screen Avengers: The Comic Heroes of the Cliffhangers." *Mediascene*. No. 19 (May–June, 1976): 4–19.

Hoffman, Eric. "Undersea Kingdom." *Those Enduring Matinee Idols*. I (December, 1970–January, 1971): 90–93.

Hoffman, Eric, and Malcomson, Bob. "Drums of Fu Manchu." *Those Enduring Matinee Idols*. II (December, 1972–January, 1973): 284–290.

Hughes, Albert H. "Outlaw with a Halo." *Montana: The Magazine of Western History*. XVII (1967): 60–75.

Hughes, William. "The Propagandist's Art." *Film and History*. IV (September, 1974): 11–15.

Jackson, Greg, Jr. "Serial World Interviews Rocketman Tris Coffin." *Serial World*. No. 10 (Spring, 1977): 3–9.

Jameux, Charles. "William Witney and John English." *Positif*. No. 88 (October, 1967).

Johnston, Alva. "Tenor on Horseback." *Saturday Evening Post*. CCXII (September 2, 1939): 18–19, 74–75.

"Judy Comes Down the Hill." *Newsweek*. XXVI (December 17, 1945): 102–103.

Kelez, Steve. "Captain America." *Film Fan Monthly*. No. 61/62 (July/August, 1966): 25–26.

King, Barbara. "Through the Looking Glass." *Liberty*. I (Spring, 1974): 8.

"King of the Cowboys." *Newsweek*. XXI (March 8, 1943): 74–75.

Knauth, Percy. "Gene Autry, Inc." *Life*. XXIV (June 28, 1948): 88–100.

Koppes, Clayton R., and Black, Gregory D. "What to Show the World: The Office of War Information and Hollywood, 1942–1945." *The Journal of American History*, LXIV (June, 1977): 87–105.

Lackey, Wayne. "Sunset Carson." *Film Fan Monthly*. No. 92 (February, 1969): 20.

Langley, W. D. "William Witney." *Films in Review*. XXVII (June, 1976): 381.

"Linda Stirling's Fond Memories of the Serials." *The New Captain George's Whizzbang*. No. 18 (n.d.): 15.

Malcomson, Robert M. "The Sound Serial." *Views and Reviews*. III (Summer, 1971): 12–26.

Malcomson, Robert M. "Sound Serials of Yesteryear." *Yesteryear*. No. 1 (n.d.): 2–6.

Malcomson, Robert, ed. *Those Enduring Matinee Idols*. I (October–November, 1969): 1 to III (Chapter 29, 1974): 9.

Malcomson, Bob, and Hoffman, Eric. "King of the Royal Mounted." *Those Enduring Matinee Idols*. III (n.d.): 338–340.

Martin, Pete. "Cincinnati Cowboy." *Saturday Evening Post*. CCXVII (June 9, 1945): 26–27, 78, 80–81.

Meyer, Jim. "Vera Hruba Ralston." *Film Fan Monthly*. No. 83 (May, 1968): 3–8.

Michael, Earl. "The Serials of Republic." *Screen Facts*. I (1963): 52–64.

Miller, Don. "Roy Rogers." *The New Captain George's Whizzbang*. No. 14 (n.d.): 18–21.

Nevins, Francis M., Jr. "Ballet of Violence: The Films of William Witney." *Films in Review*. XXV (November, 1974): 523–545.

Nevins, Francis M., Jr. *Review of Kings of the B's*, edited by Todd McCarthy and Charles Flynn. *Films in Review*. XXVI (October, 1975): 499–500.

Oates, Stephen B. "Ghost Riders in the Sky." *Colorado Quarterly*. XXIII (Spring, 1974): 67–74.

Oehling, Richard A. "Germans in Hollywood Films: The Changing Image, 1914–1939." *Film and History*. III (May, 1973): 1–10, 26.

Oehling, Richard A. "Germans in Hollywood Films: The Changing Image, The Early Years, 1939–1942." *Film and History*. IV (May, 1974): 8–10.

Page, Alan. "Mixed Bag." *Sight and Sound*. VII (Autumn, 1938): 126.

"The Painted Stallion." *Those Enduring Matinee Idols*. I (April–May, 1971): 121–123.

Parkhurst, C. M. "Parky." "The Lone Ranger Rides Again." *Those Enduring Matinee Idols*. II (April–May, 1972): 218–221.

Powdermaker, Hortense. "An Anthropologist Looks at the Movies." *Annals of the American Academy of Political and Social Science*. CCLIV (November, 1947): 80–87.

Powdermaker, Hortense. "Hollywood and the U.S.A." In *Mass Culture: The Popular Arts in America*, pp. 278–293. Edited by Bernard Rosenberg and David Manning White, New York: The Free Press, 1957.

Prylock, Calvin. "Front Office, Box Office, and Artistic Freedom: An Aspect of the Film Industry 1945–1969." *Journal of Popular Film*. III (Fall, 1974): 294–305.

Rainey, Buck. "A Conversation with Linda Stirling, Sensuous Siren of the Serials." *Film Collector's Registry*. No. 71 (December, 1976): 3–7.

Reid, Ashton. "Hero on Horseback." *Colliers*. CXXII (July 24, 1948): 27, 62–65.

"Republic Pictures Celebrates Its Tenth Anniversary." *The Independent*. (June 23, 1945): 22–24, 30.

Sanford, Harry. "Joseph Kane: A Director's Story, Part I." *Views and Reviews*. V (September, 1973): 31–38.

Sanford, Harry. "Joseph Kane: A Director's Story, Concluded." *Views and Reviews*. V (December, 1973): 17–25.

Schlesinger, Arthur, Jr. "When Movies Really Counted." *Show: Magazine of the Arts*. I (April, 1963): 77–78, 125.

Scott, Diane. "Memory Wears Carnations." *Photoplay*. LXXII (May, 1949): 34–36.

Seeley, Wallace. "A Fond Look at Movie Stuntmen." *The New Captain George's Whizzbang*. No. 11 (n.d.): 8–12.

"Serial Discussion Panel." *Those Enduring Matinee Idols*. III (n.d.): 350–355.

Shain, Russell E. "Cold War Films, 1948–1962: An Annotated Filmography." *Journal of Popular Film*. III (Fall, 1974): 365–372.

Shain, Russell E. "Hollywood's Cold War." *Journal of Popular Film*. III (Fall, 1974): 334–350.

Sherman, Sam. "Republic Studios: Hollywood Thrill Factory." *Screen Thrills Illustrated*. I (January, 1963): 24–31.

Sherman, Sam. "Republic Studios: Hollywood Thrill Factory." *Screen Thrills Illustrated*. II (October, 1963): 12–17.

Shipley, Glenn. "King of the Serial Directors: Spencer Gordon Bennet." *Views and Reviews*. I (Fall, 1969): 5–22.

Shoenberger, Jim. "A Final Visit with Reed Hadley." *Film Collector's Registry*. VII (January, 1975): 5, 9.

Shoenberger, Jim. "An Interview with I. Stanford Jolley." *Film Collector's Registry*. VI (March, 1974): 1, 4.

Sklar, Robert. "A Broad Mosaic on the Social Screen." *American Films*. II (June, 1976): 73–74.

Small, Melvin. "Motion Pictures and the Study of Attitudes: Some Problems for Historians." *Film and History*. II (February, 1972): 1–5.

Smith, H. Allen. "King of the Cowboys." *Life*. XV (July 12, 1943): 47–54.

Spears, Jack. "2nd-Unit Directors." *Films in Review*. VI (March, 1955): 108–112.

"Spy Smasher Tops Serial Poll." *Film Collector's Registry*. No. 61. (February, 1976): 4.

Stephenson, Ron. "Concerning Serials and Trends." *Those Enduring Matinee Idols*. III (n.d.): 444–446.

Stumpf, Charles. "Judy Canovall." *Film Collector's Registry*. V (July, 1973): 5–6.

Stumpf, Charles. "Weaver Brothers and Elviry." *Film Collector's Registry*. V (May, 1973): 10.

Thomas, Bob. "Hollywood's General of the Armies." *True*. XXX (July, 1966): 47–48, 86–90.

Townsend, Shepherd. "William Whitney [sic]." *Films in Review*. XXVII (March, 1976). 190–191.

Trewin, J. C. "One Thing After Another: Being a Discourse on Serials." *Sight and Sound*. XVI (Autumn, 1947): 106–107.

Tuska, Jon. "From the 100 Finest Westerns: Dark Command." *Views and Reviews*. I (Winter, 1970): 48–53.

Tuska, Jon. "From the 100 Finest Westerns: The Lightning Warrior." *Views and Reviews*. II (Spring, 1971): 49–55.

Tuska, Jon. "In Retrospect: Tim McCoy, Last of Four Parts." *Views and Reviews*. II (Spring, 1971): 12–41.

Tuska, Jon. "Overland with Kit Carson—A Cinematography." *Those Enduring Matinee Idols*. II (June–July, 1971): 146–148.

Tuska, Jon. "Overland with Kit Carson—A Cinematography." *Those Enduring Matinee Idols*. II (August–September, 1971): 163–165.

Tuska, Jon. "The Vanishing Legion." *Views and Reviews*. III (Fall, 1971): 16–33.

Tuska, Jon. "The Vanishing Legion." *Views and Reviews*. III (Winter, 1972 [1971]): 10–26.

Tuska, Jon. "The Vanishing Legion." *Views and Reviews*. III (Spring, 1972): 22–39.

Tuska, Jon. "The Vanishing Legion." *Views and Reviews*. IV (Fall, 1972): 56–79.

Tuska, Jon. "The Vanishing Legion." *Views and Reviews*. IV (Winter, 1972): 34–52.

Tuska, Jon. "The Vanishing Legion." *Views and Reviews*. IV (Spring, 1973): 28–47.

Tuska, Jon. "The Vanishing Legion." *Views and Reviews*. IV (Summer, 1973): 64–68.

Van Hise, James. "Spy Smasher." *Film Collector's Registry*. VII (February, 1972): 9–13.

Walton, Jeff, ed. *Serial World*. No. 1 (1974) to No. 10 (Spring, 1977).

Woll, Allen L. "Hollywood's Good Neighbor Policy: The Latin Image in American Film, 1939–1946." *Journal of Popular Film*. III (Fall, 1974): 278–293.

Woll, Allen L. "Latin Images in American Films, 1929–1939." *Journal of Mexican American History*. IV (Spring, 1974): 28–40.

Zeitlin, David. "The Great General Slays 'Em Again." *Life*. XLII (May 27, 1966): 93–98.

Books

Adventures of Captain Marvel. Cliffhanger Ending and Escape Pictorial. Northbrook, Illinois: Jack Mathis Advertising, n.d.

Adventures of Red Ryder. Cliffhanger Ending and Escape Pictorial. Northbrook, Illinois: Jack Mathis Advertising, n.d.

Allen, Frederick Lewis. *Since Yesterday: The 1930s in America: September 3, 1929– September 3, 1939*. New York: Harper and Row, 1939.

Alyn, Kirk. *A Job for Superman*. Los Angeles: by the author, Hollywood, California, 1971.

Barbour, Alan G. *Cliffhanger: A Pictorial History of the Motion Picture Serial*. New York: A and W Publications, 1977.

Barbour, Alan G. *Days of Thrills and Adventure*. New York: Macmillan and Company, 1970.

Barbour, Alan G., ed. *Days of Thrills and Adventure*. 2 Vols. Kew Gardens, New York: Screen Facts Press, 1968–1969.

Barbour, Alan G., ed. *Great Serial Ads*. Kew Gardens, New York: Screen Facts Press, 1965.

Barbour, Alan G., ed. *High Roads to Adventure*. Kew Gardens, New York: Screen Facts Press, 1971.

Barbour, Alan G., ed. *Hit the Saddle*. Kew Gardens, New York: Screen Facts Press, 1969.

Barbour, Alan G., ed. *Movie Ads of the Past, No. 1: The B Western*. Kew Gardens, New York: Screen Facts Press, 1966.

Barbour, Alan G., ed. *Old Movies 1: The B Western*. Kew Gardens, New York: Screen Facts Press, 1969.

Barbour, Alan G., ed. *Old Movies 2: The Serial*. Kew Gardens, New York: Screen Facts Press, 1969.

Barbour, Alan G., ed. *Old Movies 3: The B Western.* Kew Gardens, New York: Screen Facts Press, 1970.

Barbour, Alan G., ed. *Old Movies 4: The Serial.* Kew Gardens, New York: Screen Facts Press, 1970.

Barbour, Alan G., ed. *The Serial.* 4 Vols. Kew Gardens, New York: Screen Facts Press, 1967–1971.

Barbour, Alan G., ed. *Serial Favorites.* Kew Gardens, New York: Screen Facts Press, 1971.

Barbour, Alan G., ed. *Serial Showcase.* Kew Gardens, New York: Screen Facts Press, 1968.

Barbour, Alan G. *The Serials of Columbia.* Kew Gardens, New York: Screen Facts Press, 1967.

Barbour, Alan G. *The Serials of Republic.* Kew Gardens, New York: Screen Facts Press, 1965.

Barbour, Alan G. *A Thousand and One Delights.* New York: Collier Books, 1971.

Barbour, Alan G., ed. *A Thousand Thrills.* Kew Gardens, New York: Screen Facts Press, 1971.

Barbour, Alan G., ed. *Thrill After Thrill.* Kew Gardens, New York: Screen Facts Press, 1971.

Barbour, Alan G. *The Thrill of It All.* New York: Collier Books, 1971.

Barbour, Alan G., ed. *Trail to Adventure.* Kew Gardens, New York: Screen Facts Press, 1971.

Barbour, Alan G., ed. *The Wonderful World of B-Films.* Kew Gardens, New York: Screen Facts Press, 1968.

Baxter, John. *STUNT: The Story of the Great Movie Stunt Men.* Garden City, New York: Doubleday and Company, Inc., 1974.

Behlmer, Rudy, ed. *Memo from David O. Selznick.* New York: The Viking Press, 1972.

Behlmer, Rudy, and Thomas, Tony. *Hollywood's Hollywood The Movies About the Movies.* Secaucus, New Jersey: The Citadel Press, 1975.

Bergman, Andrew. *We're in the Money: Depression America and Its Films.* New York: Harper and Row, 1971.

Blair, Earl, ed. *Western Corral.* No. 1. Houston, Texas: by the author, 1976.

Blum, Daniel. *Screen World 1949.* New York: Greenberg Publisher, 1950.

Blumer, Herbert, and Hauser, Philip M. *Movies, Delinquency, and Crime.* The Payne Fund Studies Series. New York: The Macmillan Company: reprint ed., New York: Arno Press and the *New York Times,* 1970.

Bogdanovich, Peter. *Allan Dwan: The Last Pioneer.* New York: Praeger, 1971.

Bogdanovich, Peter. *Fritz Lang in America.* New York: Frederick A. Praeger, Inc., 1967.

Brosnan, John. *James Bond in the Cinema.* London: The Tantivy Press, 1972.

Brosnan, John. *Movie Magic: The Story of Special Effects in the Cinema.* New York: St. Martin's Press, 1974.

Calder, Jenni. *There Must Be a Lone Ranger: The American West in Film and in Reality.* New York: Taplinger Publishing Company, 1975.

Captain America. Cliffhanger Ending and Escape Pictorial. Northbrook, Illinois: Jack Mathis Advertising, n.d.

Cawelti, John G. *The Six-Gun Mystique.* Bowling Green, Ohio: Bowling Green University Popular Press, 1975.

Corneau, Ernest N. *The Hall of Fame of Western Film Stars.* North Quincy, Massachusetts: The Christopher Publishing House, 1969.

Dardis, Tom. *Some Time in the Sun.* New York: Charles Scribner's Sons, 1976.

Daredevils of the Red Circle. Cliffhanger Ending and Escape Pictorial. Northbrook, Illinois: Jack Mathis Advertising, n.d.

Daredevils of the West. Cliffhanger Ending and Escape Pictorial. Northbrook, Illinois: Jack Mathis Advertising, n.d.

Drums of Fu Manchu. Cliffhanger Ending and Escape Pictorial. Northbrook, Illinois: Jack Mathis Advertising, n.d.

Everson, William K. *The Bad Guys: A Pictorial History of the Movie Villain.* New York: Bonanza Books, 1964.

Everson, William K. *A Pictorial History of the Western Film.* New York: The Citadel Press, 1969.

Eyles, Allen. *John Wayne and the Movies.* Cranbury, New Jersey: A. S. Barnes, 1976.

Eyles, Allen. *The Western.* Cranbury, New Jersey: A. S. Barnes and Company, 1975.

Fenin, George N., and Everson, William K. *The Western: From Silents to Cinerama.* New York: Bonanza Books, 1962.

Fernett, Gene. *Next Time Drive off the Cliff!* Cocoa, Florida: Cinememories Publishing Company, 1968.

Fernett, Gene. *Poverty Row.* Satellite Beach, Florida: Coral Reef Publications, Inc., 1973.

Film Daily Yearbook of Motion Pictures: 1944. New York: Film Daily, Inc., 1945.

Film Daily Yearbook of Motion Pictures: 1946. New York: Film Daily, Inc., 1947.

Forman, Henry James. *Our Movie Made Children.* The Payne Fund Studies Series. New York: The Macmillan Company, 1935; reprint ed., New York: Arno Press and the *New York Times*, 1970.

Freulich, Roman, and Abramson, Joan. *Forty Years in Hollywood: Portraits of a Golden Age.* Cranbury, New Jersey: A. S. Barnes, 1971.

Gertner, Richard, ed. *1975 International Motion Picture Almanac.* New York: Quigley Publishing Company, 1975.

Gertner, Richard, ed. *1975 International Television Almanac.* New York: Quigley Publishing Company, 1975.

Golden Age of Serials, The. Catalog No. 474. New York: Ivy Film, n.d.

Greenberg, Harvey R. *The Movies on Your Mind.* New York: Saturday Review Press, 1975.

Hagner, John G. *Falling for Stars.* Vol 1. Los Angeles: El' Jon Publications, 1964.

Hagner, John G. *The Greatest Stunts Ever.* Los Angeles: El' Jon Publications, 1967.

Handel, Leo A. *Hollywood Looks at Its Audience: A Report of Film Audience Research.* Urbana, Illinois: The University of Illinois Press, 1950.

Harmon, Jim, and Glut, Donald F. *The Great Movie Serials: Their Sound and Fury.* Garden City, New York: Doubleday and Company, Inc., 1972.

Harris, Charles W., and Rainey, Buck, ed. *The Cowboy: Six-Shooters, Songs, and Sex.* Norman, Oklahoma: University of Oklahoma Press, 1975.

Horwitz, James. *They Went Thataway.* New York: E. P. Dutton and Company, Inc., 1976.

Jowett, Garth. *Film: The Democratic Art.* Boston: Little, Brown and Company, 1976.

Karpf, Stephen Louis. *The Gangster Film: Emergence, Variation, and Decay of a Genre 1930–1940.* Dissertations on Film Series. New York: Arno Press, 1973.

King of the Mounties. Cliffhanger Ending and Escape Pictorial. Northbrook, Illinois: Jack Mathis Advertising, n.d.

Kitses, Jim. *Horizons West: Anthony Mann, Budd Boetticher, Sam Peckinpah: Studies on Authorship Within the Western.* Bloomington, Indiana: Indiana University Press, 1969.

Lahue, Kalton C. *Bound and Gagged: The Story of the Silent Serials.* New York: Castle Books, 1968.

Lahue, Kalton C. *Continued Next Week: A History of the Moving Picture Serial.* Norman, Oklahoma: University of Oklahoma Press, 1964.

Lahue, Kalton C. *Riders of the Range: The Sagebrush Heroes of the Sound Screen.* New York: Castle Books, 1973.

Lamparski, Richard. *Lamparski's Whatever Became of . . . ?* Giant 1st Annual. New York: Bantam Books, 1976.

Lamparski, Richard. *Whatever Became of . . . ?* I and II. New York: Crown Publishers, Inc., 1967.

Lamparski, Richard. *Whatever Became of . . . ?* The New Fifth Series. New York: Bantam Books, 1974.

Lingeman, Richard R. *Don't You Know There's a War On? The American Home Front 1941–1945.* New York: G. P. Putnam's Sons, 1970.

Lupoff, Dick, and Thompson, Don, ed. *All in Color for a Dime.* New Rochelle, New York: Arlington House, 1970.

Lynd, Robert S., and Lynd, Helen Merrell. *Middletown: A Study in American Culture.* New York: Harcourt, Brace and World. Inc., 1929.

Maltin, Leonard. *The Great Movie Shorts.* New York: Crown Publishers, Inc., 1972.

Maltin, Leonard. *Movie Comedy Teams.* New York: The New American Library, Inc., 1970.

Maltin, Leonard, ed. *The Real Stars: Articles and Interviews on Hollywood's Great Character Actors.* The Curtis Film Series. New York: Curtis Books, 1969.

Maltin, Leonard, ed. *The Real Stars # 2: Articles and Interviews on Hollywood's Great Character Actors.* The Curtis Film Series. New York: Curtis Books, 1972.

Manchester, William. *The Glory and the Dream: A Narrative History of America 1932–1972.* Boston: Little, Brown and Company, 1973.

Martin, Olga J. *Hollywood's Movie Commandments: A Handbook for Motion Picture Writers and Reviewers*. New York: H. Wilson, 1937; reprint ed., New York: Arno Press, 1975.

Mathis, Jack. *Valley of the Cliffhangers*. Northbrook, Illinois: Jack Mathis Advertising, 1975.

McCarthy, Todd, and Flynn, Charles, ed. *Kings of the Bs: Working Within the Hollywood System: An Anthology of Film History and Criticism*. New York: E. P. Dutton and Company, Inc., 1975.

McClure, Arthur F., and Jones, Ken D. *Heroes, Heavies and Sagebrush: A Pictorial History of the "B" Western Players*. Cranbury, New Jersey: A. S. Barnes and Company, Inc., 1972.

Michael, Paul, ed. *The American Movies Reference Book: The Sound Era*. Englewood Cliffs, New Jersey: Prentice-Hall, Inc., 1969.

Munsterberg, Hugo. *The Film: A Psychological Study: The Silent Photoplay in 1916*. New York: D. Appleton and Company, 1916; reprint ed., New York: Dover Publications, 1970.

Mysterious Doctor Satan. Northbrook, Illinois: Jack Mathis Advertising, n.d.

Nachbar, Jack, ed. *Focus on the Western*. Englewood Cliffs, New Jersey: Prentice-Hall, Inc., 1974.

1956 International Motion Picture Almanac. New York: Quigley Publishing Company, 1956.

Nye, Russel. *The Unembarrassed Muse: The Popular Arts in America*. New York: The Dial Press, 1970.

Parish, James Robert, and Stanke, Don E. *The Glamour Girls*. New Rochelle, New York: Arlington House Publishers, 1975.

Parish, James Robert, ed. *The Great Movie Series*. Cranbury, New Jersey: A. S. Barnes and Company, Inc., 1971.

Parish, James Robert, ed. *The Slapstick Queens*. New York: Castle Books, 1973.

Parkinson, Michael, and Jeavons, Clyde. *A Pictorial History of Westerns*. London: Hamlyn, 1972.

Perrett, Geoffrey. *Days of Sadness, Years of Triumph: The American People 1939–1945*. New York: Coward, McCann and Geoghegan, Inc., 1973.

The Purple Monster Strikes. Northbrook, Illinois: Jack Mathis Advertising, n.d.

Ricci, Mark, Zmijewsky, Boris, and Zmijewsky, Steve. *The Films of John Wayne*. New York: Citadel Press, 1970.

Rosenberg, Bernard, and White, David Manning, eds. *Mass Culture: The Popular Arts in America*. New York: Free Press, 1964.

Rosten, Leo C. *Hollywood: The Movie Colony, the Movie Makers*. New York: Harcourt, Brace and Company, 1941.

Rothel, David. *Who Was That Masked Man? The Story of the Lone Ranger*. Cranbury, New Jersey: A. S. Barnes and Company, Inc., 1976.

Seldes, Gilbert. *The Great Audience*. New York: Viking Press, 1950.

Sklar, Robert. *Movie Made America: A Social History of American Movies*. New York: Random House, 1975.

Smith, Paul, ed. *The Historian and Film*. New York: Cambridge University Press, 1976.

Spears, Jack. *HOLLYWOOD: The Golden Era*. New York: Castle Books, 1971.

Spy Smasher. Cliffhanger Ending and Escape Pictorial. Northbrook, Illinois: Jack Mathis Advertising, n.d.

Stedman, Raymond William. *The Serials: Suspense and Drama by Installment*. Norman, Oklahoma: University of Oklahoma Press, 1971.

Stott, William. *Documentary Expression and Thirties America*. New York: Oxford University Press, 1973.

Thompson, Stith. *The Folktale*. New York: Dryden Press, 1951.

Tuska, Jon, ed. *Close-Up: The Contract Director*. Metuchen, New Jersey: The Scarecrow Press, Inc., 1976.

Tuska, Jon. *The Filming of the West*. Garden City, New York: Doubleday and Company, 1976.

Warshow, Robert. *The Immediate Experience*. Garden City, New York: Doubleday, 1962.

Weiss, Ken, and Goodgold, Ed. *To Be Continued....* New York: Crown Publishers, Inc., 1972.

White, David Manning, and Averson, Richard. *The Celluloid Weapon: Social Comment in the American Film*. Boston: Beacon Press, 1972.

Wilson, Robert, ed. *The Film Criticism of Otis Ferguson*. Philadelphia: Temple University Press, 1971.

Wise, Arthur, and Ware, Derek. *Stunting in the Cinema*. New York: St. Martin's Press, 1973.

Wofenstein, Martha, and Leites, Nathan. *Movies: A Psychological Study*. New York: The Free Press, 1950; reprint ed., New York: Hafner Publishing Company, 1971.

Wood, Michael. *America in the Movies or "Santa Maria, It Had Slipped My Mind."* New York: Basic Books, 1975.

Wright, Will. *Six Guns and Society: A Structural Study of the Western*. Berkeley: University of California Press, 19–73.

Zinman, David. *Saturday Afternoon at the Bijou*. New Rochelle, New York: Arlington House, 1973.

Zolotow, Maurice. *Shooting Star: A Biography of John Wayne*. New York: Simon and Schuster, 1974.

Zorro's Fighting Legion. Cliffhanger Ending and Escape Pictorial. Northbrook, Illinois: Jack Mathis Advertising, n.d.

Index

About the Author

Richard M. Hurst grew up in Central Indiana in the mid-1940s, where he was exposed to Westerns and serials on a weekly basis. It created an interest in these films, especially those of Republic, which remained into adulthood.

Hurst has four university degrees culminating in a PhD in American History from the State University of New York, Buffalo. He has taught New York history, museology, and popular culture on the university level as well as writing and speaking on these subjects at seminars and conferences. In 2000 he retired after forty years in museum administration. He and his wife travel throughout the world when he is not watching serials and action movies from his collection.